HERO
AND
HERO-WORSHIP

Fandom in Modern India

Edited by

Rahul Chaturvedi
Banaras Hindu University, India

Hariom Singh
Babasaheb Bhimrao Ambedkar University, India

Anita Singh
Banaras Hindu University, India

Series in Critical Media Studies

VERNON PRESS

In the Americas:
Vernon Press
1000 N West Street,
Suite 1200, Wilmington,
Delaware 19801
United States

In the rest of the world:
Vernon Press
C/Sancti Espiritu 17,
Malaga, 29006
Spain

Series in Critical Media Studies

Library of Congress Control Number: 2019951781

ISBN: 978-1-64889-232-5

Also available: 978-1-62273-859-5 [Hardback]; 978-1-64889-082-6 [PDF, E-Book]

Table of Contents

List of Figures and Tables

Figures

Tables

Acknowledgements

Many people have contributed to this book in one way or another, and we owe thanks to them all. We are extremely thankful to Argiris Legatos and her team at Vernon Press for their constant support and impeccable editorial assistance. We also express our sincere thanks to Carolina Sanchez for sending us the invite to publish our book with Vernon Press. We are grateful to all our contributors for agreeing to enrich this book with their scholarly research. The time and energy they devoted to this project have resulted in a substantial academic contribution to the field. We are also thankful to Prof. Sanjukta Dasgupta, Calcutta University, Prof. Seema Malik, Mohan Lal Sukhadia University, Dr. Amit Kumar Upadhyay, Banaras Hindu University, and Dr. Pravin Kumar Patel, Banaras Hindu University for their intellectual observations and encouraging words. We cannot thank enough to our family and friends, for without their moral support, this project would never have come to fruition.

Foreword

In modern India the concept of heroes as symbol and metaphor, and its interlinking with hero worship, fandom, *bhakt* cult, that is fan as devotee and fan clubs is about iconizing or deifying a public performer or a personality or teams of performers ranging from political icons to superstars in the fields of cinema, sports, music and spiritual counselling along with the seduction of real and imagined spaces. The given assumption is that the hero is an extraordinarily talented, handsome, masculine, cerebral brave-heart. In contemporary parlance, a hero is often addressed as an achiever and, therefore, a celebrity and superstar. The transformation of an individual from the average to the heroic is about admitting the greatness of the person concerned. Who decides who is an achiever or a hero? It is predominantly the digital fan communities that are decision-makers, in the pre-internet era the fan clubs in a more limited span, functioned similarly. In contemporary times, the rating is based often on the commercial success of a performer, a team, a place or space or a best-selling writer.

It is the fan who is the consumer of the heroic attributes and to the fan the hero becomes an inspirational icon who 'prosumes' the mind of the fan. A fan is a prosumer who consumes and produces a product. So addictive is this propensity to idolize a hero that the fan becomes completely obsessed, wallowing even in the trivia that superstardom or hero worship generates. A fan runs the risk of pathological imbalance due to obsessive besotted deification of a person that can be either edifying or self-destructive. In his book *Textual Poachers* (1992) H. Jenkins has analysed fan psychosis and referred to the 'pathological deviant subjectivities' that determine fan behaviourism. The fan, therefore, is the reader who reads and consumes the hero as text. It is the response and the reception of fans and fandom that creates, constructs and transforms outstanding performers to the stature of heroes. The concept of heroes and fans, aficionados or devotees has been present throughout human history. The heroes in religious texts and epics have been glorified and romanticized monumentally. At present, however, the common semantic usages have now reinvented themselves to such variables as leaders and followers.

In contemporary times however the reinvention of both signifiers, heroes and fans, has been primarily due to digital technology, media platforms and the rapid creation of fan communities through social networks that create digital or virtual communes where sharing is interpreted as caring, without any concerted effort. The much more sophisticated roles of heroes and fans of the 21st century are of course linked to economic globalization and the consumerist culture that the market economy has ushered in. Referring to the relevance of Carlyle's classic text *On Heroes, Hero-Worship, and The Heroic in History*, first published in 1841 and re-published as recently as 2013, the critic Brent E Kinser stated, "It is true that the inanities associated with the new social media, including Facebook, the blogosphere, YouTube, and Twitter, represent a form of triviality that is striking in its pervasive and sublunary influence...The new social media has become the engine for a digital age of revolution, the priorities of which frequently intersect with Carlyle's notion of the heroic" (Kinser 274).

According to the Oxford English Dictionary, a hero is 'a person, especially a man, who is admired by many people for doing something brave or good'. The hero may be a main male character in a story, novel, film/movie, etc., a person, especially a man, who is admired because of a particular quality or skill that he may have. Hero-worship is also defined as the feeling or expression of reverence and adoration for a deity, a person or principle. Lexically, hero worship and fandom are regarded as synonyms, the word fan emanates from the Modern Latin *fanaticus*, meaning "insanely but divinely inspired". The word originally pertained to a temple or sacred place [Latin fanum, poetic English fane]. The modern sense of "extremely zealous" dates from around 1647; the use of fanatic as a noun dates from 1650.

Carlyle was an advocate of elite excellence, a feature critiqued in one of the essays in this volume, stating that one needs to look for the heroic in the resistance of the wretched of the earth and not just among great men. So Carlyle stated, "For, as I take it, Universal History, the history of what man has accomplished in this world, is at bottom the History of the Great Men who have worked here. They were the leaders of men, these great ones; the modellers, patterns, and in a wide sense creators, of whatsoever the general mass of men contrived to do or to attain; all things that we see standing accomplished in the world are properly the outer material result, the practical realisation and embodiment, of Thoughts that dwelt in the Great Men sent into the world: the soul of the whole world's history, it may justly be considered, were the history of these..." (Carlyle 21).

Elaborating further, Carlyle stated with impassioned fervour,

> And now if worship even of a star had some meaning in it, how much more might that of a Hero! Worship of a Hero is transcendent admiration of a Great Man. I say great men are still admirable; I say there is, at bottom, nothing else admirable! No nobler feeling than this of admiration for one higher than himself dwells in the breast of man. It is to this hour, and at all hours, the vivifying influence in man's life. Religion I find stand [sic] upon it...Hero-worship, heartfelt prostrate admiration, submission, burning, boundless, for a noblest godlike Form of Man... (Carlyle 28)

The six essays of Thomas Carlyle in the book *On Heroes, Hero-Worship, and The Heroic in History* defined in detail the roles of the hero as Divinity, Prophet, Poet, Priest, Man of Letters and King respectively, and interestingly arranged in that order in the contents. Carlyle referred to Odin, Mahomet, Christ, Dante, Shakespeare, Martin Luther and Knox as heroes in his essays. In Sorenson's introduction to Carlyle's essays, he observed, "Numerous heroes of the twentieth century, among them Anna Akhmatova, Winston Churchill, Mohandas Gandhi, Vasily Grossman, Václav Havel, Martin Luther King, Rosa Luxemburg, Nelson Mandela, Osip Mandelstam, George Orwell, Franklin Delano Roosevelt, and Alexander Solzhenitsyn—pursued paths that frequently fulfilled Carlylean notions of the heroic. By their words and their actions, they inspired others to transcend self-interest in a wider battle against injustice and falsehood" (16).

The editors have provided a cogent introduction to their book and included essays on diverse aspects of heroes, hero-worship and fandom. They have outlined some of the crucial elements that define hero-worship that may be categorized as infatuation, aesthetics, self-esteem and entertainment triggering pleasure, arousal, vicarious pleasure and obsessive syndromes of hysteria. The example of the Shahrukh Khan's film *Fan* as an element of intertextuality between the Bollywood production of *Fan* in 2016 and the Hollywood film *The Fan* released in 1996, starring Robert De Niro, tracks the evolution of fandom and the cultural differences between modern India and Hollywood.

Undoubtedly, this book will provide cutting edge material in this emerging field of fandom studies to students, faculty members and researchers. Each of the 12 essays included in the book ranging from stardom, celebrity culture, fandom of Banaras and Bollywood to environmental fandom, Aamir Khan and Batman, open new doors of perception and theoretical discourse, through discursive argumentation and scholarly interventions.

Dr. Sanjukta Dasgupta
Former Professor, Dept of English
Calcutta University

Bibliography:

Carlyle, Thomas. *On Heroes, Hero-Worship, and the Heroic in History*. Eds. David R Sorensen and Brent E Kinser. Yale University Press: London, 2013. Print.

Kinser, Brent E. "Thomas Carlyle, Social Media and the Digital age of Revolution" *On Heroes, Hero-Worship, and the Heroic in History*. Eds. David R Sorensen and Brent E Kinser. Yale University Press: London, 2013. 272-282. Print.

Sorensen, David R. "Introduction" *On Heroes, Hero-Worship, and the Heroic in History*. Eds. David R Sorensen and Brent E Kinser. Yale University Press: London, 2013. 1-16. Print.

1.

Introduction:
Hero and Hero-Worship:
Understanding Fandom in Modern India

Rahul Chaturvedi

Banaras Hindu University, India

Hariom Singh

Babasaheb Bhimrao Ambedkar University, India

Anita Singh

Banaras Hindu University, India

This book has its origin in increasing usage of the word *Bhakt* in Indian public discourse, especially in relation to the political following. *Bhakt*, originally implies a devotee, a spiritual seeker of God. However, its contemporary usage in Indian public discourse has nothing to do with its etymological meaning. Rather it refers to the hyper-active followers of any political leader. Political bhakti, which is perhaps equivalent to political fandom, initially intended to constitute the core argument of this book. However, there are other kinds of *bhaktis* as well, which were originally planned to be a part of this book. The spiritual fandom of trans-national and regional *babas/gurus* (spiritual leaders) — which differs from the membership of organised religions like Hinduism, Islam or Christianity in its nature and structure— along media fandoms of 'superstars' from the cinema and cricket and the emotional over-investment of the audience in the consumerist culture of today, originally intended to constitute the fundamental premise of fandom discourse in India. Despite its limitations, the focus of the book has been throughout on understanding the fandom as a phenomenon and how it has found expression in the Indian public sphere.

I

How 'We' are not 'Them': Ethical Iconographies of Fandom

It is certainly very difficult to offer a universally accepted definition of who a fan is. Everybody, in some ways, is a fan of someone or something. Some arguments suggest that fans are, in fact, the most dedicated and ideal audience/followers. Nonetheless, in the popular opinion, a fan is a person with 'obsessive attachment' for someone or something whose admiration borders on 'threat', 'abnormality', and/or 'stupidity' (Jenkins, *Textual Poachers* 10). To be a fan, in this sense, implies to live with a stigma (this is one of the reasons perhaps that fans continue to 'refuse their fanhood' in the public space). Generally, fans are considered as people with "pathological and deviant subjectivities" (Jenkins, *Textual Poachers* 10). More than often, a fan is usually considered a potential fanatic having excessive fixation and abnormal admiration for the popular (media) figures. Fan obsessions, therefore, are mostly viewed as instances of (im)proper social behaviour which result from a programmed representation of popular celebrities on media, internet, and television intending to reinforce 'the consumerist agenda' through fandoms.

Traditionally, a fan is understood as an effect of a star. Thus imbibing an inherent passivity, a fan is understood to be unreflective and emotionally vulnerable consumer of mass media produced images who considers celebrities as heroes/role models based on an imaginary relationship s/he 'imagines' to have with the star. The model of fandom as envisioned by Jenkins in *Textual Poachers* and Joli Jenson in "Fandom as Pathology" considers fandom pathological and deems fans to be either an obsessed individual with 'a child-like subjectivity' or a member of a hysterical crowd without 'an evolved ego'. Therein, fandom refers to "individual obsessions, privately elaborated, and public hysteria, mobilized by crowd contagion" (Jenson 13). This pathological model of fan phenomenon was wittily summarised by Henry Jenkins in his *Textual Poachers* through a set of characteristics wherein fans

a. are brainless consumers who will buy anything associated with the program or its cast;
b. devote their lives to the cultivation of worthless knowledge;
c. place inappropriate importance on devalued cultural material;
d. are social misfits who have become so obsessed with the show that it forecloses other types of social experience;
e. are feminized and/or desexualized through their intimate engagement with mass culture;
f. are infantile, emotionally and intellectually immature;
g. are unable to separate fantasy from reality. (10)

Jenkins' outline of fandom suggests a moral framework of fandom which is based on the binary of 'normal audience/viewer' and 'abnormal fan'. Definition of a fan as an abnormal 'other' who is ridiculously infatuated with an individual celebrity or any cultural item/form, with the latent possibility of being violent, stands in close relation to a good, critical normal audience. Jenkins' approach to fandom is surely psychological and indicates a kind of moral dualism wherein the 'ideal' (non)fan audience lacks an abnormal psyche in apparent contrast to the 'perverse' fan-viewer. Jenkins argues that

> [T]he fans still constitutes a scandalous category in contemporary culture, one alternately the target of ridicule and anxiety, of dread and desire. . . . The stereotypical conception of the fan, while not without a limited factual basis, amounts to a projection of anxieties about the violation of dominant cultural hierarchies. (*Textual Poachers* 15-16)

Similar to the moral/pathological approach, there is another quite significant model of fandom which views fans as ignorant and uncritical people with very little brain who are vulnerable to powerful coercive forms of media. They are seen as 'cultural dopes', childlike and passive consumers of popular culture, having morbid tastes belonging to low culture. Writing about this model of fandom, Lawrence Grossberg contends that

> a second approach attempts to begin by characterizing the particular sorts of people who become fans, and the basis on which their relationship to popular culture is constructed. In this model, it is often assumed that popular culture appeals to the lowest and least critical segments of the population. These audiences are thought to be easily manipulated and distracted (not only from 'serious' culture but also from real social concerns), mobilized solely to make a profit. The various forms of popular culture appeal to the audience's most debased needs and desires, making them even more passive, more ignorant and noncritical than they already are. Fans are simply incapable of recognizing that the culture they enjoy is being used to dupe and exploit them. A second, related view of fans assumes that they are always juveniles, waiting to grow up, and still enjoying the irresponsibility of their fandom. (51)

In addition to the two aforesaid models of fandom, there can be a third approach to understand the fan phenomenon, which is slightly more liberal and emancipatory from the perspective of a fan. This model considers fans as people possessing higher creative and communicative capacities, who can engage with and interpret media texts in a variety of interesting and unexpected ways. They, as a collectivity, give birth to what can be called fan communities. Since these groups of fans participate in communal and communicational activities and do not remain isolated viewers/readers (online platforms have further consolidated their community sentiment), they constitute an interesting category of organized fandom which might be considered "a scandalous category in contemporary culture" (Jenkins 15). Due to their unavoidable (hyper)visibility, fan communities in the field of politics, religion, arts, sports, media, cinema, television, academics, etc. are no more considered merely pathological in the traditional sense rather emerge as communities with the power to intervene, influence and change the discursive space. Writing about this model of fandom which regards fans as "the most elite audience among passive consumers", Lawrence Grossberg contends that

> according to this 'subcultural' model, any of these groups would be considered fans; fans constitute an elite fraction of the larger audience of passive consumers. Within this model, the fan can discriminate between those forms of popular culture which are 'authentic' (that is, which are art, which does represent their experience, etc.) and those which are the result of the efforts of the commercial mainstream to appropriate these forms and produce tainted versions for the larger audience. Thus, the fan is always in constant conflict, not only with the various structures of power but also with the vast audience of media consumers. But such an elitist view of fandom does little to illuminate the complex relations that exist between forms of popular culture and their audiences. (52)

This view of fans rejects both the pathological and cultural dope model of fandom and posits the idea of a fan as an active audience. Thus, fans are no more considered silly, brainless and juvenile consumers of popular media texts rather appear as 'informed subjects' who are conscious of their position in the matrix of discursive structures and constantly negotiate with, and at times manipulate, the very narratives which are supposed to trick them into consumptive slumber.

To better understand how fandom is particularly productive, we may also consider John Fiske's tripartite model of semiotic, enunciative and textual productivity. Fiske considers semiotic productivity to be a "characteristic of popular culture as a whole rather than of fan culture specifically" which consists of "the making of meanings of social identity and social experience from the semiotic resources of the cultural commodity" (37). Enunciative productivity, in his formulation, can take place within immediate social relationships alone as it involves shared or face-to-face oral communication, therefore, "exists only for its moment of speaking, and the popular cultural capital it generates is thus limited to a restricted circulation, a very localized economy" (Fiske 37). Fiske further argues that fan talk is the generation and circulation of certain meanings of the object of fandom within a local community. The talk of women soap opera fans has been widely studied . . . to show how the meanings and evaluations of characters and their behaviour in the soap opera are related more or less directly to the everyday lives of the fans. Indeed, much of the pleasure of fandom lies in the fan talk that it produces, and many fans report that the choice of their object of fandom was determined at least as much by the oral community they wished to join as by any of its inherent characteristics. (38)

In his framework on fandom, Fiske lays extra emphasis on textual productivity of the fan communities, which has also been used to distinguish fan and non-fan audience:

There is, however, another category of fan productivity that approximates much more closely the artistic productions validated by the official culture, that of textual productivity. Fans produce and circulate among themselves texts which are often crafted with production values as high as any in the official culture. The key differences between the two are economic rather than ones of competence, for fans do not write or produce their texts for money; indeed, their productivity typically costs them money. Economics, too, limits the equipment to which fans have access for the production of their texts, which may therefore often lack the technical smoothness of professionally-produced ones. There is also a difference in circulation; because fan texts are not produced for profit, they do not need to be mass-marketed, so unlike official culture, fan culture does not attempt to circulate its texts outside its community. They are 'narrowcast,' not broadcast, texts. (39)

Here, Fiske is suggesting that the non-fan audience are far less likely to partake in practices of textual production, although they may certainly participate in the practices of both semiotic and enunciative productivity.

II

Understanding Digital Fandom

It's no surprise that digital space has turned out to be the most useful and fertile platform for fans to form online communities. In India, Facebook, Twitter, and YouTube are the three most powerful sites for online/digital fandom. For instance, the popularity of an actor/politician is often based on online followers s/he has. Thus, the internet has certainly altered what it means to be a star or a fan in the modern world. Fans no longer remain passive consumers and the stars are also being forced to seek ways to build personal connections with their fans, and use a variety of social media platforms to remain in constant touch with them, and at times provide support to encourage fans' creativity. Thus the stars in the new millennium face an additional challenge of keeping their fans in good humour to generate and maintain the goodwill of their fans. In return, the fans reward their stars by indulging in what is popularly known as 'fannish jobs', such as, liking, sharing, tweeting, texting, etc. With online sites dedicated to promoting fandoms, the formation of digital fan communities becomes easier, where individuals with similar interests share the same virtual space to consolidate their fan identity. Two very important things need to be mentioned here. One, we must distinguish between the sponsored fandom and spontaneous fandom. While the former category is embedded in capitalist/consumerist ideological dynamics, the latter shows the innocent obsession of an individual for his beloved star. Two, online fandoms simultaneously give rise to hatedoms as well. If fandom works to strengthen the image of the star, the opponent's hatedom of the same star may be vigorously challenging his stardom. However, in both the cases of fandom and hatedom, the star gets what he/she wants, media glare and the consequent popularity.

There is another interesting aspect that one needs to understand well: fandom is not necessarily hero-worship. Fans look for spaces of self-projection, and more often than not, have the power to influence, mould and metamorphose their hero. There can be no denying that fandom usually enables fans with a sense of self-worth/empowerment, allowing them to support their interests more successfully in their everyday lives. Therefore, the argument that fans are merely crazy idiots lacking self-esteem would surely be erroneous as many fans exhibit some sort of semiotic resistance to the star power by appropriating their images in their interest.

Further, in a society that has turned into 'a society of the spectacle', fandom can be viewed both as a symptom of perverse idiocy and therapeutic self-assertion. It is almost impossible to exactly define what fandom implies. Therefore, to say what Matt Hills has to argue would surely be more appropriate:

> I think fandom is still performative. It remains as I thought about it in Fan Cultures – that is to say, fandom is performed differently and can mean different things in different micro-contexts, in different moments of social interaction, and even on different platforms. Being a fan of Tumblr can mean one thing; being a fan at a convention can mean something else. There can be many different kinds of fandom, going well, well beyond the notion of affirmational [fandom] versus transformational [fandom] as a problematic binary. There can be all sorts – of different kinds and modes and levels and hierarchies of fandom which can be performed in a variety of ways. So, the idea that one can just come up with a definition of fandom

I think is problematized through the fact that it's performed in so many different ways and so many varied contexts. Rather than focusing on defining fandom, we need to think about how fandom is performed and for whom and in what context, and try to think, really, about what kind of subset of this vast overarching diffused category of fandom we might be dealing with. (345-46)

Thus in the digital era, fans are also using digital platforms to structure their communities limited by their individually shared tastes, wherein the audience no longer wants to remain merely as a consumer. They are also reflecting a will to collaborate, and participate in what they are being asked to consume. The fandom, nowadays, reflects how fan cultures are caught between consumerism and resistance. Elaborating this further, Grossberg has remarked

Fans actively constitute places and forms of authority (both for themselves and for others) through the mobilization and organization of affective investments. By making certain things or practices matter, the fan 'authorizes' them to speak for him or her, not only as a spokesperson but also as surrogate voices (as when we sing along to popular songs). The fan gives authority to that which he or she invests in, letting the object of such investments speak for and as for him or her self. (59)

Thus fan communities by giving expressions to their political positioning and ideological commitments institute authority in the individuals they invest in. As long as an individual fan's personal opinion is subjective and dispersed, her or his identity is only personally significant. However, the moment individual fan investments find virtual platforms like social media, they immediately form a community of 'an affective alliance'. By texting, tweeting, sharing, the heroics of any political star, and by maligning and destroying the image of the political opponent and her/his fan-followers, fan communities grant power/authority to their star. The forthcoming section tries to understand how these fan cultures form different variants of fandoms, depending upon 'the field'. In the context of this affective alliance of people, loosely understood as fandom, we intend to discuss four major kinds of fandoms that we observe in India, viz. political, spiritual, sports and cinematic fandoms.

Political Fandom

While political fandom is not a recent phenomenon, it is only in the past decade or so that scholars and social scientists have begun to consider this as a site of academic enquiry. For example, what constitutes the popularity of any political leader? What makes him acceptable is not only what he does but also a narrative that her/his fans proliferate. Historically, the core of political fandom in India has centred around a sort of fan-faith which argued that the salvation of the masses depended on the miraculous powers of an individual leader. Under the excessive faith the masses reposed in the leader, the leader is granted temporary governmental powers in excess, which transform her/him into a messianic figure. But how are we to understand this excessive political fandom? What does this offer to a fan? Like any other form of fandom, political fandom is organized around the 'ideology of pleasure in excess'. The two fundamentals of political fandom, like in any other kind of fandoms, are emotions and enjoyment. The political fan articulates and exhibits a strong obsession with the rockstar politician whose fixation is built upon a partisan identification constructed around an enemy star politician of the opponent party. Of course, charisma, character, rhetorical and communicative ability of a political candidate go into the making of a cult politician, there can be no denying that fan communities also wield enormous power through blogs, Facebook, Twitter, and YouTube to influence the democratic functioning. The political fan's relationship with his political messiah figure does not remain a normal fan-celebrity relationship wherein the former is an emotionally involved passive consumer of a given narrative, rather it constitutes the site of active engagement. The most interesting thing to note here is that a fan-celebrity relationship between voters and politicians may have the possibility of disrupting/consolidating the democratic processes. However, it also allows them to get more engaged in politics, thereby participate in democratising processes.

Spiritual Fandom

Societies continue to remain religious, and faith continues to influence lifestyles, choices, and attitudes of individuals and larger social organisation. Increasing atomisation of self and society and decreasing community contact is further resulting in experiences of emptiness and alienation, which invites intermittent doses of spirituality. In the case of India, the allegedly disconcerting encounter of the urbanites with the 'Western modernity', coupled with the loss of prestige for traditional support systems, has instilled in India's urban middle class a new kind of hunger for spiritual experience. And this has given birth to new alternative communities professing, more than often, faith in the universal brotherhood of all religions, and caring for the spiritual well-being of individuals. Middle-class urbanites, looking for someone to fill the void in their lives, are beginning to attend the religious congregations of religious godmen who lure them into their fandom by speaking on the mundane problems of humanity like their financial difficulties, marital discord, addiction to alcohol and drugs, etc. But this phenomenon cannot be reduced to the cities and middle-class alone. There are regional/local *Babas* as well, sometimes with pan-Indian acceptance, mostly having powerful local clout. Poorer people from both the cities and villages rush to them in hope of spiritual solace. These self-styled *babas* perhaps offer them an escape route. Many of these gurus help their followers, through charity in health and education and are very popular among their followers, sometimes rumoured/believed to have miraculous healing powers. Thus people turn to them for spiritual and material sustenance.

The visibility of such gurus nowadays is far higher than in the past. They have amassed huge amounts of wealth and big political clout. More than being a guru, they have turned into brands. The growth of many popular transnational devotionalist organizations along with local *ashrams* can be cases in point. And we are witnessing the avtar of the New Age *Babas*, with every possible paraphernalia of power and prominence, assisted by experience-enhancing/injecting technologies of mass deception. The number of spiritual gurus, or Babas as they are fondly addressed, is on the rise, and influential cults—similar to religious sects of the past times—are emerging as new enclaves of power. Nevertheless, the spiritual following of a *Baba* does not always remain innocent. On several occasions, the brutal nexus between a *Baba* and politicians can be observed which exploits the ignorant fan-following of the spiritual leader.

Sports Fandom

Sports has emerged as the neo-religion in modern India. It's truly amazing to reflect upon how much money, time and human emotion is invested in sports which are, after all, nothing but games. There are very few who can put themselves outside the commotion of sports fantasy. Following sports is important, however, the risk of going a little too obsessed with the player or the team that you support too requires attention. Since India is largely a one-sport society, fandom of cricket stars like Sachin Tendulkar, also lovingly called 'the god of cricket' by his fans, Virat Kohli, Mahendra Singh Dhoni, now crosses age, gender, caste, regional and religious divides. Analysing sports fandom in India, especially cricket, calls upon us to examine the underlying structures of consumption practices. It asks for closer scrutiny of mass media networks, specifically television and the internet, which led to the popularisation of cricket across all classes.

Having initially agreed that cricket and political sentiments constitute two separate realms, it is also important to understand that political undertones lie within the object of fandom. Fans may also reflect distorted sentimentalism and express specific community biases which are part of their everyday lives. Crazy popularity of the Indo-Pak cricket matches due to historical enmity between the two nations leading to virtual wars on social media platforms also leaves trails of everyday communal tensions in fan texts. The other example could be the ever-growing popularity of Indian Premier League (IPL), which might be called by its detractors polarizing Indian citizens by regional sentiments in its act of naming franchisees after cities, thus fomenting city-specific identity. Paradoxically enough, the teams are not only pan-national but international as well. And there is enough evidence to suggest that many cricket fans choose their favourite teams based on their favourite players, not after the city they belong to.

However, the possibility of a good number of fans indulging in the parochial idea of regionalism can also not be overlooked. Usually, a full-fledged 'war' is telecast widely across various media platforms before the cricket matches, and the charged vocabulary used reflects deeper ideological and normative prejudices. Therefore, the liberal notion that sports are 'merely leisure' and 'pure entertainment', having nothing to do with politics, is surely some kind of misunderstanding that fails to notice the possibility of sports diplomacy in foreign affairs and unifying/divisive capacity in affairs of the home.

Cinematic Fandom

Madhava Prasad in his essay "Fan Bhakti and Subaltern Sovereignty: Enthusiasm as a Political Factor" discussed the fan-formations around one of the most popular film stars of India, Rajnikanth. This was perhaps one of the first academic enquiry into fan studies in India. The cosmos of Rajanikant fans is enormous and there are more than 50,000 Rajanikanth fan clubs. Similarly, the mega-star Amitabh Bachchan has 3,29,02,320 million followers on Twitter, while superstar Shah Rukh Khan has been the industry's most followed hero with 3,29,41,837 Twitter followers. There are scores of such superstars from Bollywood and regional film industries, who have millions of fan-following.

On the face of it, Bollywood's fandom seems like a positive phenomenon, a symptom of cinema-going evermore popular and also suggesting some sort of democratizing that seems to put entertainment industry's controllers and its consumers on a level playing field. However, it has other sides as well. The digital fandom of the twenty-first century India, wherein fans are easier to reach than ever, fandom has become all the more fragile due to ever-increasing sea of entertainment options. It can be easily discerned that there is an undeniable solipsistic and narcissist quality to much of fandom, wherein the super-star has also turned vulnerable to the tastes of a tribe of her/his fans. Further, fan practices which verge on the boundaries of obsession and aggression, reflect more than petulant bullying of rabid fans due to the Internet's veil of unfathomable anonymity wherein any kind of fan-auditing fails to isolate genuine and fake followers. Further, the hostility between the profit-oriented commercial motivations of media moguls to monetize what fans love to consume, positions fans in critically vulnerable positions.

III

Fandom as Gendered Discourse

The questions that this segment will seek to understand consist of: Are there gendered ways of performing fandom? How are women doing their fandom in a male-dominated world or are fans gender neutral? Do women play specific roles and act differently in fan groups from men? Further, what does it mean to be 'fangirling' over a celebrity, a sports star, and a politician or media icon? Are there differences between the sexes within the fandom? A significant body of work has been done as far as female fans in sports are considered. Researchers show that sports is a gendered space that fortifies masculine identity, bonding, and relationship of power (Hargreaves; Messner) and that female fans are not considered suitably dedicated to sports (Gantz and Wenner) or that they are ignorant of the technicalities of the game (Crolley and Long) and that they are more interested in the male bodies and 'fancy the players' or the glamour that sports bring in with power and money than actual sports performance (Crawford and Gosling). Jones, in her research on female fandom, reads women's relationship to football culture and shows how women sometimes downplay their gender identities to reinforce their fan identities. For this, she interviewed 38 female fans to analyze their responses to abusive or insulting behavior by male fans. Her findings were that women used three strategies to respond to sexism and homophobia. First, they expressed disgust at abuse, sometimes redefining fandom to exclude abusers. Second, they downplayed sexism. Their third strategy was to embrace gender stereotypes, arguing that femininity was inconsistent with 'authentic' fandom and that abuse was a fundamental part of football (Jones).

Female fans are often perceived as being masculine, although frequently as de-gendered, asexual, or impotent, the eroticized fan is almost always female. The typical masculine image of fandom is of irrepressible masculine passion, a rampage of drunken destructiveness that is unbridled in response to a sports victory or defeat' but the feminine image of fandom is represented rather differently, as sobbing, swooning, and hysterical (Messner, Duncan, and Jensen). Gendered words like "passion," "craziness," "frenzy," and "obsession" are associated with female fandom (Click). Fans perceive a hierarchy of fan following. Sports fans are supposed to be virile and robust (Zubernis and Larsen). The trivialization of soaps deems the fans' cultural capital to be very low and so, "the discourse of pleasure for women is overlaid with a discourse which deems soaps to be rubbish" (Brown 204). However, soaps have usually been observed as low-grade worth, as 'fantasy and escapism for women' and televised sport for men is often seen as "a legitimate and even edifying experience" (Brown 204).

It is mostly assumed that typically female genres of fandom are media/soap operas. Women are more acceptable as media fans than as sports fans (Pope). Mohit Gahlot's recent survey "11 Most Followed Indian Celebrities on Instagram: Check Out 8th one!!" in *Bollywood Herald* goes on to show that Facebook and Twitter and now Instagram are social networking sites that succeeded in spreading their roots in India where female fan following finds its easy access to map its desires. In India, women's sports fandom is on the rise. FIFA figures for the 2014 world cup revealed a significant number of women spectators as reported in *India Times*. Advertisements also significantly targeted the new rise in viewership of females in the 15 plus age group ("In PICS: Female Fans @ FIFA World Cup" n.pag.).

Women are assuming new visible roles and we can perceive an evolution of female fandom practices, modes of engagement and fan experiencing in the wake of advanced digital technologies and the impact of global mobility. The increasing presence of women among sports crowd in cricket or football or any other game in India and the consumption of sports as entertainment has transformed traditional discourses of identity creation and mediation. This gives rise to a host of questions about feminine and masculine practices of identification and emotional investment. If any perceivable differences exist in gendered ways of doing/being a fan, along with their concomitant images of masculinity and femininity, these transform historically as a result of interfaces between the sexes within socially organized structures.

IV

This book is an attempt to understand the nature of Indian fandom. The title of this book has been borrowed from Thomas Carlyle's famous work, *On Heroes and Hero-Worship, and the Heroic in History*. The book consists of eleven insightful papers apart from the Introduction. In her paper "Discourse on Fandom in Modern India: Where do we stand?", Priyanka Shivadas by way of a series of reflections on the movie *Fan* starring Shahrukh Khan dwells on the current issues at the loci of the discourse of fandom in India vis-a-vis its western counterpart. The movie, as the paper argues, is situated at the interface of serious artwork and popular culture offering a perceptive approach to fandom depicting it primarily as pathological.

The paper "Stardom: Deceiving the Self" by Himanshu Khosla explores the nuances of engagement of men and women of today's generation with social media. Khosla highlights how one's presence on social media has become a prominent yardstick to measure one's self-worth which has induced an ever-increasing desire for a celebrity like fame in common people. The paper argues that conventional parameters of beauty have come under severe critique through online media campaigns which have resulted in people rethinking the aesthetics of beauty. Ruchi Sharma's paper "Discursive Power of Enigmatic Stars: Dynamics of Celebrity Culture", while charting the key developments in the area of star-studies, foregrounds the discursive formation of a star's value and how the audience contribute to it in various meaningful ways. The paper contends that there is a complex process through which stars acquire meaning in our society and they (un)consciously become the carriers of certain ideologies. Through the study of film stars' biographies, the paper observes that the duality of the text and the star often collapses into one. The following paper by Vishakha Sen "The Cult of Aamir Khan: A Cultural Study of Indian Fandom" portrays the evolution of fan studies in India and attempts to put one of a leading Bollywood actor Aamir Khan in perspective. The paper explores how Aamir Khan became one of the most popular actors of Bollywood. Following the classical Marxist dialectics of Base/superstructure dichotomy, the paper argues that the stars belong to the superstructure and fans in a way commodify the subjectivity of the star and function in the base. While pointing out the differences between the Western and the Indian fan cultures, the paper notes the passivity of the Indian fans and mantains that fan clubs while being pervasive in the West are significantly rare in our country. Ritika Pant's article titled "Soap Opera Stars as Corporate Commodities: The Political Economy of Television Stardom" places the phenomena of star studies in the context of television soap operas and the rise of satellite TV channels in the era of globalization. Based on her study of soap-operas or melodramatic tele-serials, she has argued that the rise of cable TV channels played a vital role in providing celebrity status to the TV artists. Through her case study of AvikaGor in *Balika Vadhu*, she highlights that the celebrity-dom of TV or small-screen artists has become an organized industry in itself which manufactures celebrities in the form of commodities through marketing, PR and promotions by the big corporate houses. The paper proceeds to argue that star phenomenon related to the small screen is more corporate-driven than being a subjective phenomenon based on the acting skills and off-screen image of the actor.

The next paper titled "Celebrity Endorsements in Advertisements: Influence on the Buying Behaviour of the Youth" by Saket Kumar Bhardwaj and Uttam Kumar Pegu discusses how in the times of information explosion and media power, advertisements play a major role in changing customer perception of brands. The paper examines the nature of celebrity endorsement which has become an essential part of today's advertisement world, especially in the FMCG sector intending to find out the impact of celebrity endorsement on the Indian youths. Shipra Tholia's paper "Bewitching Bombay: A Reflection on the Fandom of an Urban Space" captures the enigma of Bombay or Mumbai, as it has been rechristened, in all its hues and colors using the idea of 'elective belonging' through the lens of Bollywood movies like *Salaam Bombay, Chandni Bar, Citylights, Chameli,* etc. The paper looks at how the identity of a city is fashioned in the popular imagination in manifold ways through movies. Ashima Bhardwaj's "Fandom of Banaras: Beats' Guiding Star of the East" is again an exploration of a city, i.e. Banaras or Varanasi. The paper explains how the city has acquired a confluence of its numerous identities, primarily as a treasure-trove of spirituality in mythology, history, and politics. It examines why Banaras has always fascinated many tourists from abroad since time immemorial, including the Beat writers Allen Ginsberg and Peter Orlovsky.

Jamiel Ahmed's essay "Cultural Politics of War-heroes: Revisiting the Soldier Bio-icons of Jammu" analyses the iconography of war memorial sites in the Jammu region of Jammu and Kashmir. It also examines the pictorial representations of nationalism and its overtly masculine nature. Drawing on the insights of Stuart Hall's idea of encoding and decoding, the paper argues that the bio-iconic sites of soldiers present a spectacle of martyrdom and legitimize the discourse of patriotism. The penultimate paper "Indigenous Heroes of Nature and Culture: Fashioning Environmental Fandom in *Hodesum*" by Rajanikant Pandey is an insightful take on the meaning of heroism and hero-worship in the *Larka kol* tribes of Jharkhand, India. Through the first-person accounts of the struggles of Larka kol tribesmen, the paper analyses their community resistance in their native village of *Korta* in *Noamundi* against the deforestation and encroachment of their land for establishing the mining plant of Tata steel. The last paper "What my Hero Means to Me: The Confession of a Batman Enthusiast" by Amar Singh is a study in the portrayal of madness and traces the parallels between the inmates of Arkham asylum in the novel *Arkham Asylum: A Serious House on Serious Earth* by Grant Morrison and the Batman as depicted in popular culture, the most popular example being the Batman trilogy directed by Christopher Nolan. The paper deliberates on the significance of Batman as an art form and the legitimacy of fan response as an art.

Bibliography

Brown, Mary Ellen, ed. *Television and Women's Culture.* London: Sage Publications, 1990. Print.

Click, Melissa. "'Rabid', 'Obsessed' and 'Frenzied': Understanding Twilight Fangirls and the Gendered Politics of Fandom." *Flowtv.org.* N. p., 18 Dec. 2009. Web. 15 Nov. 2017. <http://flowtv.org/2009/12/rabid-obsessedand-frenzied-understanding-twilight-fangirls-and-the-gendered-politics-offandom-melissa-click-university-of-missouri/>.

Crawford, Garry, and Victoria K. Gosling. "The Myth of the 'Puck Bunny': Female Fans and Men's Ice Hockey." *Sociology* 38.3 (2004): 477-93. Print.

Crolley, L., and Cathy Long. "Sitting Pretty? Women and Football in Liverpool." *Passing Rhythms: Liverpool FC and the Transformation of Football.* Ed. John Williams. Oxford: Berg, 2001. 195-214. Print.

Fiske, J. "The Cultural Economy of Fandom." *The Adoring Audience: Fan Culture and Popular Media.* Ed. Lisa A Lewis. London: Routledge, 1992. 30-49. Print.

Gahlot, Mohit. "11 Most Followed Indian Celebrities on Instagram: Check Out 8th One!" *bollywoodherald.com.* N.p., n.d. Web. 12 Nov. 2017. <https://www.bollywoodherald.com/11-most-followed-indian-celebrities-on-instagram-check-out-8th-one/>.

Gantz, Walter, and Lawrence A. Wenner. "Fanship and the Television Sports Viewing Experience." *Sociology of Sport Journal* 12.1 (1995): 56-74. Print.

Grossberg, Lawrence. "Is there a Fan in the House? The Affective Sensibility of Fandom." *The Adoring Audience: Fan Culture and Popular Media.* Ed. Lisa A. Lewis. London: Routledge, 1992. 50-68. Print.

Hargreaves, Jennifer. *Sporting Females: Critical Issues in the History and Sociology of Women's Sport.* London: Routledge, 2002. Print.

Hills, Matt. *Fan Cultures.* London: Routledge, 2017. Print.

"In PICS: Female Fans @ FIFA World Cup." *Indiatimes.com.* N.p., 14 Jun. 2014. Web. 30 Nov. 2017<https://www.indiatimes.com/football-world-cup-2014/glamzone/in-pics-female-fans-@-fifa-world-cup-2014_-155034.html/>.

Jenkins, Henry. *Textual Poachers.* New York: Routledge, 1992. Print.

Jenson, Joli. "Fandom as Pathology: The Consequences of Characterization." *The Adoring Audience: Fan Culture and Popular Media.* Ed. Lisa A. Lewis. London: Routledge, 1992. 9-29. Print.

Jones, Katharine W. "Female Fandom: Identity, Sexism, and Men's Professional Football in England." *Sociology of Sport Journal* 25.4 (2008): 516-37. Print.

Messner, Michael A. "Sports and Male Domination: The Female Athlete as Contested Ideological Terrain." *Sociology of Sport Journal* 5.3 (1988):197-211. Print.

Messner, Michael A., Margaret Carlisle Duncan, and Kerry Jensen. "Separating the Men from the Girls: The Gendered Language of Televised Sports." *Gender and Society* 7.1 (1993): 121-37. Print.

Pope, Stacey. "There Are Some Daft People Out There!: Exploring Female Sport and Media Fandoms." *Sport in Society* 17.2 (2014): 254-69. Print.

Prasad, M Madhava. "Fan Bhakti and Subaltern Sovereignty: Enthusiasm as a Political Factor" *Economic and Political Weekly* 44. 29 (2009): 68-76. Print.

Zubernis, Lynn, and Katherine Larsen. "Fan Studies at the Crossroads: An Interview with Lynn Zubernis and Katherine Larsen (Part Two)." *henryjenkins.org.* N.p., 7 Sep. 2012. Web. 25 Nov. 2017. <http://henryjenkins.org/2012/09/fanstudies-at-the-crossroads-an-interview-with-lynn-zubernis-and-katherinelarsen-part-two.html,/>.

Further Reading

Booth, Paul. *Crossing Fandoms: SuperWhoLock and the Contemporary Fan Audience*. London: Palgrave Macmillan, 2016. Print.

Booth, Paul. *Digital Fandom: New Media Studies*. New York, NY: Peter Lang, 2010. Print.

Stein, Louisa Ellen. *Millennial Fandom: Television Audiences in the Transmedia Age*. Iowa City: U of Iowa, 2015. Print.

2.

Discourse on Fandom in Modern India:
Where do We Stand?

Priyanka Shivadas

University of New South Wales Canberra, Australia

Rudyard Kipling in his *Barrack-room Ballads* (1892) left us with, perhaps, one of the most controversial thoughts that remains to this day much reflected on. He wrote, 'Oh East is East, and West is West, and never the twain shall meet'. However, to put a spin on Kipling's particularly ominous-sounding words, West and East do come together in the same line, albeit as a point of comparison for each. This chapter, too, is concerned with a comparative study of the discourse on fandom in the West and modern India. This is not another attempt which continues to think and theorize in terms of a basic opposition between West and East, ultimately applauding one and disparaging the other, but wishes to understand the position of the latter better. The second reason for a comparative approach is that the vantage point from which I will be presenting my view on the discourse on fandom in modern India is that of the Hindi film industry, universally referred to as Bollywood, again as a cultural phenomenon studied, more often than not, vis-à-vis its Western counterpart—Hollywood. The third reason remains that much of the canonical and theoretical constructs in fan studies perused today are of Anglo-American origin. Therefore, to understand the discourse on fandom in India in isolation from the earlier and latest currents in the Anglo-American scholarship on the subject seems un-ideal, or even impossible. It may help to first present a survey of the development of fan studies since its establishment in the English-speaking Western world.

It is generally acknowledged that the publication of *Textual Poachers* (1992) by Henry Jenkins marked the beginning of fan studies in the West by taking fans as subjects that warranted serious scholarly investigation. *Enterprising Women* published in the same year by Camille Bacon-Smith has been noted as another important pioneering study in the field.[1] The most striking aspect of these two texts, according to several scholars, was not their ability to begin a critical conversation on audiences and consumers of cultural goods or popular entertainments but that they adopted an ethnographic approach.

They spoke directly to communities of fans. In *Textual Poachers,* Jenkins' focus was on one particular community. He described this community as "an amorphous but still identifiable grouping of enthusiasts of film and television which calls itself media fandom" (Jenkins 2). He goes on to add that

> this group embraces not a single text or even a single genre but many texts—American and British dramatic series, Hollywood genre films, comic books, Japanese animation, popular fiction (particularly science fiction, fantasy, and mystery)—and at the same time, it constructs boundaries that generally exclude other types of texts (notably soap opera and for the most part, commercial romance). (Jenkins 2)

Jenkins aimed to enable his readers to see what his stated subject of study—the media fans—did with the texts they came to consume ardently and quite avariciously, but in the process, he also sought to redefine "the public identity of fandom" (Jenkins 8). This meant that he first tackled the demeaning notions and misconceptions that existed around what it meant to be a fan.

In the first chapter of his book, Jenkins lists the many commonly-held stereotypes about fans. These include brainless consumers, hoarders of worthless knowledge, social misfits, feminized/desexualized, infantile, intellectually immature individuals, and finally, those who are unable to separate fantasy from reality (Jenkins 10). These stereotypes, he notes, have much to do with the etymology of the word. The term 'fan' has its roots in the Latin word 'fanaticus,' meaning "of or belonging to the temple, a temple servant, a devotee" (Jenkins 12). In time, it gathered so many negative connotations that it became difficult to shake them off. As Jenkins remarks:

> [The] abbreviated form, 'fan,' first appeared in the late 19th century in journalistic accounts describing followers of professional sports teams (especially in baseball) at a time when the sport moved from a predominantly participant activity to a spectator event, but soon was expanded to incorporate any faithful 'devotee' of sports or commercial entertainment. One of its earliest uses was about women theatre-goers, "Matinee Girls," who male critics claimed had come to admire the actors rather than the plays. If the term "fan" was originally evoked in a somewhat playful fashion and was often used sympathetically by sportswriters, it never fully escaped its earlier connotations of religious and political zealotry, false beliefs, orgiastic excess, possession, madness, connotations that seem to be at the heart of many of the representations of fans in contemporary discourse. (12-13)

Jenkins' intervention, in essence, was to communicate more meaningful and complex ways to conceive of fans. He attributes the reason for the disreputable characterization of fans to the underlying anxieties of the inheritors and vanguards of the bourgeois culture. Fan behaviour threatens them by blurring the dividing line that exists between high and low culture, reason and emotion, popular and elitist preference. Jenkins evokes Bourdieu who in his *Distinction: A Social Critique of the Judgement of Taste* has suggested that "the most intolerable thing for those who regard themselves as possessors of legitimate culture is the sacrilegious reuniting of tastes which taste dictates shall be separated" (Bourdieu 56-57). In *The Adoring Audience: Fan Culture and Popular Media*, edited by Lisa A. Lewis and published the same year as *Textual Poachers*, the first chapter titled "Fandom as Pathology: The Consequences of Characterization" by Joli Jenson brings out the same concerns and rushes to a similar conclusion. Jenson points out "the beliefs evidenced in the stigmatization of fans are inherently conservative, and they serve to privilege the wealthy, educated and powerful" (Jenson 25). To return to Jenkins, he goes a step further by articulating an answer to the problem—how do we characterize fans, after all? According to Jenkins, they are textual[2] poachers, i.e.

> Rejecting the aesthetic distance Bourdieu suggests is a cornerstone of bourgeois aesthetics, fans enthusiastically embrace favored texts and attempt to integrate media representations into their own social experience. Unimpressed by institutional authority and expertise, the fans assert their right to form interpretations, to offer evaluations, and to construct cultural canons. Undaunted by traditional conceptions of literary and intellectual property, fans raid mass culture, claiming its materials for their use, reworking them as the basis for their cultural creations and social interactions. (Jenkins 18)

This rereading of the activities of fans started a revolution, so to speak in media and cultural studies' departments which encompass fan studies.

One of the major developments in fan studies since the publication of Jenkins' discipline-shaping text has been the spread of the Internet. The Internet has allowed fan communities to evolve transmedia practices and form wider networks that operate even transcontinentally. This has led to a great many changes not only in the research methodology adopted by fan studies scholars but also in the relationship between fans and stars. As Lucy Bennett notes:

> Whereas in previous years, fans could send messages to the object of fandom via a letter in the post, which may have been filtered by management, the possibility for a direct and more immediate connection has arisen, through social media platforms such as Twitter, Facebook, and Instagram. . . . Through social media, public figures can now seemingly speak directly to their fanbase without news or management filters. (8)

Sam Ford, another scholar, has visualized a host of other developments in fan studies. These include the dichotomization of the activities of fans into affirmational and transformational, of content into drillable texts and accretive texts and secondly, the appropriation of the figure of the fan by the media and other businesses, including those in the creative industry, with the view to make money. Ford stresses that certain types of activities and texts which are referred to as transformational and drillable respectively are being given a lot more importance in fan studies scholarship than the other.[3] Secondly, with the spurt of interest in fan communities by the media and other corporations, there has been a move towards controlling fan events, activities, and even tastes. Moreover, the value of fandom comes to be gauged in economic terms (Ford). The issues raised by Ford present an adequate picture of the most pressing concerns in the field of fan studies at present. The fourth annual conference of the Fan Studies Network at the University of East Anglia, Norwich (held from 25-26 June 2016) reiterated some of these issues. The keynote address delivered by none other than Henry Jenkins sought to push "fandom studies to engage more fully with issues of race and cultural difference," linking like many have in the past fan activities and fan studies to forms of political activism and mobilization ("FSN 2016 Draft Programme").

Moving to the next section of this chapter, I want to begin by stressing that at the aforementioned conference, two papers concerned themselves with India as a socio-cultural and geographic location and both of them were, not so surprisingly, on Bollywood. In my search as well for scholarship on fan studies concerning India, the most exciting work I found has been in the realm of Bollywood. The reason for this may be very simple—Bollywood is a major cultural and entertainment industry even on a global scale, and it has an overwhelming influence on the cultural sphere of India and its people, Indian diasporic communities everywhere, and even foreigners. As early as 1991, in *Stardom: Industry of Desire*, edited by Christine Gledhill, there was a chapter called "Three Indian Film Stars" by Behroze Gandhy and Rosie Thomas. It was, however, more of a commentary on the female stars in India through the examples of Nadia (born as Mary Evans in 1910 in Perth), Nargis Dutt, and Smita Patil than the relationship between stars and fans. What's relevant to fan studies, however, is the following observation with which Gandhy and Thomas begin:

> Early each morning a saffron-robed figure appears on the balcony of a suburban house in Hyderabad. A small crowd gathers to receive the blessings of N.T. Rama Rao, the top star of the Telugu cinema, best known over the years for playing the god Krishna. That he was also elected Chief Minister of Andhra Pradesh in 1983 points to the complex way in which the relationship between divinity, film, and politics is

lived—and exploited—in India. While top Bombay stars no longer act in mythological films, as the genre has been in decline there since the 1960s, the parallels between Indian stars and the gods of the Hindu pantheon are frequently remarked upon: both are colourfully larger than life, their lives and loves, including moral lapses, the subject of voyeuristic fascination and extraordinary tolerance, and stars accept, on the whole graciously, an adoration close to veneration. (111)

Almost a decade and a half later, in 2007, in *Fandom: Identities and Communities in a Mediated World*, Aswin Punathambekar in his chapter titled "Between Rowdies and Rasikas" stating his objective says:

In this paper, I argue against framing fan activity in Indian film culture in terms of devotional excess or relation to political mobilization in south India. . . . Following this, I argue for a reassessment of the figure of the fan and the need to dismantle the binary of fan-as-rowdy versus fans-as-Rasika and, instead, locate the "fan" along a more expansive continuum of participatory culture. (199)

Punathambekar builds his case by asking us to look at fan activities on the Internet and uses the example of the online newsgroup that fans of A.R. Rahman formed on 1 January 1999. He says:

This is a space that brings together, for instance, fourth-generation Tamil-Malaysians, second-generation Indian Americans, Indians in Gulf countries like Dubai, middle-class youth in urban India, and a growing number of non-Indian fans ... The primary activity that defines this group is a detailed discussion of Rahman music ... Over the last two years, fans based in different cities around the world have begun meeting off-line to extend discussions conducted online, to help organize Rahman concerts, and, in some cases, to form informal bands and perform Rahman songs. (Punathambekar 201-202)

In the second section of his chapter, Punathambaker works to dissemble the conventional image of the fan in India as the rowdy (ill-mannered and loud) by pointing out like his predecessors that this is constructed socially to maintain hierarchies of cultural production and taste. Additionally, he urges us to locate the figure of the fan "as a construct that is not eternal and essential but rather, as shaped equally by industry practices, textual properties of film-based content that flow across multiple media, and social interactions in identifiable fan communities" if we are to broaden our understanding (Punathambekar 207). Finally, just before ending the chapter with a call to focus on transnational fan communities, Punathambekar speaks of how the predominant scholarly literature on fandom has been produced by Anglo-American contexts, and it has "moved from talking about fans as infringers/poachers (Jenkins 1992) to analyse how fans today operate as lead users, surplus audiences, grassroots intermediaries, the 'long tail,' performers, content generators, and even future talent for media companies (Jenkins 2006)" (Punathambekar 208). Punathambekar's chapter in a way is a treatise on how to move from talking of Indian fans as rowdies/*rasikas* (Rasika is translated as connoisseur) to examine their activities in more complex frameworks and in that sense is an argument that superimposes Western conceptual strategies on an understanding of fandom in India. So the question remains: is the discourse on fandom in India a sub-discipline that feeds off of its dominant other and uses the latter's categories of analysis despite the difference in contexts? In the following section of the paper, I will attempt to respond to this question with the help of none other than Bollywood or more precisely, through one of its latest productions *Fan* (2016).

Produced by Yash Raj Films and directed by Maneesh Sharma, *Fan* has Shah Rukh Khan in its lead role, rather lead roles. Shah Rukh plays both the insensitive and self-centered Bollywood celebrity Aryan Khanna and the crazed, obsessively dangerous Aryan Khanna's fan, Gaurav Chandna. The film received mostly positive responses. Reviewing the film for *The Guardian*, Mark Kermode is all praises for the lead actor who "outdoes himself twice in this dual-role psychological thriller" ("Fan review" n.pag.). Writing for *The Indian Express*, Shubra Gupta claims the film to be an "out-and-out SRK show, in which the star proves again that he can greenlight roles completely out of his comfort zone and deliver" ("Fan movie review" n.pag.). While both the reviewers are right in pointing out that it is indeed the real star that carries *Fan* to glorious heights, it is troubling that there is not enough emphasis on the figure of the fan that is, in all honesty, the true impetus for the basic plot of the film. For this chapter, let us then focus on the kind of representation the film *Fan* is of fans.

Representations are important because even when they don't come across as completely realistic, they express the worldview or cultural consciousness of a certain community of people. Sometimes representations are not only revelatory but also reinforce ideas. *Fan* is a representation of what it means to be a fan and simultaneously the representation of a man who has risen from one of the billion Indians to become the *Baadshah* of Bollywood; it is also a representation of the fan-star relationship. When the film begins, Gaurav Chandna, a little boy of not more than six or seven years of age, is shown as the quintessential fan who has made a "connection" with his idol Aryan Khanna and cannot explain why or how. He says, "*connection bhi na kamaal ki cheez hain. Bas ho gaya tho ho gaya*" (translated[4] as: when you make a connection [with someone], it is a wonderful thing. It just happens). Playing true to the most prevalent and prevailing notions on the reason for someone being a fan, Gaurav's fandom is also portrayed as an accident – it is something that he has no control over. Gaurav goes on to add, "*Jo kuch bhi usne kiya, mene use apne life mein cut, copy, paste kiya. Bas phark sirf itna hain, udhar vo star bana, mein uska fan*" (translated as: whatever he did, I did the same thing in my life with only one difference between us—while he became a star, I became his fan). This is supposed to be the moment when the film plunges its audience into the reality of Gaurav—when the gulf between the two personae that is played by the same actor becomes all too evident.

Gaurav Chandna, who has won a local talent show called Super Sitara Competition and prize money of rupees twenty-thousand by impersonating his idol Aryan Khanna, embarks on a journey to Mumbai to meet the star on his birthday. He cannot conceive of any reason why Aryan might not want to meet him. After all, the star has time and again said that whatever he is, it is because of his fans; if it wasn't for them, he would be nothing. More importantly, Gaurav has imprudently presumed that there could be no fan of Aryan greater than himself. Waiting in front of Aryan's mansion, he tries to explain to the security guard that he should be let in because he is not like the rest of the screaming mob waiting to catch a glimpse of Aryan. But when Aryan finally appears at the balcony of his mansion, the crowd goes berserk and Gaurav shrinks into a tiny speck of a human figure, disappearing into the sea of people. Following this event, he tries again to reach out to his idol. His repeated attempts to meet Aryan and spend, as he emphasizes, '5 minutes' with him, however, are thwarted, ultimately landing him in prison at the order of none other than Aryan himself. When he discovers this during a tension-fraught exchange with Aryan at the police station, Gaurav feels betrayed and worse; he feels shattered—heartbroken. Lying in the prison cell for two days, he sweats profusely, eats nothing, and finally, vomits, indicating a purging of sorts, if not of sins, but of his love for Aryan. When he comes out of prison, he is no longer the fan that he was. His unconditional love and admiration for his hero Aryan have morphed into something dangerous that borders on monomania.

The next time Gaurav meets Aryan, the fan is interested in only one thing which is a public apology for tearing down what was most precious to him. In a climax, perhaps not too unexpected, Gaurav kills himself, declaring to his idol in the last moments of his life, "*rehne de yaara, tu nahi samjhega*" (translated as: let it be, you will not understand). Thus, the plot of the film, it would seem, employs the figure of the fan, like countless other suspense films and detective shows as a stock figure that provokes terror and must ultimately be gotten rid of for the sake of the society. In 1996, Robert De Niro enacted a similar role in a film titled *The Fan*. Playing the character of Gil Renard, who lives, loves, and breathes baseball, De Niro delivers a great performance, making the film seem better than it is. When the film begins, he is shown to be excitedly awaiting the opening day when his favourite team Giants—which has just signed a forty-million-dollar contract with an extremely gifted baseball player Bobby Rayburn—will begin its regular season. Rayburn is also Renard's playing-field idol. But as the film progresses, the playing season proves to be not only an extremely challenging and humiliating time marked by losses for Rayburn, but Renard also loses his job as a salesman and gets issued a court order barring him from seeing his young son at the directions of his estranged wife. Consequently, Renard takes to stalking Rayburn with an ulterior motive to help the baseball star regain his form because he believes that somehow, he is part of the Giants team just as Rayburn is and must act to help the team win.

In an incredulous turn of events, Rayburn manages to step up his game after another player who was playing tremendously well that season is murdered by Renard. Renard believes that the death of the other player is the reason behind Rayburn's return to his original form. In return, Renard wants "a simple thank you". The rest of the film takes a rather strange turn. As Stephen Holden, a reviewer for *The New York Times* summarized, "Before it's over, Gil has kidnapped and terrorized Bobby's young son, who is the same age as his boy. The drama screeches to a ludicrous climax in which a furious rainstorm interrupts a ball game whose life-and-death agenda depends on Bobby's slamming a home run and publicly dedicating it to his stalker" ("How Baseball Becomes an Irrational Pastime" n.pag.). In the end, Renard is shot dead by policemen on the playing field in front of all the other baseball fans, almost as a warning about what happens when one of them crosses the line. On initial consideration, the Hollywood film *The Fan* and the Bollywood film *Fan* come across as similar conceptions of the stereotypical image of the fan, with the latter following in the footsteps of the former. Both the films, after all, project fans as emotionally immature psychopaths in hiding who find themselves after having crossed the point of no return left with no alternative but to die. There can certainly be found more examples of the representation of fans in the modern Indian context. The documentary *Being Bhaijaan*, directed by Shabani Hassanwalia and Samreen Farooqui, would be another good example. The documentary, purportedly more realistic than popular cinema, follows the life of a young Salman fan from the small town of *Chhindwara* in central India. The intention behind making the documentary was, however, largely to explore the different shades of Salman Khan and to understand the construct of 'masculinity' as perceived by the fans of Salman which make up a large section of the young Indian male population. For this chapter, I believe a more mainstream piece of artwork such as *Fan* with its focus on the character of the fan would be a better model to work through.

Going back to Shah Rukh's *Fan* and Robert De Niro's *The Fan,* the films have much in common thematically even with different production timelines (*The*

Fan precedes *Fan* by two decades). Thus, can it be safely argued that it is only natural that the discourse on fandom in the modern Indian context displays many of the same thematic concerns as the West? My conclusion is even though the discourse on fandom in modern India tends to do so, it should not. A deeper analysis of the film *Fan* tells us that the figure of the fan is rather complex and not quite in the way Jenkins thought fans were a complex and special set of the audience because their interaction with their object of fandom produced cultural material of significance and had other social implications. Rather, the figure of the fan is complex because in the Indian context even in the secular age, it is subconsciously and consciously likened to that of the devotee (which in itself is a complex figure) because of the commitment they each display to the object of their worship. Scholars such as Punathambekar may wish to look beyond a quasi-religious framework to locate the dynamics of the Indian star-fan relationship, but it is my argument that it is not desirable to do so considering how deeply our folk and classical traditions have been permeated by religious and mythological texts and precepts. Note that contrary to the character of Gil Renard in *The Fan*, Gaurav Chandna in *Fan* does not face a death of ignominy but in his death, he merges with the star (symbolized by the myriad bright, shining lights that twinkle in the background as he falls to the ground from the top floor of a building). Also, in the second half of the film, the fan is shown to be as good as the star in every way as almost everyone fails to tell the difference between the two.

Furthermore, in a scene in the first half of the film when Aryan is face-to-face with Gaurav at the police station and asks him why he should spare even a second of his time to meet one of his innumerable fans, Gaurav stands up to look down upon the star and says while impersonating him, "*Kyunki mein jo bhi hoon, jahan bhi hoon, jis makam pe hoon, apne fans ke vaije se hoon. Gaurav hain tho Aryan hain. Agar Gaurav nahi tho Aryan kuch bhi nahi*" (translated as: because whatever I am, it is because of my fans. If it isn't for them, I am nothing. Because there is Gaurav, there is Aryan. If there is no Gaurav, then there is no Aryan). The scene has been shot such that the audience is made to realize that the fan is as important as, if not more important than, the star. It is difficult to imagine a similar scene played out in a Hollywood film with the same emotional impact and it does not at least in the case of *The Fan*. This is because the cultural consciousness of India is not the same as that of the US. In the Indian context, everyone including non-Hindus is deeply familiar with the trope of mythology where the devotee through the power of his or her true devotion gains not just the blessings of the god he or she is devoted to but is exalted to godly status. For example, Hanuman becomes a god through his devotional service and commitment to Ram.

To conclude, I would like to stress that the discourse on fandom in India, even though it has developed in parallel to and with an awareness of the developments in the West, would do better to incorporate native categories of analysis. That is, it should recognize the continuity of Indian cultural traditions, knowledge, and beliefs even in the face of social change triggered by modernization. Secondly, it must also be noted that emotions have played a significant role in Indian aesthetics philosophy. Also, to Indian philosophers the relationship of emotion to reason was not of much importance. Therefore, to better understand the reaction of the audience or a special set of them called fans and the nature of their interaction with various artistic expressions or forms and artists, emotions have to be given serious consideration. That is, in the Indian context, it is important to emphasize the fans' emotional engagement with the object of their fandom and prioritize the study of fan emotions and their emotional experiences. If we fail to do so, fans will at some point in the future turn to the fan studies scholars of India with the words: "*rehne de yaara, tu nahi samjhega.*"

Notes

1. See the works of Sam Ford and Lucy Bennett listed in the bibliography.
2. The term 'texts' refers to a huge range of sources. For example, stars or celebrities in themselves can be considered as symbolic texts, as was suggested by Jenkins.
3. Sam Ford defines affirmational fan activities as "discussion-based fan engagement" (example: a critique of the source text) and transformational as "production-oriented" (example: fan fiction that responds to a source text). Drillable texts are those that are more or less "contained" (example: TV shows that run for a limited number of seasons), and accretive texts are those that are extremely heavy in terms of their volume (example: soap opera). His plea to other fan studies scholars is not to build "taste hierarchy" within the discipline by prioritizing one over the other.
4. The translation of Hindi dialogues of the film *Fan* that appear in this chapter has been done by the author.

Bibliography

Being Bhaijaan. Dirs. Shabani Hassanwalia and Samreen Farooqui. PSBT. 2014. Film.

Bennett, Lucy. "Tracing Textual Poachers: Reflections on the Development of Fan Studies." *The Journal of Fandom Studies* 2.1 (2014): 5-20. doi: 10.1386/jfs.2.1.5_1

Bourdieu, Pierre. *Distinction: A Social Critique of the Judgement of Taste*. Trans. Richard Nice. Cambridge, MA: Harvard University Press, 1996. Print.

"FSN 2016 Draft Programme." *fanstudies.files*. N.p., n.d. Web. 3 Apr. 2017. <https://fanstudies.files.wordpress.com/2016/05/fsn-2016-draft-programme-v2.pdf/>.

Fan. Dir. Maneesh Sharma. Yash Raj Films. 2016. Film.

Ford, Sam. "Fan Studies: Grappling with and 'Undisciplined' Discipline." *The Journal of Fandom Studies* 2.1 (2014): 53-71. doi: 10.1386/jfs.2.1.53_1

Gandhy, Behroze, and Rosie Thomas. "Three Indian Film Stars." *Stardom: Industry of Desire*. Ed. Christine Gledhill. London: Routledge, 1991. 107-31. Print.

Gupta, Shubra. "Fan Movie Review: SRK is Played to All His Strengths in the Film." *indian express.com* N.p., 4 Apr. 2016. Web. 4 Apr. 2017. <http://indianexpress.com/article/entertainment/movie-review/fan-movie-review-shah-rukh-khan-stars-2754519/>.

Holden, Stephen. "How Baseball Becomes an Irrational Pastime." *nytimes.com*. N.p., 16 Aug. 1996. Web. 20 Apr. 2017. <http://www.nytimes.com/movie/review?res=9805EFDE1031F935A2575BC0A960958260/>.

Jenkins, Henry. *Textual Poachers: Television Fans and Participatory Culture*. New York: Routledge, 1992. Print.

Jenson, Joli. "Fandom as Pathology: The Consequences of Characterization." *The Adoring Audience: Fan Culture and Popular Media*. Ed. Lisa A. Lewis. London: Routledge, 1992. 9-29. Print.

Kermode, Mark. "Fan Review—Creepy Intrigue and Big Action." *theguardian.com*. N.p., 17 Apr. 2016. Web. 4 Apr. 2017. <https://www.theguardian.com/film/2016/apr/17/fan-review-shah-rukh-khan-maneesh-sharma/>.

Punathambekar, Aswin. "Between Rowdies and Rasikas: Rethinking Fan Activity in Indian Film Culture" *Fandom: Identities and Communities in a Mediated World*. Ed. Jonathan Gray, Cornell Sandvoss, and C. Lee Harington. New York: New York University Press, 2007. 198-209. Print.

The Fan. Dir. Tony Scott. Tri-Star Pictures. 1996. Film.

3.

Stardom: Deceiving the 'Self'

Himanshu Khosla

Punjab Technical University, India

In modern times one can see the desperation of seeking attention in the number of photographs people have been uploading on Facebook. It is infinite likes and dislikes that decide the mental strength of an individual. The ever-increasing statistics of increased risk factors for an increasing suicide rate, depression, and low self-esteem are consequences of excessive attention sought after by people influenced by stars. This chapter underpins the strategic representation of star-self in the commercial world and its oft-ignored tragic aftermaths. It is essential in present times to look at the chain of exploring one's notion of 'self' through various digital and social media platforms which have with time shown an adverse effect on the lives of people in general.

With the 'Dark is Beautiful' campaign, one begins to question the deepening impact of what one is constantly reminded of about the one's self as a citizen of an erstwhile colonised nation. The campaign was launched in 2009 by *Women of Worth* to draw attention towards obsession society has with fairness. Unjust bias on the basis of skin colour leads to the corrosion of self-worth of countless people. The initiative was an attempt to celebrate hues of beauty by challenging colour-based discrimination. Earlier the obsession with fairness exhibited women wishing to be fair to fulfill patriarchal criteria for marriage. Often reflected in the newspaper, this need was then observed in the advertising industry. Later sensing an unfulfilled need, the advertising industry came out with special fairness products for men as well. The markets were flooded with face wash and face creams for fairness; acne creams were launched by numerous firms competing for better sales by developing more effective advertising strategies. In this regard, the actress Nandita Das has observed, "Now the insecurities of men are also surfacing with an equal number of fairness products for them. Such pressure and so little public debate around it!" (Chopra n.pag.).

Film stars are the faces influencing modern India. Thus, a new demand for fair men has a powerful impact on a color-conscious culture. For the first time, gender stereotypes are not restrained to women. Shahrukh Khan, John

Abraham, Sushant Singh Rajput, Virat Kohli, M.S. Dhoni and so on are a few star names that show youth a path to stardom. Interestingly, it was through the mindless and robotic conduct of following the rat race that invites larger audiences to enslave themselves like drug addicts in the world of fair-complexioned role models. The impact, however, is deep-rooted, affecting the producer, actor, and audience. The induced fear followed by careless advertising has drawn varied responses.

Groysberg, Lee and Nanda have discussed the 'visible professionals' at length in their research which looks at performance and public recognition as two variables of success. The forecasts of new stars are based on the accuracy of their refined sense of these two variables. This further helps them establish relationships with the audience who estimate the probability of their exit from the industry based on the performance of the competitor star. Greater is the visibility of the star, easier it is for them to achieve prominence. However, the vulnerability of the one newly anointed as the star is no less than the normative expectations held by the established stars. Looking at the dimensions of this concept, the debate pays attention towards the process of transforming ordinary people into celebrities. The social and cultural rooting often is pitted against the compromise stars have to make because of the star culture that manifests commodification.

Commodification stretches power by making most celebrities the symbols of social cohesion. Generally, this power helps many of these stars to achieve political success. Many prominent stars like Amitabh Bachchan, Jaya Bachchan, Shatrughan Sinha, Jayaprada, Rekha, Dara Singh, Dharmendra, Hema Malini, Kiran Kher, Moon Moon Sen, Paresh Rawal, Gul Panag, and others have cautiously used their celebrity image to win elections. It is symptomatic of how fans and the majority of the people interpret celebrity culture. The masses are mostly driven by the star-image. Stardom affects the general community when people make these stars their reference points. Blurring the distance between the ordinary and what is implied by being a celebrity, people are influenced to follow the notion of individuality as showcased by their favourite stars. Remarkably, when one looks at the paradox of celebritisation, one precisely refers to the process of transforming the ordinary into celebrities. The essential porters of this transformation include both visible and non-visible professionals like media, stylists, and critics who legitimise the fantasies of society by creating the star one consequently becomes. Dyer says celebrities are both labour and the thing that labour produces. In the process of looking at this fragmented division of the self that emulates individualisation of star-self, the challenge is to trace the starting point of the transformation.

It is, therefore, crucial to look at the challenges of time that cannot be measured within the normative starting or endpoint. The question remains how one's understanding of fame stretches within the star culture of a nation. Encircled within the national boundaries, one finds an overlapping patchwork of star culture within the small space of television and larger canvas of the cinema. Although fame has been defined and discussed in previous ages, the relative lack of historical star culture against the modern star culture merely looks at it as an expanding phenomenon proclaimed within the given time frame.

Concerning public awareness of the time period and star culture, veteran actor Shabana Azmi posted on her Twitter account on 15 April 2017` how at Cannes Film Festival 1976 the film was important, not the clothes (Sharma, "ShabanaAzmi's Photo From Cannes" n.pag.). *Nishant* was officially selected in 1976 and, in 2017, her film *The Black Prince* has been screened with Satinder Sartaj walking the red carpet for the first time in a turban. Running in its 76th year, Cannes Film Festival today shows the obsession stars have with the red-carpet appearances diverting the point of appreciating cinema to appreciating the attires and styles of representative stars.

At Festival de Cannes 2017, Anupama Chopra interviewed Nandita Das for a popular media firm *Film Companion*. Nandita showed her concern towards the growing obsession of star culture digressing from the significant success pillar of performance towards variables that affect not only Indian cinema economically but also the quality of films that could have made to the list of selected films at the festival. She aptly stated, "You have to be truly local for a film to be to be Global, local in its flavour and its context. What you are trying to say can be universal. . .stories that are rooted are universal. . .emotions are universal" (Chopra n.pag.). She pointed towards theatre artists turned into commercial actors like Nawazuddin who still struggle for sponsors for their films. The standards set by industry have been restricted to the financial gains one can make out of a commercial film outrightly as against the art film that might truly be a great contribution to the history of Indian cinema made by gifted thinkers of and about society.

A series of biopics made by directors in 2016-17 shows how real-life heroes have been the first choice of directors to evade the gap created in the past because of celebritisation. The popular films like *Dangal, Mary Kom, Sachin, M.S. Dhoni* were based on the lives of common men and women, making it large in the sports world. However, by the end of 2018, there are 14 real-life stories with their cinematic adaptation to be released the following year.

Manto based on the life of the writer Sadat Hasan Manto, *Daddy* based on the life of don turned politician Arun Gawli, *The Accidental Prime-Minister* based on the life of India's former Prime Minister Manmohan Singh, *Haseena: The Queen of Mumbai* based on Dawood Ibrahim's sister Haseena Parker's life, *Jhalki* based on the life of Kailash Sathyarthi, Nobel Peace Prize winner 2014, *Padman* based on the life of Padma Shri winner Arunachalam Muruganantham, *Mogul* based on late music baron Gulshan Kumar's life, *Gold* based on the life of hockey player Kishan Lal under whose leadership the Indian Hockey team bagged the Gold Medal at the 1948 London Olympics, *Manikarnika: The Queen of Jhasi* depicting life of Rani Lakshmibai and *Saare Jahan Se Achcha* based on the life of India's first astronaut to have landed on the moon are a few films to look forward to.

It is interesting to note how modern media participates and presents an event transforming it into a manifestation of stars without the essence of the image availed for the consumption. Much of this manifestation involves what the recipients expect. Generally, the factors affecting include popular culture transmitting the opinions of the modern elite. The word 'modern' here adequately refers to the commercial population that is inclusive of media and the young audience who eagerly reach out to multimedia platforms. Multimedia platforms, however, capture the popular culture.

The purpose of composing and capturing reality has now been commercialized. Mirroring representation of society, the process of both commercialization and commodification creates a star. Stars as individuals who are much more than the accumulation of their public image. Embodying the onscreen and off-screen images of their complicated personality, they often deceive their 'self'. In projecting the expected reality of not lacking anything, many times stars are stressed. Being the face receiving constant overviews from the public, media and fans, their predilections perhaps primes into restrictive behaviour patterns.

Lately, newspapers have been emphasizing on the stars and how they had been dealing with depression. The list includes famous stars like Ranvir Singh and Deepika Padukone. Deepika battled with anxiety and depression at the peak of her career while she was attaining national and international recognition. Several articles state how hard it is to accept that a smiling star and a successful actor found herself 'choking' and 'broke into tears.' Eventually, she launched a social campaign with the 'Live Love Laugh Foundation' that encourages to break through the stigma, come out and seek help.

Another take at the old age of the stars can be noticed in how veteran actress Geeta Kapoor, who starred in the film *Pakheezah*, was abandoned by her son in a Mumbai hospital. The list includes the cinema's some of the greatest actors like Vinod Khanna, Raj Kiran—who was abandoned by his wife and children and was found in a mental hospital in America—and Satish Kaul (who was rescued by the Innovative Artist Welfare Association). It is essential to pay particular attention to ways in which stars demand heightened emotional and personal attention. It could be argued that stardom or star phenomenon depends majorly on the popular reception their films get. Denigrating reviews of the films make them vulnerable and eventually destroy their critical and commercial success as the star in later years of life.

Today the digital platform is full of articles written about body shaming. But what has gone unnoticed is how body-shaming did not begin in a day. It was injected like the drug abuse into our country. On the one hand, where the Kapoors of the film industry are considered to have a typical Punjabi body structure, it is an entirely different story for the audience to strive to look like the young charming Ranbir Kapoor. The long-standing connection between Bollywood and body-shaming can be seen in the articles written about Sonakshi Sinha, Parineeti Chopra, and Vidya Balan. Since stardom has distinctly followed the culture of presenting stars with the perfect body, Kareena inspired many to lose weight by sparking the trend for size zero. Young followers' desire to look like the star demonstrates their negatively changing satisfaction that they have with their bodies. There are several reports that state health hazards faced by stars like Kareena, Nicole Ross and others who fainted or collapsed on the set as they suffered from malnutrition.

It is significant to look at extreme cases of Uruguayan twenty-two-year-old model Luisel Ramos and her eighteen-year-old model sister Elina who died due to fasting and malnutrition. Eventually, in 2006 there was a ban on size zero at Uruguay Fashion Week. Marisol Touraine, France's Minister of social affairs and health, showed her concern towards anorexia, unrealistic body images promoted by beauty idols. Consequently, to protect the health of models, stars and the influenced youngsters, France has a law banning unhealthily thin fashion models. In 2015, the French National Assembly considered the health reform bill where the law was backed up by French MPs, who supported punishment for employing underweight models. Newspaper reports stated that those violating the law would be fined up to 75,000 euros or imprisonment for six months. The law also undertakes 'retouched photographs' or 'digitally altered photographs' of the models to avoid manipulation of the model's appearance. The models will have to provide a doctor's certificate with regard to their measured and regulated body mass index (BMI). France followed the suit after a similar law was passed by Spain, Italy, and Israel.

With various rumours circulating about stars and star kids, one of the most popular ones is how easy it is for them to drop a dozen pounds. With celebrity-nutritionists helping stars sculpt their bodies, the audience often ignores accumulated fitness time spent in exercising. The body transformation including both weight loss and weight gain have lately been pulled as bad influences. As discussed, breaking old traditions some stars have steered a debate around weight issues and how it could disturb good health, both mental and physical. The fragmentary and selective account given about stars on social media platforms has now witnessed a shift with blogging websites. With actors having a willingness to have dialogue, readers can now find their attitude towards life in their comments and blog writings. Bollywood actor, Fardeen Khan, states in his reply to his haters for trolling him for his weight gain:

> This worldwide behavioral pattern on the internet is disturbing even though I believe in absolutely free speech and opinions. Being a realist, I will caution that all we can hope to achieve by speaking out...is that the next time a person trolls purely for their amusement, he or she pauses to consider their own moral and ethical code. I also want them to honestly answer to themselves a very relevant question. Would they still feel empowered to troll if the anonymity offered by social media platforms on the internet did not exist?... I just want you all to know that after a very long time I am in a great space in my life. All I ask is for you to be happy for me and expect not to be disappointed for long. ("Not ashamed or offended" n.pag.)

The problem arises with constant reminders of dissatisfaction with one's own attributes. However, the disatisfaction is reflected in the constant striving one has for what one has not or could never have. For instance, the possibility of having a lighter skin tone has often led to using cosmetic products that have resulted in disastrous chemical reactions. Worldview justifications given by and to media about the stars have been changing the understanding of their 'selves'.

Sometimes the vision of the self is a reduced vision of one's life which is a consequence of undermining periods of crowning glory in the star's career. Transmitting the ideas and experiences of stars as the foreground of the subject, the theory of 'self' concerns with identity. Notwithstanding the binaries of cultural differences unsettling conditions of stars, working both locally and globally is found constrained within the parameters of their self. We have seen lately how the use of the word 'I' by stars in their speeches and thoughts reflected in their writings on digital platforms has been highly deceptive. In various ways, the social interaction has entangled star power over larger fans they have for the masses. Shahrukh Khan lately mentioned the controversy cooked up on the birth of his third child AbRam in his TEDx Talk. He clarified that his three-year-old son AbRam is not the 'lovechild' of his first son, Aryan. Problems like these can be defined as the problems of the star subject and their complex world often highly charged for their charisma. To look at the same act with a different analysis of selfhood, readers and viewers may understand how exhaustive their analysis of the star could be costing them both.

Sometimes the stars seek to present their subjective-self, forgetting the privileged position of availing freedom and setting the change in society. However, the challenges faced are often negotiated against the intense focus of them belonging to the class of society known for defying the norms. This can be seen in how inter-faith marriages or divorces or multiple marriages or changing one's own religion are accepted as the norm. On the contrary, the audience's perception of a star is open-ended yet known, understanding of their selfhood attained or understood by their meticulously maintained personality in the world of appearance.

Representation of a perfect male body with six-pack abs has led to an increase in the intake of steroids like decadurabolin, prednisone, and proteins. The common people have drawn a comparison in what is a mere representation of their lives or characters like them in cinema. What has gone unnoticed is that the actors or stars thrive and survive in the industry because of their looks, for it is their face and body that gets them going in the industry. This is, however, an irreconcilable representation of the common man who survives not on the basis of his appearance as much as he does on the basis of his performance at the workplace. The demands sought after are different for people working in different industries. The advertising industry has thinned this line of difference by blurring the depictions on television and other social media platforms.

While some stars like Aamir Khan embody respectable values with their concern towards honest citizenship on their show *Satyamev Jayate*, others exercise their individual rights with objective analyses of country's law treating stars as big as Sanjay Dutt equally. What makes the star-self a fragmented personality is the speculative choices made in life that test them for the truth and knowledge they gain about living. Influential contribution, thus, is another form of investigation in popular humanist culture in contemporary times. The goal to reach and discover the self looks at the stories that tell us how stars have been busy in meaning-making of varied cultures by adopting villages or by fighting battles against cancer and sharing the victorious story of them being survivors. Manisha Koirala has been confident in giving an explanation for self-contained emotions that formulated her unique and mysterious model of self-understanding. She told at TEDx Jaipur:

> Life had planned something else for me. That I would be thrown into a whirlwind of things where slowly I would lose it all. Initially, it started with a bad film like when I signed a bad film. I had developed an unhealthy lifestyle which was attracting a lot of bad companies…I used to have an entourage of friends, a huge circle of friends. But today I have a handful of them. (Sharma, "Manisha Koirala's TED Talk" n.pag.)

The insight that even stars are fallible and seek to understand fierce ideologies and dogma associated with stardom has perhaps given us flashes of how they seek resting-place in other humans. Indeed, even when we look at prominent suicide cases of actresses, such as Jiah Khan and Pratyusha Mukherjee, we see how they refused to encounter challenges that stardom pinned down for their better selves. The most crucial of all discussions is to protect the star self from a definitive destructive situation of a pretentious life. Of course, the schematic treatment of schizophrenia getting the better of Parveen Babi's personality or inconsistencies with which Meena Kumari or Madhubala moved from one wrong relationship to another until their death, reveal the story of the stars' private life. These actresses draw attention to the crucial absence of a true relation in their life. Most of their families have specifically been affected by their inability to provide a sensible model of family. Splitting the difference from a good relationship as against a bad one can be mapped through a sequence of relations Bollywood stars have been indulging in. The issues or discord in family relations at the personal front is seen as the bedrock of stars' widespread influence on the public. The hot-headed stars move into a different world away from the reality where the world is an embodiment of their desires, and not that of others.

The intense pressure of social living affects the love-lives of the stars at the core. Broken marriages and relationships do not come as a surprise under such social and cultural pressures. Justifying contemporary critical thought on these relations, Kangana Ranaut became a vehement opponent of how relationships are merely looked upon as a temporary replacement of one for another. Nilanjana Basu quotes her saying

> The letters that I might have written were brutally exposed to the world. How did I feel like a human being because every letter that you've written to your lover holds a lot of vulnerability? You are exposing part of your soul or yourself, not to the world but to an individual. I felt extremely naked in front of the world. I cried for nights in my room. People make fun of me. But I never answered to that brutality in the same spirit. I think that makes me see myself as a winner. (n.pag.)

Her point of contention was the crisis one faces in perpetual self-evaluation that is often a result of fundamental instability. As the stars enter the industry, this leads to them throwing everything in doubt since they become the bone of contention in media for most of the debates. Consequently, the way stars put 'I' in most interviews today is the beginning of a new understanding that reflects strengthened selfhood developed out of being bold in sharing the experience.

In the modern era, the commitment to attain the ideal of a stable relationship emerges in the thinking process which makes one a self-aware person instead of the star being. Petrifying the illusion that makes their world of fixed categories as professional and personal, the star-self is expected to control and regulate itself in the public sphere which most likely blurs the very difference between the two. The self is harassed until separated from other spontaneous roles played both on-screen and off-screen. In the process of tracking down the self, the axes of self's perspective reflect how success is counted against the career and money one has. Following their passion, they find their authentic selves. However, most often in due course, one realizes that the star-self has been buried beneath the expectations and demands of the audience.

Therefore, the study of 'self' seen as mediated in cinema can be noted as located in the socio-cultural context. Going beyond the politics of location, the star studies has been adopting a genealogical discourse. This discourse locates star-self in a specific context and situates cultural differences that explicate and trace the trend followed by the larger audience. The audience keenly observe stars as humans prone to impulse and sensation that distinguishes mind and soul. Many people have written about confessions and memoirs where the star justifies himself or herself. Stars like Dilip Kumar, Naseeruddin Shah, Rekha, Rishi Kapoor, and Karan Johar have put their selves at the centre to tell an original story in their memoirs, autobiographies, and biographies.

To name some of the popular autobiographies, one could read *The Substance and Shadow: An Autobiography* by Dilip Kumar, *And Then One Day: A Memoir* by Naseeruddin Shah, *Moments of Truth: My Life With Acting* by Roshan Taneja, *Mamta Kulkarni: Autobiography of an Yogini, Prem Naam Hai Mera* by Prem Chopra, *Romancing With Life* by Dev Anand, *Quiver* by Javed Akhtar, *Bonding: A Memoir* by Vyjayantimala, *Khullam Khulla: Rishi Kapoor Uncensored, The Style Diary of a Bollywood Diva* by Kareena Kapoor, and *An Unsuitable Boy* by Karan Johar. Some interesting biographies include *I want to Live: The Story of Madhubala, Meena Kumari: The Classic Biography, Rekha: The Untold Story,* and *Smita Patel: A Brief Incandescence.*

Furthermore, what unites these books in understanding star studies are the disparate and muddled places and events mentioned in the writings. The unity of such works is grounded in the feeling of being the star, living with the fragmented self, fighting petty squabbles and rivalries within. These events give a complete picture of the 'I' writing about life's interest without omissions. The inclusive phenomenon in these autobiographical and semi-autobiographical works is the way the writings avoid distortion in the dynamic unity of the celebrity culture.

The writings reflecting and representing stars in the state of more or less perfection leave readers engulfed in prejudice. In the attempt to liberate their true selves, a new star is born out of the writings. Contemplating the fallen nature of humankind, the writings trace the journey of a star in pursuing their ambition. This perhaps connects them with the thinking self, uniting them all in the self-conscious attempt of writing. The purposeful sense of selfhood attained in present times entitles them to dynamic processes essential for the emergence of a star and his or her talent. A systematic study of star biographies and their works helps us determine how the self-regulatory choices are a consequence of the stability they have financially, emotionally and socially. Self is then a mental construct, much affected by the degree of sensitivity that attunes the identity of the star.

The identity and the notion of self is moderated by cues given and received both by the star self and their fans or audience. The cues are nothing more than the evaluative cognitive signs that describe the star in a positive light making him or her different from the rest. The focus for one is to become the ideal while the other looks at becoming like the ideal. The evaluative judgment of the ideal is based on a series of perspectives forming goals and values of an individual. Interestingly, some fans have taken it to another level by having a star as an idol in the temples. The list includes a temple for the actor Amitabh Bachchan in Kolkata, for the actor turned politician Karunanidhi in Vellore, Tamil Nadu, for the actress Mamta Kulkarni in Nellore, Andhra Pradesh, for the actress Nagma in Tamil Nadu, and for the actor Rajinikanth in Kolar, Karnataka (Ajjampudi). Generating artistic legitimacy another list of Bollywood stars at Madame Tussauds wax museum has shown the social capital generated out of the cultural value created after their screen performances.

Taking the relational perspective of the star and audience within the cultural interface, the definitions and understandings of 'self' are distilled. In this way, self and identity remain connected as explanatory factors. Embodying the star-self, the stars are widely respected for their unique position. Stars can thus be understood as mesmerizing objects, constantly being watched and reviewed. However, the position of control is set across flashing surfaces applauding their performance. The sense of worth and competence is based on identity developed out of focus and commitment one has towards work. It is noticeable how the inner essence of the character that serves the actor in the long run as against the ephemeral star-self.

Beginning a massive publicity campaign, the discourse of star studies has also resulted in productive films on the subject that reflects striking it lucky phase in life. The audience can trace a journey of representation of 'self' in films like *Saransh, Fashion, Udta Punjab, Dear Zindagi,* and many others. These films have a common theme of dealing with the life problems in effective and affective ways to reach larger audiences. However, each of these films raises pertinent issues regarding the representation of 'self' that looks at the self through a three-gaze theory including the director's, the actor's and the viewer's notion of self-being created and reaffirmed in the process of receiving the film. In this process of observation, one can establish the connection star studies have with audience studies and the fact that star image is an idea culturally produced and reproduced routinely.

Bibliography

Ajjampudi, Vamshee. "List of Indian Actors Who Have Temples To Their Name" *Pycker*. N.p., 28 Feb. 2018. Web. 27 Jun. 2018. <https://pycker.com/articles/did-you-know-that-these-stars-have-temples-in-their-name/>

Basu, Nilanjana. "Kangna Ranaut On Leaked E-Mails To Hrithik Roshan:Felt Naked, Cried For Nights." *Ndtv.com*. N.p., 17 Dec. 2016. Web. 27 Jun. 2017. <http//:movies.ndtv.com/bollywood/kangana-ranaut-on-leaked-e-mails-to-hrithik-roshan-felt-naked-cried-for-nights-1638913/>.

Chopra, Anupama. "Nandita Das Interview Cannes Film Festival 2017." *Facebook.com*. N.p., 23 May 2017. Web. 2 Jun. 2017. <https://www.facebook.com/filmcompanion/videos/1205154129607873/>.

Dyer, Richard. *Heavenly Bodies: Film Stars and Society.* London: MacMillan, 1986. Print.

Groysberg, Boris, Linda-Eling Lee, and Ashish Nanda. "Can They Take It with Them? The Portability of Star Knowledge Workers' Performance." *Management Science* 54.7 (2008): 1213-1230. Print.

"Not ashamed or offended: Fardeen Khan on being trolled for weight gain" *Deccanchronicle.com*. N.p., 27 May 2016. Web. 10 Jun. 2017. <https://www.deccanchronicle.com/entertainment/bollywood/270516/not-ashamed-or-offended-fardeen-khan-on-being-trolled-for-weight-gain.html/>

Sharma, Isha. "Manisha Koirala's TED Talk On Finding The Meaning Of Life When Reality Hits Is A Must Watch." *IT Entertainment*. N.p., 5 Jun.2017. Web. 6 Jun. 2017.<http://www.indiatimes.com/entertainment/celebs/manisha-koirala-s-tedtalk-on-finding-the-meaning-of-life-when-reality-hits-is-a-must-watch/>.

Sharma, Isha. "ShabanaAzmi's Photo From Cannes 1976 Is Going Viral & It Has A Legit Reminder For All Of Us."*Indiatimes.com*. N.p., 22 May 2017. Web. 24 May 2017. <http//:www.indiatimes.com/entertainment/celebs/shabana-azmi-s-photo-from-cannes-1976-is-going-viral/>.

Further Reading

Kameshwari, A. "Deepika Padukone in Tears as She Talks About Depression: If It Wasn't For My Mother, I Wouldn't Be Here." *indianexpress.com* N.p., 10 Oct. 2016. Web. 31 May 2017. <http://indianexpress.com/article/entertainment/bollywood/deepika-padukone-in-tears-as-she-talks-depression/>.

"Shabana Azmi Shares a Throwback Picture From Cannes 1976 When 'The Film Was Important Not the Clothes'."*iDIVA.com*. N.p., 22 May 2017. Web. 26 May 2017. <http://www.idiva.com/news-entertainment/shabana-azmi-shares-a-throwback-picture-from-cannes-1976-when-quot/>.

4.

Discursive Power of Enigmatic Stars:
Dynamics of Celebrity Culture

Ruchi Sharma

Chitkara University, India

Seminal work of Richard Dyer, *Stars* (1979) established a new arena of research called star studies. This study looks at the contribution of stars in creating the meaning of the film-text. From the 1970s onwards, the narrative of films provided a serious arena of film research. By the twentieth century, cinema narratives redefined performance space concerning the performer. Eventually, on-screen and off-screen presence of the performers was captured in varied forms like biographies, both written and documented on celluloid and newspaper reports that mechanically reproduced reality. It was at this time that Butler observed, "meaning did not exist in the actor's performance, but rather in the manipulation of performance through editing" (342). Therefore, it is imperative to study interpretive efforts of the spectator or audience and the process of the star becoming a sign and text in itself.

Stars have been contributing fundamentally to the meaning of film-text, adding significant value to the present society. Film scholars in the 1940s and 1960s were trained in literary criticism. Scholars like Dixon paid attention to the performance of the star and thus explored fascinations adequately expressed for the star of all ages. Dyer's book and his established consideration of stars generating the meaning through the process of cinema creation has provided a new gateway to the study of stars. Today a star is much more than the representative of popular exception with his/her ideological discourses. Moreover, the determined star intentionally chooses to become a sign to posit the meanings he or she represents as an individual.

The stages from star production to star reception have been reshaped in every decade. This chapter looks at the star as an icon of an era, who in the process of deserving admiration and celebration becomes a cultural sign. The critical gravity of the study provides further scope for introspection to academicians and scholars of audience studies, culture studies, and literary studies. The increase in the collection of accounts of the lives of stars in India has imperatively helped scholars track down the historical moment of making and breaking a star. The collective experiences of female stars in the 1980s have succinctly summed up the tragedy of their lives. More importantly, biographies written about actresses have created a pastiche that carves out or captures the leap visible in the glamorous lifestyle they follow. Placing stars in a constellation of actors who have seen stardom provides much information about how stardom shapes the perception of culture the audience develop. The value of stardom and celebrity status comes as a seamless transition from the enigmatic reputation of a star with his or her performance and persona.

Vinod Mehta, in his book *Meena Kumari*, has shown how an actress became a repository of star culture. He has given a heart-rending story of challenges seldom quoted by media that called her 'great tragedienne'. Meena sympathized with Marilyn Monroe's inconceivable pain. Therefore, it comes as no surprise that Marilyn's husband, Arthur Miller, had passing similarities with the love of Meena's life, Kamal Amrohi. She found herself often dragged in life with her only wish to strive to be happy in love. Believing someday her lover would come and facilitate her redemption, she carried on with her indelible marks of emotional turmoil. With a moonlike face, Mahajabeen was made Meena in Bollywood who bid farewell to pleasantries of childhood too soon. From being Baby Meena to being one of the most wanted actresses of her time, she moved to the top as an actress while at personal front, her marriage was steadily going downhill. Her biography marks memories, personal history, silences and screams of the star celebrity. Meena Kumari's stardom pointed to new hopes for working women for the choices they made. This, however, was years later to give stars of the industry the public prominence that would bring forth a new generation of media critics. The public life of stars was eventually presented on the screen within the cycle of quasi-film noirs that presented the biting reality of film criticism.

Stars were presented in the cinematic adaptations exposing the personal life of a star with spotlight thrown on the coping mechanisms they had for dealing with their work. Bereft of hope they poured their loathing into glasses filled with alcohol. Many have given their precious years to drug abuse. Films and biographies present emphatic and somewhat antiquated focus on negotiations the stars made. This representation juxtaposes the onscreen portrayal of the stars with the off-screen practices of the film industry. Madhur Bhandarkar has been directing films like *Fashion* and *Heroine* that perpetuate representations of stardom.

The sequence comes from the meaning that emerges within the context of the characters' collision which further makes the star a text in himself/herself. Interestingly, such films can be seen as counter-narratives of Bollywood stardom while understanding movie stardom as a dazzling illusion. With an all-encompassing authority, the director and writer of these narratives present the image of an exploited and victimized film star. However, scholarly indications lately have reflected a different take on how Bollywood is ready to take a responsible place within the community of artists.

Contemporary actress Kalki Koechlin unearths the subversive history of cyberbullying in her fourteen-minute short film *Naked*. The film was released on International Women's Day, 8 March 2017. Director Rakesh Kumar pulls the theme from filmic examples of actresses as well as from their biographic information. The film demonstrates how the invasion of privacy by social media has deeply affected the stars, leaving them with emotional scars. Stars being major social, political and entertainment dignitaries are often presented with a series of unforeseen events. Cross-media stardom has hurtful past representations that are put aside by films like *Naked*. These films speak for respectability and equality against gender discrimination.

Spreading across optimistic hope, Kalki was perfectly positioned in a web series made by Y-Films called *Man's World* in 2015. The series features other stars including Parineeti Chopra, Richa Chadha, Rhea Chakraborty, Shweta Tripathi, Pritish Nandy, Soni Razdan, Aditi Singh Sharma, Cyrus Sahukar, Meiyang Chang, Anupama Chopra, Aditi Mittal, Naveen Kasturia, Miss Malini, RJ Malishka, and Priyanka Bose. Most importantly this web series confirms and resonates with the gradual acceptance of new performative spaces like YouTube that promote such web series and short films. Having the potential of fetching into the category of art films, celebrities have lately been promulgating ideological objectives through short films. The list of such films includes Huma Qureshi's *Ek Dopahar*, Manoj Bajpayee's *Kriti*, Naseeruddin Shah's *Interior Café Night*, Jackie Shroff's *Khujli*, and Anupam Kher's *Kheer*.

Studying stars and stardom in a different context, as can be inferred from the short films mentioned above, has given an insight into the inter-textual discourses thus developed. The fabrication of the star as a sign ascertains their scrutiny within the social spectral. The initial reservations of the censor board with a challenging subject can be seen concerning the problems of public relations. Such problems include less understood or misunderstood performances of the stars.

Receiving mixed critical reception, the film *Lipstick Under My Burkha* takes into account online visitors who become superfluous audience members as they scroll down online pages of varied social media platforms. Serving to highlight the moral policing of women, this film thwarts social stereotypes. Lately, an actress from the film, Ratna Pathak Shah talked about the changes observed in the films directed by females in the last decade. Journalist Archana Nathan cites her as saying that "the numbers can improve even further, yes, but the attitude of these new female filmmakers who are confident and are saying, judge a film for what it is worth and not because it is made by a woman – now that's beautiful" (Nathan n.pag.).

Ethereal representations of female stars on-screen and off-screen have institutionalized textual discourse of the modern women of India. Over the last decade, women characters have seen a shift in the portrayal of the feminine. Female stars, being the celebration of ideological power, have shown with a blend of everyday and the exceptional roles played both onscreen and off-screen. More pertinently, the emotional power is invoked and provoked with the help of a digital context that advertises trailers of films. More befitting visual culture, eventually, helps stars in achieving heightened awareness of the conscious audience.

In contemporary times, the popular trend is to explore women's unique idiom which is presented in mythological texts and represented in their cinematic adaptations. In 2016, Neena Gupta acted in the award-winning short film *Mama's Boys* that critiques social disparities and marks the relevance of a woman's voice. At the core, this film is a possibility of how the retelling of myths can be an instrument of change. Exploring women's form and way of communication in the *Mahabharata*, this film challenged established notions of womanhood and her desires ("Mama's Boys: An Irreverent Take on India's Mahabharat" n. pag.). Thematically revolutionary, this film is based on Chitra Banerjee Divakaruni's novel *The Palace of Illusions* (2008). Divakaruni has written another version of the *Mahabharata* from Draupadi's perspective in her novel that questions the patriarchal structures of society. Conspicuously, Kunti and Draupadi do not find their voice in the narratives given to us traditionally, which the novel and the film foreground. Director Akshat Verma paves the way for a modern take on the tale of Panchali. It traces the shift from whether she wanted it or not, how Draupadi was "like a communal drinking cup . . . passed from hand to hand" (Divakaruni 120) to the modern version where "she's excited at the prospect of multiple husbands and actively seduces them" ("Mama's Boys: An Irreverent Take on India's Mahabharat" n. pag.). Starring Aditi Rao Hydari, Neena Gupta, and Amol Parashar, this retelling involves women's perspective and hitherto neglected woman supremacy. This film provides an opportunity for women characters regardless of the discriminatory practices prevalent in times then and now.

Neena Gupta's character, as a controlling and demonstrative mother Kunti, raises questions of political correctness of being a mother-in-law as against being a woman. In the charged atmosphere, the viewers find Kunti regarding Draupadi as her adversary. To observe changing power relations within the boundaries of home, one can look forward to the characters' quest for identity. The film echoes illusory authority imposed by women characters over 'food wars' in the kitchen and at the dining table. Redefining the traditions, the film begins in the kitchen symbolizing the 'fireplace' of the house which is linked to anxieties and desires of women. The dynamic interaction of characters eventually leads to complex questions of repetition of history, myths, chores and monotony of life at large.

Neena Gupta was questioned for her choice of being a single mother 27 years back. In her interview, when asked about her reputation as a tough woman, she says "because of media, who have made my reputation of being a strong woman. And a strong woman is a bad woman in India. In reality, I am very vulnerable and honest, so people feel scared of me" (Gupta n.pag.). She emphasizes the importance of marriage and the marital status of a woman for her social and emotional well-being. However, in times of crisis, she has been an inspiration to many single mothers in the country. Instead of being an insecure individual, she chose to find her identity as a single parent. While some women rigidly adhere to social constructs, women like Neena Gupta have changed the definition of the strong woman.

Miss Universe Sushmita Sen's life has also been a testimony to the ideology of self-entitled independence and her determination to be "an embodiment of how to live like a boss" (Taragi n.pag.). At the age of 25, she was single and adopted two girls to be a role model of the modern collective female solidarity. Fighting legal battles for adoption at 23, she realized that her choice as a single mother shall be sought by many women to celebrate motherhood. This determined the relation women should have with themselves as self-sufficient individuals. Having beauty and intelligence, she has been a living example of a woman's sense of liberation. With a stunning move towards establishing *I AM Foundation: The Power of One*, a charity organization, she has made the best use of her celebrity status by providing opportunities to the vulnerable section of the society. With a vision to strengthen the nation, she has succeeded in changing the world for providing a better version of women's reality. It is important, in particular, to see how stars are constructively challenging the value structure of patriarchy. This means creating a new culture of equality by being a responsible face of society. Stars thus empower society by being progressive citizens to publicly raise social issues and reaching out to the masses. There are many campaigns that have gained currency in the nation because of the celebrity stars who directed their noble intentions for the larger good of society.

To begin with, among the actresses taking up films that created a new audience, the best foot put forward has always been that of Shabana Azmi. As an actress, she has dared presenting before the public diverse representations of women in her films like *Masoom*, *Neerja*, and *Fire*. She has been actively carving out an important place for female actresses in the world of heroes.

She has made it to the list of 'sheroes' coming to the fore with her active attempts in voicing her opinion on women's rights and objectification of women. Her performing abilities as an activist have been an addition to her prestige as an artist. Garnering positive notion of stardom Shabana Azmi, Konkona Sen, and Girish Karnad lately participated in the protest *Not in My Name*. This silent uprising points towards the urgency of the protest after the killing of 16-year-old Junaid. Filmmaker Saba Dewan used Facebook to show resistance against lynchings. *Times Now*, in an online news article, quoted her as saying that this protest was an attempt to "reclaim the Constitution" and "resist the onslaught" on rights (Issar n.pag.).

Lives of stars dominate the celebrity culture that is constantly evolving. An NGO in Mumbai called *Akshar* has begun a campaign called 'Hashtag Rewrite Songs.' The co-director of the campaign Nandita Shah has emphatically pointed towards developing a sensitization towards the right and wrong lyrics. The result is a short film *Gaana Rewrite All Films* where quite a few popular songs have been sung by females with new words producing new meanings that empower women. The film ends with a question of why lyrics are not written like this. Perhaps, social media has now witnessed an increasingly widespread reform articulating the emergence of a new image of femininity.

The film industry today concentrates on crafting consciousness that suits society the best as the celebrities pave the way for discovering and embracing empowered beings. A great boost has been given to women-centric issues that have subsequently led to ideologically committed actresses winning the national awards for their contribution to the society. Stars have been coming to the fore as exemplary beings who have conveyed changing the meaning of success and status. Considering the celebrity status, a fundamental paradox for stars is the process of how their image is built and rebuilt in society. Image building also includes their constant efforts, yet sometimes conscious struggle to maintain that image of a popular performer in the film industry leads to annoying comparisons.

On certain occasions, stars have been seen as challenging the conventional ways of society. The marriages of star icons fundamentally present the audience with the ideal couple image often romanticized by fans. Ironically, an interfaith marriage between stars breaks the conventional nature of marriage in society. A divorced star marrying again is not expected to have conventional standards. Even though the stars seem to show their front as an effortless embodiment of their day to day dealings, the reality leaves them no less than a mortal, vulnerable, broken and threatened in crucial times. In this sense, the fascination of the audience lies with how their favorite star deals with misery. Thus the star becomes the subject or the text that introduces the change in the social structure.

The stars like Farhan Akhtar and Hrithik Roshan have exploded the restrictive capacity of a broken marriage. Leaving an impact on the social milieu, they have moved beyond the fragmented personal lives. Offering the possibility of making work and personal happiness a priority, they have reduced the gap between personal and public fronts. As one unveils the complex layers of star image, the contextualized meaning of the star is laid bare. Certainly, the image of the star will be perceived and received differently by the audience at different times. Yet reconstructing the image of the star in a particular context will only help academicians demystify the dynamics of celebrity culture. There are limitless possibilities of the star being an embodiment of various meanings produced at different times and roles played both onscreen and off-screen. Indeed, a definite impact is processed within the dynamics of interactive sites that have the star as a passive recipient or as an active agent inducing change. Stars are thus made and re-made by the roles played by them.

The undue emphasis on the appearance of women bruises the confidence they develop. Furthermore, loosening the professional constraints gets critical acclaim for stars. The politics of acting often hinges on recognition of unwanted pressures that usually have open-ended conclusions drawing attention to celebrity culture. Nandita Das, as an activist has had a larger impact being the co-founder of an advertising organization, *Leapfrog*, which emphasizes making socially conscious advertisements. Kavitha Emmanuel, founder-director of *Women of Worth*, began 'Dark is Beautiful' campaign with Nandita in 2009. These campaigns challenge the idea of beauty driven by the obsession Indian society has with fair skin. Because of certain stereotypes, it seems impossible for women to have an empathetic connection with their emotional selves.

Myntra, the ethnic wear brand has launched its digital campaign titled *Anouk—Bold is Beautiful* which has a series of short films, *The Visit, The Move, The Calling, The Whispers,* and *The Wait.* Gunjan Soni, Chief Marketing Officer and Head, International Brands Business, Myntra, has been stressing that "Anouk's campaigns have always exemplified how the Indian woman can voice her opinion and craft her destiny . . . Through these campaigns, the intent has been to deliver the brand message in an impactful but non-intrusive manner" ("Myntra's in-house brand Anouk gets bolder" n.pag.). The issues highlighted in the films range from homosexuality, single parenting, the joys of staying single, prejudices faced by women while exploring career opportunities, and discriminatory behaviour during maternity. Such campaigns establish women's personae too noticeably so that these films exemplify the premise of gender equality by breaking stereotypes.

In 1990, Naomi Wolf showed similar concern in her book *The Beauty Myth* as to how the beauty myth "countered women's new freedoms by transposing the social limits to women's lives directly onto our faces and bodies" (270). The new wave has gained ground with dark and dusky being the new beautiful. With women magazines gaining power in mainstream media, images of stars on the cover pages have been undoubtedly attracting the changing definitions of beautiful. Lately, Serena Williams has graced the cover of the magazine *Vanity Fair* which features her "nude, pregnant, and glowing" (Lubitz n.pag.) breaking the stereotypes of beauty. Ironically, the political importance of the word 'vanity' grows clearer as the women on the cover page choose to define themselves, taking charge of their health, both physical and emotional. The word 'fair', however, makes enough space for equality achievers. Providing a rare platform, the magazine acknowledges fleeting female realities, women's burden in varied role-plays. The cover invited several comments that include Sylvia Obell's assertion, 'I Met God, She's Black'. These magazines are the product of popular culture and take women's concerns seriously and present the star as the brand.

Reflecting on the anxious and uneasy truce in which stars are made to appear flawlessly beautiful, the magazines split reality into what is a surreal idea of beauty as against the mechanisms to escape this stereotype of beauty. What is seldom acknowledged is the popularized idea of beauty being managed at the cost of hours spent in the makeup room and as Sonam Kapoor remarked that money is invested in "generous servings of the Photoshop" (n.pag.). Seen in this light, the actress Sonam Kapoor decided to be the instrument of change by writing an article, "I Didn't Wake Up Like This". The essay is self-expression about apprehensions and intensified fears reinforced by media. She writes: "The ball is in the media's court to celebrate fit bodies rather than thin ones, and to know the difference . . . pursue prettiness for yourself, by your definitions – not to meet culturally preset notions of 'flawless.' Flawlessness is a dangerous, high-budget myth, and it's time we shatter it" (Kapoor n.pag.).

Beauty is a 'mobilizing and socializing force,' for women are often drawn as an intangible concept within the social realm in the advertising industry or cinema. Fortunately, the beauty index has been changed by the Indian comic book *Priya's Shakti*, first of its kind that won the 2014 Gender Equality Champion award from UN Women. Dan Goldman, writer and the illustrator of comics has carefully chosen Bollywood actress Rekha to be the model for Shakti's character. Offering a new template, the comic con offers dusky and dark protagonist Shakti in the same hue. *Priya's Shakti* is an oracle speaking to the readers challenging mass-market of demanding socialization. When young girls read the comic book of feminine culture, the myth regarding fairness norms of beauty is subverted.

There is always a risk that comes with celebritization and the subject position star holds and what the star endorses has high stakes. Aishwarya Rai Bachchan, the former Miss World and a celebrated Bollywood actress, is the national ambassador of brand *Kalyan* jewellers. In 2015, she was featured in an advertisement representing the aristocracy, "bejeweled, poised, and relaxing" with a child "very dark and emaciated" trying to hold an oversized umbrella over her head (Bhalla n.pag.). The advertisement courted controversy after an open letter was sent to her from a group of feminist activists and a former chairperson of the National Commission for Protection of Child Rights. The open letter read: "As an influential member of the Indian film industry and a popular star with a large fan following, we trust that you wish to use your image in a manner that promotes progressive thought and action, and would not knowingly promote regressive images that are racist and go against child rights" ("Aishwarya Rai Bachchan Slammed" n.pag.).

Eventually, the jewellery brand withdrew the advertisement having its publicist's statement addressed to Farah Naqvi, Nisha Agrawal, Enakshi Ganguly, Bharti Ali, Madhu Mehra, Shantha Sinha, Harsh Mander, and Mridula Bajaj, who signed the letter posted online:

> At the onset, we would like to thank you for drawing our attention to the observation of the perception of the advertisement. Here is an attachment of the shot taken by somebody during the shoot . . . The final layout of the ad is entirely the prerogative of the creative team for a brand. However, I shall forward your article as a viewpoint that can be taken into consideration by the creative team of professionals working on the brand visual communication. Thank you once again. ("Aishwarya Rai Bachchan Slammed" n.pag.)

Going back to the impact made by stars in previous years, we can think of the actor and activist Aamir Khan and some of his works, e.g. his decision to volunteer for Narmada Bachao Andolan (Save Narmada Movement) and Bhopal gas tragedy victims with Medha Patkar in 2006, and his take on social affairs with his television debut *Satyamev Jayate* in 2012. However, embedded in the dutiful structure, stars often have perfect image-correlation. Directors like Shoojit Sircar have shown their concern towards the rising popularity of reality shows featuring children. He wrote on Twitter: "Humble request to authorities to urgently ban all reality shows involving children. It's destroying them emotionally and their purity" (Sircar n.pag.). As reflected in the process of improvisation and visualization of the star-text on-screen and off-screen, the emphasis is laid on the collective functioning of celebrity culture.

Star studies in contemporary times generate a mode of representation of cultivated personalities. The desired goals for the star centre on the text they become in the process of celebritization. The ability to pull off a coherent performance of the star as a celebrity in life makes him or her an important variable to be studied by contemporary academia. This chapter has traced the star's journey towards becoming an agency that empowers society at large. A star evolves through the exchange of personal and public discussions throughout the process of celebritization. Thus, attaining stardom can be studied by deconstructing star-text which precisely is a process of tracing the revision of social values in any given age.

Bibliography

"Aishwarya Rai Bachchan Slammed Over 'Racist' ad, Actress Says Image Changed." *Economictimes.indiatimes.com.* N.p., 22 Apr. 2015. Web. 20 Jun. 2017. <https://economictimes.indiatimes.com/magazines/panache/aishwarya-rai-bachchan-slammed-over-racist-ad-actress-says-image-changed/articleshow/>.

Bhalla, Nita. "Kalyan Jewellers Pulls "Racist", "Slave-Child" ad With Aishwarya Rai." *Reuters.com.* N.p., 23 Apr. 2015. Web. 25 Jun. 2017. <https://www.reuters.com/article/india-bollywood-childslavery/kalyan-jewellers-pulls-racist-slave-child-ad-with-aishwarya-rai/>.

Butler, Judith. *Gender Trouble: Feminism and the Subversion of Identity.* New York: Routledge, 1990. Print.

Devineni, Ram, Lina Srivastava, and Dan Goldman. *Priya's Shakti.* Mumbai: Rattapallax, 2014. Print.

Divakaruni, Chitra Banerjee. *The Palace of Illusions.* New York: Picador Random House Inc., 2008. Print.

Dixon, Simon. "Ambiguous Ecologies: Stardom's Domestic Mise-en-Scène." *Cinema Journal* 42.2 (2003): 81-100. Print.

Dyer, Richard. *Stars.*London: British Film Institute, 1979. Print.

Gupta, Neena. Interview. "Neena Gupta :I Want to Tell All Women That If You Want to Live in India and in Society, You Have to Marry." *Timesofindia.indiatimes.com.* N.p.,9 May 2015.Web. 28 Jun.2017. <http://timesofindia.indiatimes.com/entertainment/hindi/bollywood/news/Neena-Gupta-I-want-to-tell-all-women-that-if-you-want-to-live-in-India-and-in-society-you-have-to-marry/articleshow/>.

Issar, Vritti. "Not In My Name: A 'silent' Uprising Against the Lynch Brigade." *Timesnownews.com.* N.p., 29 Jun.2017. Web. 25 Mar. 2018. <http://www.timesnow.tv/india/article/not-in-my-name-a-silent-uprising-against-the-lynch-brigade/>.

Kapoor, Sonam. "I Didn't Wake Up Like This." *Buzzfeed.com.* N.p., 28 Sept. 2017. Web. 27 Mar. 2018. <https://www.buzzfeed.com/sonamkapoor/i-didnt-wake-up-like this? utm_term/>.

Lipstick under My Burkha. Dir. Alankrita Shrivastava. Prakash Jha Prod. 2016. Film.

Lubitz, Rachel. "Serena Williams Graces the Cover of 'Vanity Fair' Nude, Pregnant and Glowing." *Mic.com.* N.p., 27 Jun.2017.Web. 27 Mar. 2018. <https://mic.com/articles/180919/serena-williams-graces-the-cover-of-vanity-fair-nude-pregnant-and-glowing/>.

"Mama's Boys: An Irreverent Take on India's Mahabharat." *Bbc.com.* N.p., 14 Sept. 2016. Web. 27 Mar. 2018. <http://www.bbc.com/news/world-asia-india-37340277/>.

Mama's Boys. Dir. Akshat Verma. 2016. Web. Film.

Man's World. Dir. Vikram Gupta. Y Films. 2015. Web. Film.

Mehta, Vinod. *Meena Kumari: The Classic Biography.* Mumbai: Harper Collins Publishers, 1972. Print.

"Myntra's in-house brand Anouk gets bolder with new ad film." *Exchange4media.com.*N.p., 25 Aug.2016. Web. 20 Jun.2019. <https://www.exchange4media.com/advertising-news/myntra's-in-house-brand-anouk-gets-bolder-with-new-ad-film-65708.html/>.

Naked. Dir. Rakesh Kumar. Scud, AOC and Live Signages. 2017. Web. Film.

Nathan, Archana. "Ratna Pathak Shah on Lipstick Under my Burkha." *scroll.in.* N.p., 1 Jul.2017. Web. 30 Mar. 2018. <https://scroll.in/reel/842043/ratna-pathak-shah-on-lipstick-under-my-burkha-my-hope-is-that-men-take-lots-away-from-the-film/>.

Sircar, Shoojit. 8.24 am, 4 Jul.2017. Web. <https://twitter.com/ShoojitSircar/status/882070022629318656/>.

Taragi, Geetanjali. "8 Times Sushmita Sen Became A Role Model For Women Across The World & Made Us Look Up To Her." *ScoopWhoop.com.*N.p., 28 Jun.2017. Web. 20 Jun. 2019. <https://www.scoopwhoop.com/sushmita-sen-a-role-model/?ref=social&type/>.

Wolf, Naomi. *The Beauty Myth: How Images of Beauty are Used against Women.* London: Vintage Books, 1990. Print.

Further Reading

Devineni, Ram. "Stand with Priya --A Survivor of Rape and First Comic Book Hero to Fight Sexual Violence." *Indiegogo.com.* N.p., 21 Dec. 2015. Web. 25 Jun.2017.

The Cult of Aamir Khan:
A Cultural Study of Indian Fandom

Vishakha Sen

University of Lucknow, India

In the postmodern decades, Indian cinema and fandom have reshaped the creative media space where the proliferation of identities along with the understanding of cultural essence occurs persistently. It exploits the themes of religion, socio-political attributes of caste, creed and folk culture massively. Such cultural reflection directly connects the film actors to mass audiences. This leads to the emergence of enthusiastic fans. In 1992, Henry Jenkins' seminal work, *Textual Poachers* established fandom studies in the ambit of technological development and social media, reframing it for contemporary readers, and reappraising its contributions to the entertainment industry. With the digital revolution, the accessibility of famous individuals as icons has become a new text of exploration for the audience and readers. Fandom studies are not limited to the formation of a star's image. It also highlights fans' gaze, desire, and expectation towards a celebrity who have actively immersed themselves in creating star's national and global value. This phenomenon has accelerated with the YouTube revolution. Such fandom is also witnessed by Indian film celebrities, who play the role of institutions in structuring meaning and crystallizing ideologies. The film industry along with the institutions of journalism, mass media, and social media provides easy interpretive tools to fans for the promulgation of Indian socio-cultural customs. In the Indian star-fan equation, actor Aamir Khan has worked implicitly on distilling earnest issues concerning Indian sensibility through his choice of films, productions, and social service through creative expression. The paper thus discusses the engagement of Indian fans and Aamir Khan's stardom to understand and examine Indian cultural production.

Fandom refers to a group of fans of a particular work of fiction. The word 'fan' is derived from 'fanatic' which means an ardent worshipper of a particular media text. It can be an artefact or a person in a genre of art or/and recreational forms like cinema, television, music, videogames, sports, etc. Members of fandom are typically interested even in infinitesimally small details of the plot, characters, themes, or setting of these texts. Fan fiction is by its nature always a 'work in progress', and it is futile to understand fan fiction outside the social relationships it helps to facilitate. Fans can be interested in the biography of a film star or can be inclined to social critique by journalism and media. There are two types of relationships which fans share with a star or celebrity, the sociological and linguistic. The sociological relationship occurs because fans and the star partake in the same sociological, cultural space. The political and economic changes affect both fans and the star in different proportions. The fans are influenced by the biographical persona of the star. His narratives of struggle and failures create celebrity construct which is internalized by fans. In the Freudian context, the fans objectify the subjectivity of the star. The linguistic relationship involves semiotic activities of fans who give ever new interpretations to the text a star is a part of. The public image of the star, their appearances and opinions also affect how fans respond.

To critique Indian fandom, it is necessary to first analyze the origin of fandom on the world map. Fan fiction began with the 1990s technological evolution as a response of an audience to fictional or filmic texts like *Sherlock Holmes, Star trek*, etc. Transformation of audience into fans became directly proportional to the available intermediality of the text. The entertainment industry now has an organized facility for production, distribution, and reception of culture. It has been dependent on changing material formats and technologies- manuscripts to printed books, mural painting to photography, and architecture to virtual creations on a gadget screen. Such texts are based on varied genres like fantasy, cartoon, and adventure. Their commonality lies in an engrossing plot, user or audience entertainment, mass viewership and readership. Genre-wise, these narratives are an evolved form of epic. The texts which interest fans most are the ones with a hero, who begins a quest through an overwhelming journey. This phenomenon of a hero or a group into adventurous pursuit can be traced in video games like *Link* from *Zelda* games, *Mario, Cloud Strife* of *Final Fantasy VII, Sonic* series' *the Hedgehog, Master Chief* from *Halo* series, *Kirby, Solid Snake* from *Metal gear* series, *Ezio* from *Assassin's Creed, Pikachu* in *Pokemon, Dante Devil May Cry* series; fantasy adventure films- *Wizard of Oz, Harry Potter* series, *Lord of the Rings* series, *Clash of the Titans, Transformers* series, etc; TV and web series *Supernatural, Breaking Bad, Game of Thrones, Flash*, etc. Josef Adalian in his article "The 25 Most Devoted Fan Bases" argues that

> for most consumers of pop culture, fandom is a lower-case concern. They are 'fans' in the sense that they may like a particular movie, TV show, band, or personality but don't think much about it when not experiencing it firsthand. Capital-F Fandom is something else

altogether. It goes beyond 'like' or even 'love' and straight to 'devoted.' Their Fandom is all-consuming, a jumping-off point for a deep dive into fan fiction, convention-attending, recap-writing, role-playing, costume-making, language-learning, and more. There is a passion to this kind of Fandom that binds enthusiasts in the manner of people who share a secret — this secret just happens to be shared with millions of others. (n.pag.)

In all the above mentioned intermedial genres and mediums, the protagonist undergoes a metamorphosis. In the fiction itself, they live in the parallel worlds of the outer world and inner hidden world, just like the muggle and wizard world of *Harry Potter*, the normal life of the protagonist, crime scene investigator Barry Allen, and his superhero world as *Flash* of *DC comics*. The fans are attracted to such conventions of the plot which are similar to the epic form of poetry. A member of one of the largest fan fiction community Fanfiction.net, Aura ChannelerChris' *The Subspace Emissary's Worlds Conquest* is the longest work of fiction ever written. This fanfiction has surpassed Marcel Proust's *À la recherche du temps perdu* (*In Search of Lost Time*) and is 3,548,615 words long. That's three times longer than Proust, and six times longer than *War and Peace*. Jason Mittell in a review of *Fandom: Identities and Communities in a Mediated World* elucidates:

Fandom pushes the boundaries of fan studies in bold directions, incorporating high culture fandoms, global fan cultures, fan technologies, and antagonistic anti-fandom, while rethinking the core tenets of fan studies concerning aesthetics, place, intellectual property, and interpretive communities-all presented with a lively, accessible, and engaging writing style. (n.pag.)

John Fiske in "The Cultural Economy of Fandom" (1992) discusses three kinds of fan productivity which are semiotic, enunciative and textual. Semiotic productivity demands an understanding of media text, while enunciative productivity concerns with the propagation of specific star artefacts, fashion, food, clothing trends, etc. This further relocates the interest of fans beyond the text. And textual productivity ultimately focuses only on dedicated fandom groups bringing in exclusive fan fiction, sponsorship and opportunities for a core fan group. He also highlights the appropriation of official cultural artefacts by fans in the production of derivative texts and objects (Fiske). The following Table 1 depicts key motivation platforms where fans interact with stars on social media. Facilitating interaction is a key construct in relationship marketing.

Table 5.1: Engagement of Star with Fan at Different Intermedial Levels by Vishakha Sen.[1]

Intermediality-same Text in Multiple Media		Trailer Release, Promotional Techniques	Interactive Fan Response
Personal	Whatsapp	Photographs, posters, video of film shoot scenes	One to one and group sharing, reviewing
Social	Youtube	Teasers, trailers	Fans watch, like and share
Network	Facebook	Create film page	Fans watch, like, comment, share
Network	Twitter	Photographs, contests, dumbmash.com videos	Fans connect to star personally
Film merchandize		Collaborate with brands, advertisements	Fans play consumer role
Multiplex offers		Ticket discount, tax-free, and other perks	Fans instantly buy such offerings and become easy bait
Film campaign		Interviews and involvement of media foraudience, target audience tours	Fans participate and respond to such campaigns

Thus strategies like viral marketing, telefantasy, synergy, direct market co-optation, gameplay, marketing, etc. influence the way fan groups interact with the star. The configurations of popular narratives are necessarily identical with varieties of fans. They are fans of specific films, television personalities, rock performers, sports teams or soap operas, etc. It concurrs that differences and similarities of experience among fan groups arise from their specific historical locus within the cultural hierarchical inclinations in various forms of entertainment. Hence, when fandom becomes an economic production, a sense of specificity is required to define the fans as Karen Hellekson in an interview by Henry Jenkins reveals:

> I am not interested in expanding the notion of the fan to include all aspects of what may be termed fannish behaviour. Fans of stamp collecting or sports may engage in a sort of fandom, but they don't tend to call it that. They may also configure their engagement and their passion differently. The word *fandom* may properly be applied to these activities, but to my ear, the connotation isn't right. Broadening fan studies to all aspects of 'fanatic' behaviour merely because the activities match what the term denotes is certainly a valid point of view, but it's not my point of view because I am interested in what it *connotes* and how fans work to build that connotation. The term also comes out of SF literature fandom, which I have studied, and in some ways I want to acknowledge fan studies' outgrowth from SF fandom. (n.pag.)

The digital technology has commoditized the way fans express their fandom. Fans play the role of the reader/audience and become the facilitator in cultural production within the fandom.

The fandom processes can be compared with superstructure and base activities defined by neo-Marxist Louis Althusser in "Ideological State Apparatuses" from *Lenin and Philosophy, and Other Essays* (1971). The entertainment industry and celebrity culture constitute the activities related to the superstructure, ideological state apparatus (ISA). The private image of a star, media releases, and interviews create an imaginary ideology that interpellates fans. Marx in the preface to *A Contribution to the Critique of Political Economy* opined that "it is not the consciousness of men that determines their living, but, on the contrary, their social being that determines their consciousness" (2). Stars get involved in the proliferation of social and cultural codes. They belong to superstructure functioning at the ontological level. The activities of fans can be accommodated in Repressive State Apparatuses (RSAs) based activities in the public domain. Such activities include following film stars on social media like Twitter, Facebook in an attempt to familiarize themselves with their personal lives, watching the films, keeping track of production and future projects of favorite stars. They function in the epistemological production not only of fan fiction, but also responses for the star. The comments, compliments, and trolls that fan create in daily activities are similar to base activities of raw material production which as Althusser defines, are controlled and regulated by social platform authorities. Just like the failure of raw material can hamper production, the opinions, negative trolls, comments of fans about the release of film or acting can affect the response of the star.

Figure 5.1: Neo-Marxist Relations Between Celebrity as Star and Audience as Fan by Vishakha Sen.

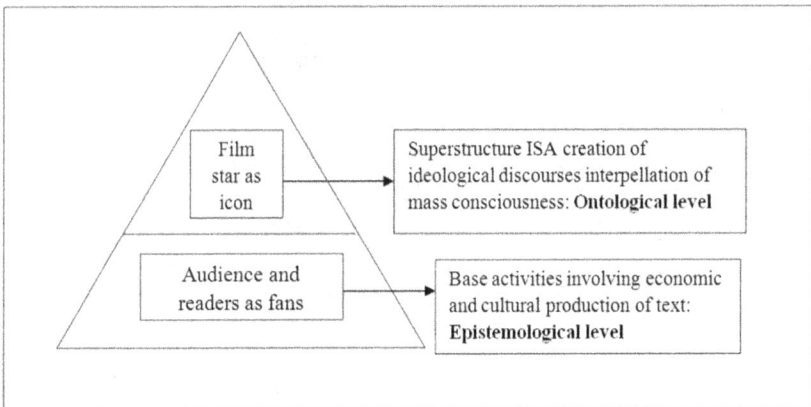

The Indian scenario of fandom is entirely different from its western counterpart. In the western tradition of the star-fan equation, the fans are more creatively advanced and technologically adept. They are active in the production of textual memories of fan fiction, such as of J.K Rowling's *Harry Potter* series or *Avenger* comics. Coppa notes the creative fan works for Western live-action shows and connected fandoms. It involves literary production of fan fiction about famous contemporary games, novels, films, and TV series. Whereas Indian literary production does not attract such fandom discourses, there are no significantly organized nationwide networks of fan clubs, interpretive communities in Indian literary scenario. For instance, in the case of Indian English novels, the readers can be divided into broad categories like college industry readers and elite bureaucrat readers.

The college industry readers read Indian English literature as a curriculum of the college syllabus. A large percentage of marketing and engineering students usually choose novels by Chetan Bhagat, Durjoy Datta, Nikita Singh, etc. Such readers have no idea of specific literary genres. They are less involved in the literary and cultural production of book fairs, literature festivals. Publishing houses only cater to huge marketing investment by financially stable authors. The elite reader group includes university professors, scholars, bureaucrats, page three denizens, artists, hoteliers, veteran filmmakers, and playwrights. They usually end up either reading literature by western authors or resorting to marketing trends. They do incline to Amitav Ghosh, Anita Desai, Shashi Deshpande, etc. Yet serious fandom has not developed. Their interest is short-lived. Their fandom ends with buying more novels. Similarly, while shifting from fictional text to filmic text, the situation is worse.

Unlike the western fandom whose bulk percentage is enthusiastic about fiction, films, television series, Indian fans are more connected to the star image than the film text. Fans follow the stars on Instagram, their personal lives and daily routines. Actors like Amitabh Bachchan, Shahrukh Khan thus become mere brands for such fans, as the star-fan relation exists as a commodity-consumer relation. As long as box office tickets sell in billions, the objectified actors like fans are just consumers and nothing more than that. Indian fandom in a star-fan relationship does not share intellectual, creative space. Aamir Khan has, to a certain extent, transcended this trend in Indian fandom. It is suggested by contemporary television and media critic P. David Marshall who in *The Celebrity Culture Reader* (2006) discusses that most music, television and film stars should emerge from the distanced nature of their screen image. Their aura of distance and distinction has been evaporating due to digital proximity. They create an entrepreneurial and presentational self in the process.

Indian fandom on game culture consists of western video games. In India, the fandom of cricket is the most passionate compared to any other realm. As discussed earlier, the basis of fandom is the intermedial availability of the entertainment text. Indian middle class cannot afford video games. They use the pirated versions. There has been no Indian fan community on any video game character. It is cricket that is easily accessible to all classes in India. One can watch it on TV, listen to a radio broadcast, and most accessible is *gully-cricket* (cricket played on streets). Cricket is one such sport which can be played anywhere. It does not need a net or closed premise like badminton or tennis. It does not need optimum stamina, heavy workout or proper diet as in tennis, football, weightlifting or boxing. It does not need large space, proper playground and other facilities as in track and field sports. Fans can save money and watch Indian Premier League (IPL), state-level cricket and national level cricket. The purchasing capacity of a fan is often within his means when it comes to cricket. Indian films or Bollywood, along with Tollywood (south Indian film industry) movies, are maximum earners. Here too, the fans are passive. They are only active in watching films and adoring the stars. In extreme cases, they turn into stalkers.

Hence Indian fandom is passive. The parameter for an Indian fan to adore a text or an icon is money, quality, and availability of the medium. Western stars, production houses, and fandom have a good network of fan clubs. The production houses and directors keep a tab on suggestions by the fans in the introduction of characters as *Game of Thrones, Supernatural*, etc. They update their episodes and seasons as per the creative, fictive inputs by their fans. Whereas in India there exist no such fan communities, and fans' suggestions are never acknowledged. Western fandom keeps track of the fans through the fan community whereas Indian films, sports, and TV industry keep track of box office earnings solely. They do not build any fan base neither care nor appreciate the contribution of fans. Indian fans are only mentioned when box office collections of movies like *Bajrangi Bhaijan, Sultan, Dangal* reaches billions. The western fans continuously react and respond to the text- novels, films, and video games. The relationship between the western entertainment industry and the fan is much stronger than the Indian star-fan relationship.

Aamir Khan is an Indian actor who has received four National awards and an Oscar nomination for *Lagaan* (2001). Apart from romantic films, he has acted in broad genres of films based on patriotism like *Sarfarosh* (1999), *Lagaan* (2001), *Mangal Pandey: The Rising* (2005), *Rang De Basanti* (2006), religious-cultural unity *1947: Earth* (1998), *Fanaa* (2006), *PK* (2014), youth-centric like *Holi* (1984), *Taare Zameen Par* (2007), *3 Idiots* (2009), and *Dangal* (2016). Aamir Khan productions has made path-breaking films like *Lagaan, Peepli Live* (2010),

Dhobighat (2010), *Dangal* (2016), *Secret Superstar* (2017), etc. The actor made his Bollywood debut as a child actor in *Yaadon Ki Baaraat* (1973).

He is the first Indian actor to create awareness about social issues, bias, domestic violence and public crime plaguing India through his conceptual talk show *Satyamev Jayate* (2012-14) on *Doordarshan*. It received unprecedented positive reviews from its viewers living across 165 countries. Aamir Khan and his production house work intensively to merge rich phases of Indian culture and grave phenomenon, blending aesthetic with commercial in the Indian society. He targets all kinds of communities that feed on Indian cultural discourse. Indian fans can be categorized in such communities, which are interpretive, imagined and virtual. The fans who participated in the show act as an interpretive community. Through projections of real-life incidents and surveys, *Satyamev Jayate* has focused on specific active interpretive families and common man in general. Aamir Khan works on the historicity of issues inductively, from specific to general. The concept of show *Satyamev Jayate* consists of introducing a broader social issue through the narration of an individual's real experiences. This is followed by logistics and facts revealing how serious and appalling the situation is. Then Khan as the host proceeds to discuss such surveys with prominent journalists, social activists, government officials, or social group representatives.

The emotional connection that fans build during the show is chiefly due to the common people, and the victims. The people who were inspired by various social issues discussed are invited to share their inputs and feedbacks. This simultaneously brings a transformation in the star-fan relationship. The star's emotional involvement during the instances where victims burst into tears genuinely creates a cathartic effect which is as powerful as the agro-effect of the British playwright Edward Bond when he showed violence to evoke the deepest consciousness of people. For instance, the narration of domestic violence suffered by the victim who has been invited in the show is both a presentation (filmic) and representation (dramatic) in terms of performance to arouse awareness and empathy in the audience/viewers. The victim is representative of all such women, girls who suffer from physical abuse in India. Fans who view the episodes become immediate receptors similar to interpretive communities (coined by Stanley Fish) as they are "are made up of those who share interpretive strategies not for reading ... but for writing texts, for constituting their properties and assigning their intentions" (219). Only here the medium is not reading but audio-visual. Each fan base and audience interpret the stories of atrocities in a unique way within Indian culture.

The audience witness a tiny fraction of their actual personalities onscreen. To bring out the live effect and decrease this host-audience/ star-fan imaginative distance, *Satyamev Jayate* has worked tremendously to connect the audience with real-life philanthropists who have worked on deadening issues of female foeticide, child abuse, domestic violence, dowry, honour killing, etc. The episodes also discuss issues involving men as the victim and culprits. Aamir Khan as a star has utilized his stardom to reform Indian society. He has used his star-image to voice the silence which creeps in as dark shadows of marital abuse, sexual abuse, and gender bias. But his demeanour on the show is that of a common man. This kind and generous host frame has influenced millions of fans.

The show focused on another misconception in star-fan affiliation. Psychologically, *fausse reconnaissance* or false recognition about the star that whatever role they enact in films is permissible in real life is false. In *Satyameva Jayate's* last episode of Season 3, Aamir Khan invited actors Amitabh Bachchan, Deepika Padukone, Kangana Ranaut, etc. to clear this misconception that the violence or rowdy behaviour of heroes in films is solely for entertainment and it should not be the yardstick of the behavior in real social scenes. Aamir Khan's role as a sensitive host opens with emotional interviews of common people, who were brave enough to participate in this social reformation. When the stardom is reciprocated as an interviewee, it changes the dynamics of understanding. The guest becomes the new celebrity and such instances develop into a cult of positive fandom. This trend has been adopted by other reality shows post *Satyamev Jayate.* Until now, most reality shows were concerned only with creating stars. Today they bring families and parents of the participants to become a part of the show. More the common masses are represented onscreen, more the desire to be like the participants ignites among potentially talented viewers. The viewers and fans now relate to the reality of the participants. They witness their struggle towards stardom. It is commendable how "Aamir Khan Production crafts an image of a small, independent, artisanal production house that handpicks projects reflecting 'Khan's social conscience, intelligence, creativity, and authorial vision'" (Punathambekar 191). During a conversation with Sonia Singh in the episode of *NDTV Dialogues* (2015), Aamir Khan says:

> I need not stop at just entertaining people. I can take one step further which is to try and affect people's minds and how they think and look at things. I understand I am able to connect with people, I have an emotional bonding with people, and my strength lies in my ability to tell stories and to touch people's hearts and to move them . . .my attempt is to look at problems that face us as a society and see if I can address those. (n.pag.)

Contrary to the assumption that the audience expect a certain social, personal message from Aamir Khan's film or show, he believes that people do not know what to expect from him because he does not follow a pattern. This is the reason he did a film like *Ghajini*, a totally different film just after *Taare*

Zameen Par. He has also produced dark comedy films like *Delhi Belly* which has nothing to do with customary social cause as expressed in NDTV interview. Being plausible, Aamir Khan saves himself from being type-casted. This behavioural pattern is crucial for an actor. A fan exactly expects unconsciously that his favourite actor should only do certain specific roles. It is at this point an actor should not buy such expectations; else his aesthetic value will stagnate with stereotypical roles. He should keep trying new roles and, at the same time, contribute to a social cause outside the screen. With social media platforms like Twitter and Instagram becoming popular, whatever social, creative welfare causes an actor takes up off-screen, is under constant scrutiny by fans and media. Today's digital fans should realize this difference.

Satyamev Jayate can be called social *agitprop*. Though the western world considers it having a negative connotation, a*gitpróp*, a portmanteau of 'agitation' and 'propaganda' is political propaganda, especially the communist propaganda used in Soviet Russia, that is spread in the general public through popular media such as literature, plays, pamphlets, films, and other art forms with an explicitly political message. There have been films showcasing corrupt officials and chaotic governance, but the daily TV series could never create such strong ripples nationwide as done by *Satyamev Jayate*. In the last episode of the last season "When Masculinity Harms Men," two gory cases of male violence were discussed. Two young boys lost their lives in two different incidents originating from the violence of masculinity. In the first instance, a father-son duo killed an innocent young boy by beating him with a helmet just because their bike got scratches during a minor accident. On the show, Aamir Khan and feminist activist Kamla Bhasin discussed how the misconception that masculinity lies in commanding power resulted in such murder. The father repeatedly instructed his son to continue beating the boy. He challenged onlookers with grave consequences if anybody intervened. In another incident, a boy committed suicide due to ragging. Ten to twelve seniors tortured him sexually in such a barbaric way that he was even unable to share it with his parents. Acid attack on Laxmi Agarwal in 2005 was also narrated in the first person. Laxmi shared with the audience how she could see her own skin melt like burning plastic. She was attacked with acid just because she refused a 32-year-old man's proposal. She kept asking for help but no one came forward to rescue her. It is to be noted that Bollywood films use violence as props in harsh extremities. Either the heroes become stalkers, harassing, eve-teasing the heroine, or become insanely violent post murder or rape of the heroine. The stagnant and flawed plots are not critically censored by the board. Ethical cultural production suffers due to industrial profit. In *Satyamev Jayate*, the audience realizes how mass consciousness is conditioned by generational consumption of violence, in its myriad silhouettes and structures. Such discourse of multi-faceted perspectives associate fans not only with host Aamir Khan but also with the victims. This further helps the audience re-evaluate their conduct, and shared responsibility in different dimensions of real life. It makes uplifting and evaluating the multiple identities of citizens possible. In this regard, Aamir Khan in an interview with *News18* has contended that "through this show, we understand the problem of the people; we are not here to make a change. I am no one to change anything. I don`t think I am in the position to change anything else. I feel understanding a problem and feeling it or holding one's hand or hugging is also important. I may not have the solution, but at least I can hear and understand" ("Amir says he was jittery" n.pag.). Ritu V Singh of *IBN Live* also states that

> Aamir Khan deserves applause for bringing up such a sensitive issue and presenting it in a hard-hitting way. The amount of research Aamir and his team has put into the show was visible with the facts and figures presented. Every aspect of the issue was covered with great diligence . . . *Satyamev Jayate* is not just a show; it's a movement to change people's mindset. (n.pag.)

Parmita Uniyal from *Hindustan Times* praised the content and format of the show and said, "Aamir Khan has to step in to do what journalists are supposed to do – make a difference. The show is a classic example of that" (n.pag.). Gayatri Sankar in her review from *Zee News* described the show as an "eye opener" and commented that "*Satyamev Jayate* will make you unlearn all the wrong you have learnt and discover that compassionate human your soul wishes to be. The show grips you and leaves you dumbfounded! You will be left asking for more and would wish the show never ends" (n.pag.).

It is after *Satyamev Jayate* that serials like *Savadhaan India* (2012), *Hoshiyar: Sahi Waqt, Sahi Kadam* (2016) are being aired on the prime television networks. Although these serials lack substantial background research yet focus on crime. However, the media needs to emphasize realism in the script. To pen a crime scene is far easier than to research true incidents and then show it to a larger audience. Aspects like the balance between facts and fiction, the degree of fiction that can be blended in facts while filming/shooting, is quintessential for creative production. *Satyamev Jayate* had this quality of optimum research on such minute details. Apart from this, the show also used broadcast tactics to reach the maximum mass audience of India in Indian languages via *Doordarshan*. It also had a toll- free number and SMS service for people to contribute to different NGOs and respond to the ongoing discussions related to the episodes. The official website put up the 'Speak Up' section where audience and fans could upload videos related to social issues and *Satyamev Jayate* became the most searched word on the first day of its telecast (Sheikh). In the last season, the response from government and civic bodies has been praiseworthy, as they also have become an indirect part of positive fandom. For instance, in response to curb female foeticide, Rajasthan CM called for stringent action against this social malaise. In a negative response against honour killing episode, the 'Khap panchayats' appealed to put down the broadcast of the show.

It is crucial for the star-fan equation to strike a balance between fan legitimacy and the hero's power to control the amount of social media involvement. It is both a celebrity's right and duty to filter what to share and how much to share— creativity, personal life, private occasions, and public occasions. The role of intermediality is crucial in star-fan culture. Fans connect to stars in all forms of mediums. Shared readership demands legitimate broadcasting within multiple media where intermediality aims to keep the essence of text pure. Khan is very particular about avoiding discrepancy in such intermedial flow of creative information as on IBN live. He once insisted that he doesn't want to talk much about how the show will be, and about its format. The selection of linguistic mode and cultural code when a star interacts with fans is another factor in Indian fandom that is usually being overlooked. The choice of words even while promoting a consumer product or while interacting with media, has a huge impact on the psyche of fans and viewers. At times, media plays a foul and creates an intermedial difference in the actual statement of an actor. With easy gadget and app modifications, a consumer has also become part of information production. It has led to problem of fake news, disinformation like spreading a hoax, through morphed content for creating wrong political opinions and public outrage. According to cultural critic Stuart Hall, "things and events in the real world do not contain or propose their own integral, single and intrinsic meaning, which is then merely transferred through language. Meaning is a social production, a practice" (67). Hence, fandom studies bear a social responsibility to be aware of the language while interpreting a star's creative discourse.

Before the onset of fandom studies, the Indian audience and fans were just concerned with the reflection of a film star in their individual personality. They would follow film stars to groom their own individuality. Gradually, now the fans demand more than just grooming. With unlimited access to Instagram, Facebook, TikTok, and YouTube handle, they are ready to observe and follow what a star had to share beyond personal grooming. Fans nowadays are interested to know about the star's spiritual inclination, health, fitness and nutrition choices. They feed on everything from personal, casual, formal, and social to the overall routine. Akshay Kumar has become another icon for positive government-centric propagandist roles. This trend entrusts stars to involve in social welfare and activism to keep their fan record high. It is up to the star to differentiate between welfare and publicity. Stars conform to fans in a way Ludovica Price describes as:

fan fiction and fan art have been a mainstay of fan output for several decades now (the well-known 'Mary Sue' phenomenon can be traced back to 1973). But in an era where different cultural forms are converging, remediation activities are increasingly visible and varied in scope, and fans are often at the forefront of such creative endeavours (take, for instance, modding, cosplay, gamics and machinima.) (Price 2)

Perceptions and behaviours of communities and individuals no longer hold a relation to their physical, territorial and social contexts. Industry has impacted entertainment and fandom in the form of personalized interaction. Thus, fandom calls for a larger exchange of creative ideas between the text and the subject. It is only through regulated fandom and star relationship that real-time travel, stage concerts, and social blogs become relevant to erase the misconceptions, presumptions of the same on and off-stage image about famous personalities. Aamir Khan has been successful in filling this gap between cinema, television's portrayal and fans' understanding not only of the medium, but also their duty for Indian culture and society as a whole. Today Indian fandom has shown convalescent transmutation in its comprehending of emerging genres, the low-budget high purpose films, and embracing the creative and social efforts of stars. They are now supporting better creative and personal experience. A star holds deeper liability as citizens and humans. Their outlook unconsciously commands a million fans. Hence, it becomes imperative to look for fluidity in fandom for cultural developments in fan creativity in the sphere of media, art and democratized social engagements.

Notes

1. Table has been created to categorize star's interaction with fan at personal, professional and social level.

Bibliography

Adalian, Josef. "The 25 Most Devoted Fan Bases." *Vulture.com*. N.p., 25 Oct. 2012. Web. 23 Apr. 2017. <www.vulture.com/2012/10/25-most-devoted-fans.html/>.

Althusser, Louis. *Lenin and Philosophy and Other Essays*. London: New Left Books, 1971. Print.

"Amir says he was jittery when he signed up for TV." *Zeenews.india.com*. N.p., 25 Oct. 2012. Web. 27 Apr. 2017. <https://zeenews.india.com/entertainment/celebrity/aamir-says-he-was-jittery-when-he-signed-up-for-tv/>

AuraChannelerChris. "The Subspace Emissary's Worlds Conquest." *Fanfiction.net*. N.p., 2008. Web. 23 Apr. 2017. <www.fanfiction.net/s/4112682/1/The-Subspace-Emissary-s-Worlds-Conquest/>.

Coppa, Francesca. "Writing Bodies in Space: Media Fan Fiction as Theatrical Performance." *Fan Fiction and Fan Communities in the Age of the Internet: New*

Essays. Ed. Karen Hellekson and Kristina Busse. Jefferson: Mcfarland, 2006. 225-244. Print.

Fish, Stanley E. *Is There a Text in This Class?: The Authority of Interpretive Communities.* Cambridge, Mass: Harvard University Press, 1980. Print.

Fiske, J. "The Cultural Economy of Fandom." *The Adoring Audience: Fan Culture and Popular Media.* Ed. Lisa A Lewis. London and New York: Routledge, 1992. 30-49. Print.

Hall, Stuart, and Paddy Whannell. *The Popular Arts.* Boston: Beacon, 1967. Print.

Hellekson, Karen. "Where Fandom Studies Came From: An Interview with Kristina Busse and Karen Hellekson (Part One)." Interview by Henry Jenkins. *Henryjenkins.org.* N.p., 17 Nov.2014. Web. 23 Apr. 2017.

Khan, Aamir. Interview by Sonia Singh. "NDTV Dialogues: In Conversation with Aamir Khan." *Ndtv.com.* N.p., 30 Mar.2015. Web. 31 Mar. 2017. <www.ndtv.com/india-news/ndtv-dialogues-in-conversation-with-aamir-khan-full-transcript-750208/>.

Marshall, P. David. *The Celebrity Culture Reader.* New York: Routledge, 2006. Print.

Marx, Karl. Preface. *A Contribution to the Critique of Political Economy.* Moscow: Progress, 1970. Print.

Mittell, Jason. "Review of *Fandom: Identities and Communities in a Mediated World.*" *nyupress.org.* N.p., n.d. Web. 14 May 2017. <https://nyupress.org/9780814731819/fandom/>

Price, Ludovica. "Fanning Flames: A Review of *The Adoring Audience.*" *The Comics Grid: Journal of Comics Scholarship* 3.1(2013):1-3. Print.

Punathambekar, Aswin. *From Bombay to Bollywood: The Making of a Global Media Industry.* New York: New York Univ P, 2013. Print.

Sankar, Gayatri. "Review: Aamir Khan's 'Satyamev Jayatev' Stirs Souls." *Zeenews.india.* N.p., 6 May 2012. Web. 23 Apr. 2017. <zeenews.india.com/entertainment/idiotbox/review-aamir-khans-satyamev-jayatev-stirs-souls/>.

Satyamev Jayate. Dir. Satyajit Bhatkal. Perf. Aamir Khan. Doordarshan. 6 May 2012-9 Nov. 2014. Television.

Sheikh, Aminah. "Satyamev Jayate a Hit on Social Media." *Livemint.com.* N.p., 6 May 2012. Web. 14 Apr. 2017. <www.livemint.com/Consumer/nii5FdRGS IrvbEkZFwXEM/82162Satyamev-Jayate8217-a-hit-on-social-media.html/>.

Singh, Ritu V. "Satyamev Jayate: Aamir's TV Show is a Movement." *news18.com.* N.p., 6 May 2012. Web. 24 May 2017. <https://www.news18.com/news/india/satyamev-jayate-aamirs-tv-show-is-a-movement-471650.html/>

Uniyal, Parmita. "TV Review: Aamir Khan strikes the right chord with Satyamev Jayate." *Hindustantimes.com.* N.p., 7 May 2012. Web. 23 Apr. 2017. <www.hindustantimes.com/tv/tv-review-aamir-khan-strikes-the-right-chord-with-satyamev-jayate/story-y2Gjc23awNh5bBihk871MP.html />.

Further Reading

Fiske, John. *Understanding Popular Culture.* Boston: Unwin Hyman, 1989. Print.

6.

Soap Opera Stars as Corporate Commodities: The Political Economy of Television Stardom

Ritika Pant

University of Delhi, India

In the year 2010, when a leading Hindi entertainment channel Colors' flagship television programme *Balika Vadhu* (*The Child Bride*) was poised to take a five-year leap, the child actor Avika Gor who played the protagonist Anandi was to be replaced by an older female actor. Since Anandi as a character had gained immense popularity and love from the audiences, the channel bestowed the onus of choosing the new Anandi onto the audiences. For the first time on the Indian Television, the protagonist of a soap opera was to be chosen through public voting. The channel mounted three fresh faces for an audience poll to choose the new Anandi from the chosen three. The on-ground activation for the same was carried out in five major Hindi Speaking Markets (HSMs) – Jaipur, Lucknow, Indore, Nagpur, and Ahmedabad in two phases by Candid Marketing, a strategic brand activation agency. The first phase was designed to "engage consumers on-ground, so as to spread awareness and build curiosity around the revelation of the new face. In the second phase, on-air participants were given a chance to meet the actress who was finally chosen to play Anandi".[1] The two-step strategy adopted by the broadcasters not only helped to dismantle the older image of Avika Gor as Anandi but also built curiosity around the new face.

The anguish of Gor leaving the soap was transformed into an inquisitiveness amongst the audiences leading to queries like 'Who will be the new Anandi?' Devika Sharma, Vice-president, Client Servicing, Candid Marketing in an interview with an online portal said, "We were able to reach at least thirty-thousand people across these five cities through the activity".[2] After many speculations in the media and a unique SMS campaign, Pratyusha Banerjee was chosen to play the new Anandi. Banerjee, although a fresh face in the television industry, received immense recognition via such a campaign much before she could prove her mettle as an actor. She was warmly embraced as the new Anandi by the audiences and became a popular face even before she ventured into the gates of stardom.

The above example brings to our attention the many paradigms that form the star-image on the small-screen. First and foremost, the innovative marketing strategy of the channel which made Banerjee popular as a star; second, the onus on the audiences who elected and accepted Banerjee as the new Anandi; and third, the character-driven stardom that Banerjee was bestowed upon by Gor as soon as she donned the role of Anandi. In this complex replacement of actors, it becomes important to note that both Banerjee and Gor were positioned as 'commodities' that were sold to the audiences with the branding of the fictional character Anandi. The channel's conscious efforts to maintain the popularity of the brand Anandi depicts not only its revenue-oriented strategy but also the character-driven and corporatised form of stardom that the television actors attain through various corporate strategies while offering themselves as commodities. Referencing the above example, this paper looks at the political economy of stardom in the Indian television industry and examines how female stardom on the small screen is constructed through various corporate industrial practices.[3]

Locating the Political Economy of Television Stardom

Theodor Adorno and Max Horkheimer, in their study of the culture industry, observe that the production of cultural content in capitalist societies satisfies the larger needs of the capitalist economy. For them, the culture industry "remains the entertainment business" that produces factory goods like films, songs, and advertisements (15). In a similar vein, Barry King produces a critique of the "commodity-centered politics of visibility" and observes stars and celebrities as the vehicles of capitalism (7). Richard Dyer's reading of stars as "property" and Graeme Turner's designation of them as "celebrity-commodities" signifies the economic importance of stars in the film business (Dyer 5; Turner 13).

The political economy of stardom on the small screen, as Turner suggests, needs to be understood in a broader cultural and economic context of "globalization and media convergence" (33). In India, globalisation was a result of the new economic policies introduced in the early 1990s that not only changed the economic sector but also transformed the political, social and cultural matrix of the country. Television stardom in India can also be contextualized within the framework of globalisation. While the process of globalisation introduced Indian audiences to private satellite channels like Star TV and Zee, it also brought along Western programming formats adapted to the needs of Indian audiences with it (Kasbekar). In a technologically-driven globalised society, the extremely competitive private media entrepreneurs created the environment for media convergence resulting in "the same content being delivered by way of different media platforms" (Turner 35). Unlike the earlier soap operas like *Hum log* (*We, the people*) and *Buniyad* (*The Foundation*) which had minimal promotions limited to a single public service broadcaster *Doordarshan*, the soap operas of the post-satellite television era find promotions across myriad platforms that include but are not limited to radio, print, new media and outdoor media partners, etc. This direct promotion of the soap operas and indirect promotion of the soap opera stars across several media platforms becomes critical to the phenomenon of stardom on television in the post-globalisation era.

The television industry, like all the other divisions of the culture industry is a business enterprise that employs entertainment as a tool to generate revenue and increase its profits. To begin with, this paper will examine the function of the three legs of the corporate machinery— Marketing, Promotions and Public Relations in mounting the 'star image' on the small screen. The television channels, via extensive marketing and promotional campaigns of the soap operas, serve as catalyzing agents in the transformation of ordinary television soap actors into TV stars. Not undermining the individual caliber of television actors, the paper thus argues that 'television stardom' is a 'corporatised' form of stardom that rests more on corporate mechanisms than on individual star personae. In doing so, the television channel(s) exploit(s) the television actors by strategically promoting them for its own benefits for a specific period of time (generally, the period when a television star's soap opera is on-air), recycling them through reality shows and other formats to increase the respective channel's brand value and discarding them after an exhaustive use. Thus, in a relatively short life-span of their acting careers, the television stars oscillate between hyper-visibility and complete obscurity. At one instance a soap opera star becomes an omnipresent televisual entity performing in his/her show, promoting the respective broadcaster's upcoming TV shows, participating in reality TV formats, endorsing consumer products for TV advertisements, etc. and in another instance, the star is abruptly bundled into anonymity, thus being replaced by new faces and new stars. This vicious cycle of discarding old stars and introducing new ones is specific to the small-screen and explains the short-lived stardom of TV actors. Following the marketing and promotional strategies of the three leading Hindi General Entertainment Channels (GECs) – Star Plus, Sony, and Colors, I will scrutinize the corporate practices of building star-images for the small-screen and demonstrate how these entities build star-images that fluctuate between hyper-visibility and complete obscurity. But before I move on to disentangle the complex phenomenon of the formation of the star-image on television; it is essential to understand the constitution of a television star's image.

Small-screen and the Star-Image

Referring to film stars, Richard Dyer points out that they are "images in media texts" (10) and these images "have to be made...by the media industries" (85). He asserts that a film star's image is a complex synthesis of his on-screen and off-screen images which includes his/ her films along with the promotion of those films and the star through "pin-ups, public appearances, studio handouts...interviews, biographies, and coverage in the press of the star's doings and private life" (Dyer 85). Television, however, positions its stars in a distinct manner from film stars. Differentiating the two, P. David Marshall observes that while a film celebrity "plays with aura through the construction of distance . . . the television celebrity is configured around conceptions of familiarity" (119). He, further, notes that the domesticated positioning of the television set, the insertion of commercials as part of the programming pattern, and the star's close connections with the broadcasting organization are all reasons which lead to decay in the aura of a television celebrity.

Furthermore, John Ellis moves away from the prevailing lexicon and posits that due to its immediacy and intimacy what television offers are not stars but television personalities: "The personality is someone who is famous for being famous and is famous only in so far as he or she makes frequent television appearances" (314). Attributing one of the key characteristics of television personalities, Graeme Turner observes them to be operating "within a different semiotic economy" where they seamlessly perform to "eliminate the distance between their performance and themselves" (17). Talking about soap opera stars, in particular, Marshall notes that the soap operas by their function are intimate; they draw the audiences to the bedrooms and living rooms of the characters and often invite them to understand the "psychological make-up of characters" (128). For Marshall, "the full sense of knowledge of the individual soap opera character by the audience impedes the possibility of the actor in a soap opera becoming known beyond his/her role" (252). In the Indian context, Pramod K. Nayar speaks of a "sympathetic identification" with the television stars as opposed to an "auratic identification" with the film stars (32). Further, "It is in their (the television stars') familiarity of characters and situations that their recognisability and star value exists" (Nayar 32). While numerous television scholars explain the discourse around television stardom to be centrally located in the actor/character dichotomy, the discussion about the economic apparatus that establishes such character-driven-stardom on the small-screen, especially in the Indian context, finds insignificant attention. This paper delves into a dissection of the corporate apparatus that produces character-based-stardom on television and thus, proposes the idea of a 'corporatised stardom' on the small screen. While my argument about a 'corporatised' form of stardom is primarily about television stars, it may be extended beyond the medium of television. With the yesteryear film production houses operating in a studio-based economy and the contemporary film production houses turning into corporate business firms utilizing lucrative marketing techniques alongside a parallel emergence of artiste management companies, film stardom may also be conceived of as falling under the category of corporatised stardom. This, however, is material for a different study.

Although the terms 'celebrity', 'television personality' and 'stars' have blurred boundaries, yet I would prefer to use the term 'stars' for television actors for various reasons. First, the expansion of cable television in India in the last two decades has led to a tremendous increase in the popularity of television actors almost at par with film stars. Second, the techniques of marketing and promotions have become a quintessential factor for television programming which has not only benefitted the broadcasters but has also promised a greater exposure to small-screen actors that often leads to hyper-visibility. Third, with the convergence of different media, film stardom itself has been redefined, as film stars, now, are often seen making use of the small-screen to promote themselves and their films. Therefore, the small-screen itself has emerged as a powerful medium in the contemporary visual milieu in which small-screen actors are glorified as television stars.

The 'Corporatised' Star-Image

Graeme Turner notes that the celebrity status of soap opera actors in the United States was a result of "their exposure in a particular, low-prestige vehicle…maximized through an industrial structure that vigorously exploited cross-media and multiplatform promotions" (196). Turner mentions that the broadcasting networks which commissioned the soap operas also owned a chain of magazines that frequently featured the soap opera stars on the cover page. As discussed in the earlier section, the star status that the Indian soap opera actors acquire is also a result of similar visibility that the broadcasting channels provide them with across diverse media. Through the paper, I will analyse various platforms that the television channels create for the marketing and promotion of their fiction properties which in turn become lucrative for the television actors to acquire popularity through their on-screen characters and thus help them attain stardom.

The marketing and promotions of television soaps are as crucial as their production. While the programming team in any channel is responsible for producing the creative content of the soap operas, it is with the help of the marketing team that the real numbers in terms of Television Rating Points (TRPs) are delivered. The marketing team in any television channel ensures that a show on their channel reaches a maximum number of audiences before the launch, and sustains its audiences post-launch. Gaurav Seth, Senior Vice President of

Sony Entertainment Television (Sony, hereafter), during my field interview, explains the functioning of the marketing of a soap opera in Hindi GECs:

> The marketing of a soap opera depends on its core appeal and the target audience. Once we figure that, we then start propelling that soap into our TG's (a term used for target audience) minds using a variety of media available to us. We create promotional campaigns or the promos which highlight the story using the strengths of the character. Typically, whoever is the protagonist of the soap is then front-footed onto the promotional campaign. This then goes on to the off-air campaigns and takes the form of billboards, hoardings, print advertisements, radio, internet, mobile depending on how best to reach the target audience. (Seth)[4.]

Sonia Huria, Associate Vice President – Communications and PR, Colors explains that the promotions of the TV shows are mainly targeted in the 23 Hindi Speaking Markets (HSMs) where the main audiences for Hindi GECs reside. She further adds:

> When we launch a show, we prioritize the markets depending on where the show will appeal more. But now we are going deeper due to the extension of TAM (Television Audience Measurement) meters. Now smaller towns like Ranchi and Kanpur also have TAM meters. So, it becomes very important as to how you are introducing a star to them and building connectivity with the viewers. (Huria)

The promos of the soaps are the first audio-visual packages of promotion that introduce a soap opera to its audiences. While the On-air Promotions Team (OAP) is responsible for producing promos at the creative front, the Marketing team decides the reach and frequency of the promos to be played on air. The promos are strategically placed in between successful prime-time soaps so that they reach out to a wider audience. They are played not only on the broadcasting channel but also on a wider network to which the channel belongs.[5] Looking at the launch promo campaign of a soap opera, I will analyze how the female protagonist of the soap is front-footed while the concept of the soap opera is simultaneously revealed to audiences.

Kehta Hai Dil . . . Jee Le Zara (Live a Little...the Heart Says) is a prime-time soap opera that was launched on Sony TV on 15 August 2013. The soap unfolds the story of a strong and independent thirty-four-year-old Sanchi (played by Sangeeta Ghosh) who has dedicated all her life to take care of her family (that comprises her brother, sister and maternal and paternal grandmothers) and has completely ignored her individual priorities in life. The on-air promotional campaign for the soap is divided into three promos, each promo of 45 seconds duration. The first promo is narrated by the protagonist Sanchi and introduces the audience to Sanchi and her family. The promo opens with Sanchi introducing us to her sister while she helps her sister choose a dress followed by her brother asking Sanchi for his pocket-money, and then her maternal and paternal grandmothers and finally her workplace – her factory. At last, Sanchi looks into the camera and introduces herself to the audiences saying *"Main hoon Saanchi aur yeh hai meri zindagi, mera sab kuch"* (I am Sanchi, and this is my life, my everything). The first-person narrative in the promo indicates that the soap is primarily the story of Sanchi while all the other characters are peripheral and help her in her journey of life. The second promo is a conversation between Sanchi and her two grandmothers who are trying to convince her to get married saying that she is thirty-four years and that they have been a burden on her ever since and now she needs to live her own life. The third promo is the point-of-view of the male protagonist Dhruv (Ruslan Mumtaz), where once again we are introduced, not to Dhruv but to Sanchi through him. The voice-over of the promo which goes as follows introduces us to Sanchi in a more intricate manner, leading us to various facets of her day-to-day life:

Dekhne mein kisi aam ladki si lagti hai,	When I see, she looks like a common girl
Par sochta hoon toh khaas lagne lagti hai	But when I think of her, she appears special.
Kabhi hukum chalati hai	Sometimes, she orders everyone
Toh kabhi rob jamati hai	And at other times she throws tantrums.
Par nazrein milau toh nazrein pher leti hai	But when I look at her she looks away;
Ghar aur business dono khud sambhalti hai	she manages her home and business all by herself,
Par khud ka khayal rakhna aksar bhoool jaati hai"	But she forgets to take care of herself!

The promo ends with a tagline *"apno ki zindagi mein har rang hai bhara, ab toh apne liye jee le zara"* (You've lived enough for your family, now live a little for yourself too). Looking at all the three promos individually and in entirety, the audiences get an idea about the concept of the soap and how critical the character of Sanchi will remain in unfolding the narrative of the soap. Even before the soap opera goes on air, the audiences build an image of Sanchi as a modern, independent, strong, ambitious and self-sacrificing woman who balances perfectly between her personal and professional life. On the one hand, the promos of the soaps showcase the stories they will offer to the audiences and on the other, they also create a curiosity about the characters and make them popular much prior to the telecast. While the promos are direct communication related to the story of the soap, there are also various indirect communications that help build the popularity of the soap opera characters. The following sections of the chapter will look at various other devices through which the soap opera characters are made popular and projected as stars.

Public Relations and the Construction of a Fictional Star

In a television channel, the Public Relations (PR) team often operating under the umbrella of the marketing team that promotes the soap operas and its characters through diverse media tie-ups with electronic and print media.[6] The PR strategies for a TV soap are often extensive and are handed over to external PR agencies that work for the television channels.[7] Senior Manager, Communications and PR, Star Plus, Pooja Kumbhare explained that the key to promoting a TV soap is to put the protagonist at the core of all promotions.

> The basic PR brief for any soap opera is that we need to build in character. Everything revolves around the character, and the story comes in later. The initial PR campaigns introduce the character, frontload the show and drive the audiences towards the tune-in of the show. So, we end each campaign with the Date, Day, Time (DDT format) of the launch. (Kumbhare)

Talking about a popular soap opera *Jassi Jaisi Koi Nahi (There's No One Like Jassi)*, Kumbhare adds that the entire PR for *JJKN* revolved mainly around Jassi.

> Till about two years Mona's (the actor who played Jassi) identity was hidden. She only appeared as Jassi to the media. Her braces, her pink umbrella became famous amongst the audiences. Even in the Press Conference, no one had seen her real self. We made the character so adorable that when she actually transformed into a pretty damsel, the audiences stopped identifying with her and the show ratings dropped. (Kumbhare)

On a similar note, Huria explains how PR stories on the soap *Balika Vadhu* mainly focused on the social evil of child marriage, but many of the stories were built around the protagonist, Anandi, as she says "When we cast Avika Gor for Anandi, we built stories about the effort that went into getting into the skin of the character of playing the little Anandi. How she met real child brides and how she rehearsed her lines, all this became fodder for the press" (Huria). However, she adds, "After the launch, we started promoting other characters also - *Dadisa* (grandmother) as the grey character, Bhairo Singh as the righteous father. The soap's impact was such that it became cool to wear *ghagra choli* (long skirt and blouse), gold jewellery and to use words like *'Dadisa'* and *'khamagani'* ('Hello' in Rajasthani dialect) in the day to day conversations" (Huria).

The basic PR plan for any TV show is to promote it across media including television, print, radio, digital and outdoor in the specific target markets. The PR strategy for a TV show across Hindi GEC is to make an official announcement about the show with a press conference, providing opportunities for photographs, interviews/ audio-visual bytes by the key characters to all the media. From time to time, the PR team circulates print/electronic stories about the soaps and its characters to keep the buzz going. The journalists are often invited to the sets where they can interact with the actors and interview them. Such stories, however, are almost always about the 'reel' life of the actors and do not enter the realms of their off-screen lives.[8] Listed are a few examples of the headlines of news stories published in various newspapers and websites that elucidate how the channel PR teams strictly allow for the circulation of only character-driven stories:

- Ram Priya's love story to be revived in *Bade Achche Lagte Hain* (*The Times of India*, 6 February 2014)
- Are Anandi and Shiv ready to adopt a disabled child in *Balika Vadhu*? (www.entertainment.oneindia.in, 9 January 2014)
- *Balika Vadhu's* Anandi to finally divorce Jagiya (*The Hindustan Times*, 19 April 2012).
- Priya to leave Ram's house in *Bade Achche Lagte hain* (www.tellychakkar.com, 20 November 2013)

The stories about the private lives of television stars which are incoherent with their on-screen characters find little weight on the broadcaster's front and have had disastrous effects for the television channels in the past. Maintaining the anonymity of a TV actress who played the protagonist in a prime-time soap opera on Star Plus, Kumbhare explains how the ratings of the show dropped drastically when the newspapers covered stories of the actress being found smoking in a lounge and being escorted by the policemen:

> As a channel PR, I will never want the press to cover such a story because it impacts my audiences. The story came out at a time when there was a high point coming on the show, but it all got brushed off. Every month you get the most loved characters report. The said actor was on top for so many weeks, but after this, her ranking suddenly dropped. (Kumbhare)

Furthermore, television news channels cover news stories about the soap opera storylines and characters typically in the 2:30 pm afternoon slot in programmes like *Saas Bahu Saazish* (ABP News), *Saas Bahu aur Betiyaan* (Aaj Tak) and *Saas in the City* (Headlines Today). Kumbhare explains that in such shows, apart from giving out regular stories about the storyline of the soap, the PR team often promotes the characters by having them host one of the segments of the show as anchors but in their character appearances. These shows bring to us the para-texts of a television show, often including 'Behind the Scenes' footage, stories from the personal lives of the TV stars but mostly address the actors with their character names. These shows cover myriad aspects of a television star's life maintaining a thin line between the character and the actor. The programming format includes segments on the narrative progression of a soap by giving a glimpse of the forthcoming episodes, the celebration of festivals like Diwali and Holi with the stars, or a day out with the stars covering their reel and real lives both on the sets and even at their homes. While these shows reveal interesting facts from the inner lives of the television stars they also refer back to the on-screen character in subtle ways, thereby maintaining a fair balance between the reel and the real lives of the television stars. Apart from circulating stories across various media, the PR department in collaboration with the Marketing team also ensures to organize other activities like on-ground events, city visits, contests, meet and greet sessions with the television stars to increase the exposure of the soap operas and also of the star faces.

These 'on-ground activations' are typically executed within the HSMs in public spaces like a mall, a housing society, a school or even a consumer's house. The protagonists of a particular soap are taken to audience markets like Lucknow, Jaipur, Kanpur, Indore, Nagpur, etc. where they 'meet and greet' the audiences. These activities happen during the launch of a soap opera, but also at times when the soap has achieved a milestone. The channel's purpose of an on-ground activation is to build a consumer connect and to attract more eyeballs. However, I see these on-ground events or any such PR initiatives as activities that help to build and further catalyse the television actors' stardom. While the television channels use the television actors' popularity for monetary benefits, the actors themselves use this platform to reach out to a vast audience. Another important factor that counts in making these events successful is the media presence. Any PR activity is termed successful as long as it gains maximum media coverage. Pramod Nayar considers media as an important element of celebrity ecology that has enormous "symbolic power" (34). Therefore, I look at all of these PR activities, specifically the on-ground activities as what Nayar terms the "media rituals" that help in the construction of stardom (Nayar 34). Substantiating my argument with an example, I will examine how various on-ground events create character-driven stardom for small-screen stars.

Star Parivaar - Aapka Star Aapke Shehar (*Star Family - Your Star in your City*) was a major consumer engagement initiative led by the entertainment channel Star Plus in the year 2012 before the commencement of its annual award ceremony, Star Parivaar Awards. The series was also televised on Star Plus as a curtain-raiser to the upcoming awards. The Marketing and PR team designed an on-ground activity where they took the key characters of the leading soap operas to a few important HSMs. The actors visited these towns, interacted with their fans, engaged in fun activities with them and invited them for the annual awards. The actors were chosen to visit the target markets where their soap operas were fictionally set. Star Plus' prime-time soap *Diya aur Baati Hum* (*We are the Lamp and the Light*), set in Rajasthan had its lead pair Sooraj and Sandhya visit Jaipur. Interestingly, the actors conducted these activities as the characters they played on-screen, dressed in their character costumes, often addressing each other by their character names. The entire event when viewed on television as a half an hour episode appeared as a staged performance of mediated frenzy created by well-choreographed shots of television stars passing through huge crowds of fans who were eager to get a glimpse of them. Unlike film stars, who their fans can desire from a distance, television stars engaged with their fans in acute proximity.

Television Stars as Financial Assets

With an emphasis on the economic importance of celebrities, Turner notes that they are a "financial asset to those who stand to gain from their commercialization – networks, record companies, producers, agents, managers, and finally the celebrities themselves...As the asset appreciates – as the celebrity's fame spreads, so does its earning capacity" (193). The following section of the chapter will argue that television stars are also financial assets for the respective television channels which the channel produces for its own advantage and later puts to optimum usage for monetary profits. I will thus argue that in due course, the star often loses her identity as an actor and instead becomes a commodity that is sold for the host channel's financial interests.

Seth, Senior VP- Marketing, Sony, observes that the lead character of the channel's most successful show always has a larger impact on audiences. He further adds, "We try and push all other properties through one show. We want people to get hooked on to the entire prime time and not just one show" (Seth). Kumbhare from Star Plus is also of the same opinion and says,

> By default, everyone knows the show leads. We don't strategise that we should build one star and then introduce another through her. The thought is to make every character iconic – so that each character represents an ethnicity. If Sandhya from *Diya Aur Baati Hum* and Akshara from *Yeh Rishta Kya Kehlata Hai* (What is this relationship called?) are Rajasthani, they hold the Rajasthan market very well. Gopi Bahu (*Saath Nibhana Saathiya*) is very big in Gujarat. For us, every character is important in various geographies. But if one show does extremely well you piggyback on that protagonist. (Kumbhare)

While this division of geographies provides the television channels a uniform presence over all the leading HSMs, it often leads to uneven popularity of the television actors in specific regions. This phenomenon, I term 'regional stardom' on television where a star becomes very famous in a particular region of a country while not so much in the other parts. While there are iconic characters like Jassi or Anandi who have a national appeal, there are other characters like Akshara, Archana or Gopi who, although popular country-wide, hold a strong market force in specific regions. With the soap operas set up in a particular village or a region, the characters embrace certain physical characteristics and diction that belongs to that region. Talking about the protagonist Archana from *Pavitra Rishta* (A Sacred Relationship) telecast on Zee TV, Kumbhare says:

> People identify with one character. Archana, being a Maharashtrian girl is very famous in the Maharashtra market. The way she wears her nose-pin, ties her hair, or even uses Marathi words like *'aayi'* (mother) and *'baba'* (father) in her regular conversations, makes the Marathi audiences identify with her more than they could with any other character. (Kumbhare)

Huria agrees that there is regional stardom, but the stardom of the actor is not directly related to the markets where her soap opera is set. For instance, she explains that although *Balika Vadhu* is set in Rajasthan, the highest ratings of the show are received from Madhya Pradesh. The reason for this, she says, is the marketing strategy. "The channel does a plus one strategy. For *Balika Vadhu* (set in Rajasthan), we target a strong market for the show like Rajasthan for promotions, and we also target a weaker market to get the inactive audiences" (Huria). This weaker market might later on garner more ratings thus making the soap opera popular in that region. Kumbahre's analysis of the audience identification with the character traits of a specific region and Huria's analysis of an uneven marketing approach bring home the fact that while there can be characters with national appeal, there are also characters with regional appeal who acquire regional stardom.

I will now explore some examples to understand how television channels bank on the key characters of their leading soap operas to promote both fiction and non-fiction properties. The year 2008 changed the landscape of television programming on Hindi GECs when it's newly entrant member, Colors, gave respite to the audiences from Ekta Kapoor's Balaji Telefilms' never-ending *saas-bahu* sagas. First in its bouquet of television soaps was *Balika Vadhu* that launched in July 2008 and was received very well by audiences. The child protagonist Anandi became a household name in just a couple of weeks. By the time, the channel was preparing for its second big fiction property, *Uttaran* (*The Discarded*), both Anandi and *Balika Vadhu* had acquired immense popularity. Huria explains that promoting *Uttaran* through *Balika Vadhu* was a safe bet for the channel as it had a large viewership:

We promoted *Uttaran* through Anandi. She was the face of the channel and the communication for *Uttaran* was done through Anandi wherein she invited the audiences saying *–Aapne dekhi meri kahani, ab dekhiye Ichcha ki kahani* (*You saw my story, now watch Ichcha's story*). So, we tugged the audiences to Ichhcha (*Uttaran's* protagonist) through Anandi. We continue to do so for all our shows. (Huria)

Reality TV show *Bigg Boss- Season 7* Grand Finale episode on Colors also witnessed the show's host Salman Khan introducing the protagonists of the two upcoming soaps *Rangrasiya* (*Beloved*) and *Beintehaa* (*Limitless*) which were to replace *Bigg Boss*. Such in-show promotions or plug-ins (as they are termed in the industry) work successfully because the broadcasters don't have to incur an additional cost for promotions as they are the host channels. Also, promoting a new property through a platform like *Bigg Boss* ensures them not only maximum eyeballs but also a loyal audience who faithfully watch the channel the next day even though their favourite show (*Big Boss*) goes off-air.

One of the most successful non-fictional shows of Star Plus, *Masterchef India*, also promoted the launch of the second season through its fictional characters. One launch promo of *Masterchef India season 2*, used the popular face of the female protagonist Akshara from *Ye Rishta Kya Kehlata Hai* (*What is this relationship called?*) making the *Masterchef* show logo with her hand while the voice over played *"Ab Badlo India apne khane ka andaz"* (*India, Now change the way you eat*). The domesticated and traditional figure of Akshara was in perfect synchronization with the *mise-en-scene* of a cooking talent hunt show and invited women audiences to watch it as their favourite *bahu* Akshara endorsed the show. Sony Entertainment Television's December 2013' launch *Main Na Bhoolungi* (*I will not Forget*) also had one of its most successful prime-time soap, *Bade Achche Lagte Hain's* (*It Seems So Beautiful*) protagonist Priya (Sakshi Tanwar) do a cameo in the first episode and introduce to the audiences, the protagonist, Shikha Gupta (played by Aishwarya). Seth explains that since *Bade Achche...*is a successful show, "the protagonists Ram and Priya have a brand value and they sell very well. So, all brand-related work is done by them" (Seth). Thus, the usage of popular fictional characters to promote other fiction and non-fiction properties of the broadcasting channel is a widely used strategy that serves a dual function of garnering revenue for the host channel and increasing exposure for the television stars.

In the year 2010, when Star Plus completed its ten years, the channel underwent a major rebranding with the tagline *"Rishta Wohi Soch Nayi"* (*Same Association, New Outlook*). The campaign center-staged all the key female faces of its successful shows dressed in red (which was to be the colour of the new logo of Star Plus) on hoardings, on-air promos and the digital platform. While the on-air campaigns included promos, the off-air campaigns had print advertisements in newspapers, and hoardings across HSMs.[9] The channel aired many versions of a ten-second promo that showcased a few of the protagonists of the successful soaps. One of the promos had Suhana, the protagonist of *Sasural Genda Phool* (*My Husband's Home is like a Marigold Flower*) looking into the camera and opening her palm to let out the new red star logo. Another had Akshara, the protagonist of *Yeh Rishta Kya Kehlata Hai* looking into the camera and revolving around the red star logo. Both the promos ended with the tagline *"Rishta Wohi Soch Nayi."* These promos that played not only on Star Plus but also on the other channels of Star Network and various news channels helped in building a strong connection between Akshara/Suhana - the character and Star Plus – the brand. Therefore, one can see that at one level, Hina Khan, who played Akshara, did get famous, but her fame was not independent of the popularity of the character Akshara or the brand Star Plus. With such a campaign, her association with Star Plus became so strong that any other channel would not offer her a new show then because she was the 'face' of Star Plus. Also, it is interesting to note that the entire campaign was driven by the female protagonists of the channel and their male counterparts were almost absent from all promotional drives. Another point that is noteworthy is the absence of female protagonists from the day-time soaps in the campaign. All the faces that promoted the campaign were protagonists of the prime-time soap operas as the afternoon soap protagonists were not given enough importance by the channels. Therefore, the revenue-oriented drive of the channel also compelled it to exploit its most popular faces to promote the new brand image while obscuring others.

A closer look at the promotional music videos of the Star Parivaar Awards over the past few years, explains how the 'face of the channel' is also an example of a continuously shifting paradigm of stardom. Star Parivaar music videos are shot and aired annually before the main event as a precursor and an invitation to the audiences for the final award ceremony. Every year the music video has a freshly written and composed song, shot along with a few important actors of the channel. The Star Parivaar audio track and signature tune remain more or less similar every year; however, the faces which are featured on the video keep altering. Drawing a contrast between the music video of the year 2009 and 2012, I observe that all the actors featuring in the 2009 video had been replaced by fresh faces. The 2009 music video opened with four leading couples - Akshara- Naitik from *Yeh Rishta Kya Kehlata Hai*, Heer-Prem from *Kis Des Mein Hai Mera Dil* (*In which Land is my heart?*), Ragini- Ranvir and Saadhna - Aalekh from *Sapna Babul ka –Bidaai* (*Departure: The Dream of a Father*) heartily thanking their audiences for giving their love and support to the channel. The 2012 video, however, featured Gopi-Ahem from *Saath Nibhana Saathiya* (*Be With Me, My Beloved*), Pratigya-Krishna from *Mann Ki Awaaz–Pratigya* (*The heart's voice - Pratigya*),

Sandhya-Suraj (*Diya aur Baati Hum*) and Khushi-Arnav from *Iss Pyar ko main Kya Naam Doon* (*What Shall I Call this Love* ?) as the leading faces of the channel. While there can be an explanation that most of the soaps around 2009 went off-air by 2012 and hence fresh faces were used for a fresh music video, there was also disappointment amongst other actors who were not showcased in the music video despite their shows being on air (the absence of afternoon soap opera actors). Though I will maintain the anonymity of such actors, I would like to assert that my field research did demonstrate that the actors are well aware of the strategies of the channels and they realize that at any point in time the channel promotes only a set of actors belonging to the successful soaps that can fetch some brownie points for the broadcasters, particularly the prime time soaps while completely ignoring the others.

Too Much Too Soon: The Hyper-visible Star Body

Discussing the role of Marketing and Promotional strategies in the construction of small-screen stardom, television Producer Rajan Shahi explains that the broadcasters have a lot at stake in building a brand image of the channel or in making an actor a star:

> Now, channels play a major role in the promotion of a star. They spend huge amounts of money sending them for city-visits, on-ground events, overseas events, marketing and promotions to make the character popular. They make big brands of the characters through the actors and ensure that they become household names. So, a Suhana from Star Plus is a brand who has certain equity. The channel will not want her to be seen in short dresses as it distorts the image of an ideal *bahu* that the channel wants to emphasize upon. (Shahi)

In contrast, with reference to film actors, Turner observes that while promoting a film, the personal interests of the stars differ from that of the producers. "The stars promote their latest work as a means of enhancing their commercial value in general and so it is possible that they will be reluctant to closely tie this publicity to the particular performance vehicle" (Turner 195). In other words, while the film star promotes the film, she simultaneously also promotes herself through other projects for other producers. However, a television star's commitment to one project at a time does not grant her the liberty to do the same. While a television star also attempts to promote her (self) as she promotes the television show, she lacks the agency of doing the same that the film star possesses. This lack of agency often ends in frustration for the star where she constantly negotiates the reel/real difference by masking her own identity behind the fictional character she plays. Television Producer, Rajan Shahi discusses the agitation in the actors that come with such frustration over a period of time: "You help the actors create a character, they become popular because of that and then they want to fight that image because they want to move over that image" (Shahi).

Furthermore, Shahi observes a 'too much too soon' phenomenon for television actors wherein they become so popular within a limited time-frame that they are suddenly everywhere – advertisements, inaugurations, ribbon-cutting ceremonies, *dandiya* performances (a dance form), etc. This hyper-visibility of the actors enables them to quote exorbitant prices for public appearances, promotional events and at times for their soaps which made them stars. Apart from the financial aspect, their appearances on platforms other than their soap operas create a non-negotiable tension between their on-screen character roles and other appearances that the audiences do not comply with. Writer-producer Zama Habib and Rajan Shahi explain that lately, the channels have started to realize the real commercial value of television stars and hence are making strict moves towards controlling the star's professional involvements:

> Now, for the past two years, a few channels have initiated a tri-party contract. Earlier the contract would be between the actor and the production house. But now the channels have also become a stakeholder as they have realized the actors' commercial value. The channels exploit them to promote their own shows and to build their brand-image. Maintaining the image of the character is, therefore, crucial for the channels. (Shahi)

Taking into account the contractual labour and extreme working conditions of the actors, I drive my argument further by taking into consideration the 'use and throw' economy of the television industry where the stars reach two extremes of their careers from hyper-visibility to complete obscurity in a very short time-span. While a show is on-air and receives good ratings, a television actor becomes the 'face of the channel' and is exploited by the channel to an optimum usage where she is used to endorse or promote possibly everything on the channel, or even the network (as in the case of Star TV, Viacom 18) from a new soap opera, a non-fiction show, an Award function or even a Corporate Social Responsibility-led activity. All the brand-related endorsements are conducted by the actor who is the 'face of the channel' since her face acts as a strong brand recall for consumers/audiences. Whereas the actors of the soap operas that do not have a large viewership or cannot deliver ratings (especially day time soap operas) have to bear with the partial nature of the broadcasters and hence are provided least visibility or promotion by the broadcasters.

Huria explains that when in *Balika Vadhu*, the old Anandi was being replaced by a new one, Colors did not let go of Avika Gor, who played the old Anandi, and instead put her on another show *Sasural Simar Ka* (*Simar's In-*

laws) as Roli because she was still a selling property. Avika Gor was kept alive but as Roli. But in most cases, the popular faces of television channels are discarded once their soaps are over and are taken up by other channels in other characters after a certain gap of time. This time-gap acts as a cooling-off period for the audiences to shed the previous character image and accept the actor in a new image.

The association between a specific channel and an actor is often strong and difficult to dismantle. However, there have been instances when one actor who was strongly associated with a channel appeared in another soap opera on a competing platform. A prominent example of this is Sakshi Tanwar who was associated with Star Plus for eight years in the image of Parvati Bhabhi in *Kahani Ghar Ghar Ki* (*The Story of Every House*) and is currently the face of Sony TV as Priya in *Bade Achche Lagte Hain* (*It Seems So Beautiful*). However, it is worth pointing out that the two shows happened within a gap of almost three years, thereby giving enough breathing time to audiences to accept Parvati as another character, Priya. Other actors like Sara Khan, Sanaya Irani, Jia Manek and Ragini Khanna have also worked across competing platforms, but it is noteworthy that their first screen image is the most impactful one that overrules their other performances. Smriti Irani, one of the most prominent female stars ever on the small screen with her character Tulsi in *Kyunki Saas Bhi Kabhi Bahu Thi* (*Because the Mother-in-law was Once a Daughter-in-law*), also could not sustain her popularity through other characters that she later played. All her other efforts on the small-screen were ineffective as audiences found it difficult to rid themselves of her image as Tulsi. However, her image of an ideal *bahu* did help her to create new career opportunities in politics with the right-wing Bhartiya Janata Party offering her a ticket to contest the Lok Sabha elections in 2004 and again in 2014 and 2019.[10] While on the one hand, a broadcaster's deep investment in the promotion of a particular soap opera and its actor(s) enables the small-screen actors to attain stardom, on the other the small-screen stardom is often confined within the fictional realms of the soap opera narrative.

Conclusion

Although the chapter argues that a television star's image is corporatised, I will not take away from the fact that the television actors' contribution to their individual stardom is immense. Functioning within a restricted economy and a short career-span, a television star's career fluctuates in two contrasting directions – from hyper-visibility to complete obscurity. The after-life of a soap opera star is both challenging and eventful as she constantly tries to dismantle the corporatised character-based stardom and negotiates with the reel/real dichotomy. While the early years of a soap opera actor may be observed within the framework of corporatised stardom, the after-life of a soap opera star could open up new discourses on the 'agency' of the star-figure in the field of television stardom studies.

Notes

1. See "Balika Vadhu leaves footprints on ground too," 29 July 2010, accessed from http://www.afaqs.com/news/story/ on 5 March 2014.

2. See "Balika Vadhu leaves footprints on ground too," 29 July 2010, accessed from http://www.afaqs.com/news/story/ on 5 March 2014.

3. By the term 'television industry', I limit my discussion to only Hindi General Entertainment Channels – Sony, Zee, Colors, Star Plus. My research might be applicable to but is not involved with the News Channels, regional channels or other Lifestyle channels.

4. The interviews with Gaurav Seth, Pooja Kumbhare, Zama Habib, Sonia Huria and Rajan Shahi were taken during my field trip to Mumbai in December 2013.

5. If a soap opera is launched on Star Plus, the promos of the soap will also be played across other Star Network channels like Life OK, Star World, Star Movies, Star Utsav, Channel V and so on.

6. While PR is mostly referred to as 'free publicity', PR teams in GECs spend a huge amount of money in buying media space/time to promote specific television shows and characters.

7. In my interviews, I found out that all the three channels under my study, have handed over their work to external agencies like–Hanmer MSL(StarPlus), Genesis (Colors), Value360 Communications (Sony Entertainment Television).

8. This is not to say that the stories about the private lives of television actors do not interest media. The real-life stories, however, are always dug out by the journalists themselves and the channel PR team does not initiate any such publicity unless it is in the commercial interest of the broadcasting channel.

9. The channel tied up with the women's Hindi Magazine *Grihshobha* in order to promote the rebranding. The magazine cover had the protagonist *Pratigya* (Pooja Gor) dressed in a red saree, while the bottom left corner of the page had the red star logo along with the date and time of the telecast of the soap *Pratigya*. It also had the message "samaj sudhar ki pehel ghar se" (beginning of the social change from home).

10. Irani currently heads the Ministry of Women & Child Development and the Ministry of Textiles in the Narendra Modi-led Bhartiya Janata Party government after the party had a landslide victory in the 17th Lok Sabha elections in May 2019.

Bibliography

Adorno, Theodor, and Max Horkheimer. "The Culture Industry: Enlightenment as Mass Deception." *Hollywood: Cultural Dimensions: Ideology, Identity and Cultural Industry Studies.* Ed. Thomas Schatz. New York: Routledge, 2004. 3-37. Print.

Bade Achche Lagte Hain. Prod. Balaji Telefims. Perf. Sakshi Tanwar. Sony Entertainment. 30 May 2011-10 Jul. 2014. Television.

Balika Vadhu. Prods. Sunjoy Waddhwa and Comall Sunjoy W. Perf. Avika Gor. Colors. 21 Jul.2008-31 Jul.2016. Television.

Beintehaa. Prod. Farhan Salaruddin. Perf. Preetika Rao and Harshad Arora. Colors. 30 Dec. 2013-21 Nov. 2014. Television.

Bigg Boss-Season 7. Prod. Endemol Productions. Perf. Salman Khan. Colors.15 Sept. 2013-28 Dec. 2013. Television.

Buniyad. Prod. Amit Khanna. Perf. Alok Nath. Doordarshan. 1986-87. Television.

Diya aur Baati Hum. Prod. Shashi Sumeet Productions. Perf. Anas Rashid and Deepika Singh. Star Plus. 29 Aug. 2011-10 Sept. 2016. Television.

Dyer, Richard. *Heavenly Bodies.* Oxon: Routledge, 2004. Print.

Ellis, John. "Stars as a Cinematic Phenomenon." *Star Texts: Image and Performancein Film and Television.* Ed. Jeremy G Butler. Detroit, Michigan: Wayne State University Press, 1991. 300-315. Print.

Humlog. Dir. P Kumar Vasudev. Perf. Vinod Nagpal and Jayshri Arora. Doordarshan. 7 Jul.1984-17 Dec. 1985. Television.

Iss Pyar ko main Kya Naam Doon? Prods. Gul Khan, Nissar Parvez and Rajesh Chadha. Perf. Barun Sobti and Sanaya Irani. 6 Jun. 2011-15 Dec. 2015. Television.

Jassi Jaisi Koi Nahin. Dirs. Tony Singh and Deeya Singh. Perf. Mona Singh. Sony TV. 1 Sept. 2003-4 May 2006. Television.

Kahani Ghar Ghar Ki. Prod. Balaji Telefilms. Perf. Sakshi Tanwar. 16 Oct. 2000-9 Oct. 2008. Television.

Kasbekar, Asha. *"Television": Pop Culture India!*California: ABCCLIO, 2006. Print.

Kehta Hai Dil...Jee Le Zara. Prods. Shrishti Arya and Goldie Behl. Perf. Sangeeta Ghosh and Ruslaan Mumtaz. 15 Aug. 2013-8 May 2014. Television.

King, Barry. "Stardom, Celebrity and the Money Form." *The Velvet Light Trap (University of Texas Press)* 65.1 (2010): 7-19. Print.

Kumbhare, Pooja, Sonia Huria and Gaurav Seth. Personal Interview. Ritika Pant. 28 Dec. 2013. Audio.

Main Na Bhoolungi. Prods. Yash Patnaik and Mamta Patnaik. Perf. Aishwarya Sakhuja. 23 Dec. 2013-15 Aug. 2014. Television.

Mann Ki Awaaz–Pratigya. Prod. Pearl Grey. Perf. Pooja Gor. 7 Dec. 2009-27 Oct. 2012. Television.

Marshall, P. David. *Celebrity and Power: Fame in Contemporary Culture.* Minneapolis: University of Minnesota Press, 1997. Print.

Master Chef India - Season 2. Prod. Colosceum Media. Star Plus. 2011-12. Television.

Nayar, Pramod K. *Seeing Stars: Spectacle, Society and Celebrity Culture.* New Delhi: Sage, 2009. Print.

Pavitra Rishta. Prods. Ekta Kapoor and Shobha Kapoor. Perf. Sushant Singh Rajput and Ankita Lokhande. Colors. 1 Jun. 2009-25 Oct. 2014. Television.

Rangrasiya. Prod. Saurabh Tewari. Perf. Ashish Sharma and Sanaya Irani.Colors. 30 Dec. 2013-19 Sept. 2014. Television.

Saath Nibhana Saathiya. Prod. Rashmi Sharma. Perf. Jia Manek. Star Plus. 3 May 2010-23 May 2017.Television.

Sapna Babul Ka...Bidaai. Prod. Rajan Shahi. Perf. Sara Khan. Star Plus. 8 Oct. 2007-13 Nov. 2010. Television.

Sasural Genda Phool. Prod. Ravi Ojha and Zama Habib. Perf. Jay Soni and Ragini Khanna. Star Plus. 1 Mar.2010-21 Apr.2012. Television.

*Sasural Simar Ka.*Prod. Rashmi Sharma. Perf. AvikaGor. Colors. 25 Apr.2011-2 Mar.2018. Television.

Shahi, Rajan, and Zama Habib. Personal Interview. Ritika Pant. 22 Jul. 2013.Audio.

Star Parivaar - Aapka Star Aapke Shehar. Prod. Key Light. Star Plus. Television. 19-23 Mar. 2012.

Star Parivaar Awards. Prod. Optymistix. Star Plus. 3 Jul. 2003. Television.

Turner, Graeme. *Understanding Celebrity.* London: Sage, 2004. Print.

Uttaran. Prods. Pintoo Guha and Rupali Guha. Perf. Tina Dutta. Colors. 1 Dec. 2008-16 Jan. 2015. Television.

Yeh Rishta Kya Kehlata Hai. Dir. Rajan Shahi. Perf. Hina Khan. Star Plus. 12 Jan. 2009-present. Television.

Further Reading

Ellis, John. *Visible Fictions: Cinema Television Video.* London and NY: Routledge, 1982. Print.

7.

Celebrity Endorsements in Advertisements: Influence on the Buying Behavior of the Youth

Saket Kumar Bhardwaj

Tezpur University, India

Uttam Kumar Pegu

Tezpur University, India

India is one of the most rapidly emerging economies in the world. In the present dynamic and competitive condition, ever-expanding buyers' desires and requests power advertisers to adopt progressively innovative publicising practices, for example, celebrity support to impact buyers' purchasing conduct. India is a developing nation that is overflowed with various brands. With such a large number of items flooding the market, the organisations think that it's hard to differentiate their products based on their inherent product features. Truth be told, advertising is a viable publicising tool accessible to advertisers to create and spread awareness about their products. To make the advertisement progressively appealing and maintain a strategic distance from the media mess, organisations use celebrities to endorse their products. The interest for instant recall, brand awareness, and emotional bonding with clients has made big name supports the most recent pattern. Famous people add new dimensions to a brand.

Big names have a lot of impact on the decisions of the common man. What's more, that is the reason most brands pick different Bollywood celebrities to embrace their items infrequently. It might appear to be a costly issue for the organisation, however, on the off chance that it works, and after that, the value never again matters. Also, turning into a brand ambassador is probably the sturdiest approach to keep up the celeb's fame. Here are some of the celebrities and their endorsement valuations:

As per a report published in the *Economic Times* on 1 November 2016, which assess the commercials from September 2015 to August 2016, Bollywood star

Shahrukh Khan and Cricketing star Virat Kohli are the two famous people with the lion's share of the support advertising. Deepika Padukone and Priyanka Chopra are the main female celebrities in the rundown of the top ten brand endorsers (Shambhavi). The main five segments which use celebrities for endorsements are personal care, food and beverages, automobiles, e-commerce, and jewellery. Top 10 Fast Moving Consumer Goods add up to 41% portion of celebrity endorsement. Among them, the soft drink industry alone covers the 8% of the stake, after soaps with 6% of share, and toothpaste with 5% share.

Table 7.2: Top 10 Celebrity Endorsers in 2016.

Name of Celebrity	No. of Brands Endorsed	Valuation (in million dollars)
Shahrukh Khan	22	131.2
Virat Kohli	21	92.5
Deepika Padukone	18	86.1
Salman Khan	15	58.3
Priyanka Chopra	09	44.9
Ranbir Kapoor	10	36.6
Ranveer Singh	16	35.5
Hrithik Roshan	12	34.1
M. S. Dhoni	18	31.1
Amitabh Bachchan	9	26.4

Source: US consultancy firm Duff & Phelps (Jain n.pag.)

The act of celebrity endorsement has multiplied over time. Celebrity endorsement is inevitably increasing in the Indian advertising business when contrasted with the US as they have a genuinely huge effect on shoppers' purchase decisions. Over half of the Indian advertisements have superstars in them as against 20% in the US, the report said. A report by the *Business Standard* in 2017 says that the all-out estimation of the top 15 celebrity brands in India is more than $691 million ("At $144-mn net worth" n.pag.). Celebrities are commonly connected with a high status because of their wide acknowledgment in the public, as well as publicity, which is given to them by media. Indian film stars impact the youth in India. Thinking about the fame, size, and reach of the big names in India, it can be said that they have the ability to impact the frame of mind and conduct of individuals, especially the youth.

An organization utilizes superstars to embrace their merchandise so as to make advertisements progressively appealing and this has turned into an unavoidable component in the advertising industry and communication management. Advertisers use celebrity endorsers to impact the buying attitude of customers so as to increase their sales and extend their market shares. Today celebrity endorsement has developed as a billion-dollar industry with organizations signing deals with celebrities planning to stand apart from the messiness and give them an unmistakable and substantial situation in the brain of buyers. Over the world, celebrities have been utilized for an assortment of brands.

Everyday buyers are exposed to many advertisements for FMCG products of different brands. Fast Moving Consumer Goods (FMCG), products are commonly purchased essential or non-essential goods, such as food, soft drinks, and disposable diapers, etc. Some of the best- known examples of Fast-Moving Consumer Goods companies include Procter & Gamble, HERO Group, Colgate-Palmolive, H. J. Heinz, Cadbury, Reckitt Benckiser, Sara Lee, Nestlé, Unilever, Coca-Cola, Pepsi, and Wilkinson.

Famous people in advertisements are regarded as referents by customers, which alludes to nonexistent or real people imagined to have a significant bearing on the shopper's assessments, desires, and conduct. The ads endeavor to take a clueless individual as an ideal opportunity to advise him or her regarding various characteristics of an item. The challenge of the advertiser is to discover a snare that will hold the subject's consideration and for these organisations to contribute colossal sums for procuring the big name.

Indian purchaser's dispositions are changing at a quick pace and they are winding up increasingly mindful of the items that they use to characterize their 'self'. The study is carried out to acquire a view among the Indian customers about big-name underwriting. Is it as positive as it thought to be? Most commercials, be they of any structure, significantly focus on the young generation. Additionally, the exploration of celebrity endorsement is helpful for marketing, as it investigates the impression on Indian buyers of celebrity endorsement. In India, an enormous measure of cash is put into the publishing industry. Henceforth, the study gives a plan to firms whether endorsements return them a better benefit or the quality, accessibility of the items get a better perception in the market. This study concentrates on looking at the impression of the Indian customers about the celebrity endorsement process and the ensuing effect on their buying behaviour. The research also investigates different FMCG products. *TAM media research* (2011) expressed that 65-70% of the promotion of FMCG items includes celebrity endorsement ("Synopsis of Celebrity Endorsement" n.pag.).

The Indian soft drinks market enlisted a more grounded twofold digit off-exchange esteem development rate than the compound yearly development rate (CAGR) for as far back as five years. The soft drinks advertisements have constantly highlighted various celebrities to draw in the customer's attention. Consequently, it is fascinating to assess the impact of celebrity endorsement in the customer purchasing attitudes. These FMCG items have consistently focused on the young section of society. Additionally, the study illuminates the distinction of impact among the young people concerning celebrity and non-celebrity promotions.

In recent years many Bollywood stars are endorsing different soft drink brands. For instance, Katrina Kaif's *Slice* advertisement, Ranbir Kapoor in *Pepsi* advertisement, Kareena Kapoor with *Limca*, Asin in *Miranda*, and Parineeti Chopra and Imran Khan in *Mazza* advertisement. Celebrity endorsements can be widely seen in advertisements of soaps, and toothpaste, hence these Fast Moving Consumer Goods (soft drink, soap, toothpaste) are selected for gauging out the impact of celebrity endorsement on buying behaviour.

As the market has now turned out to be exceptionally aggressive and with such a significant number of celebrities endorsing different brands, it is fundamental to comprehend the Indian shoppers' conduct and buying behaviour through the impact of these celebrity endorsements.

Celebrity Endorsement: An Indian Perspective

Celebrities are individuals who enjoy open acknowledgment and who have particular traits, for example, the allure and reliability (McCracken; Silvera and Austad). The term celebrity introduces us to a person who is well known to the general society, for example, on-screen characters, sports figures, performers, and others for their accomplishments in their respective areas (Friedman and Friedman). As indicated by McCracken in "Who is the Celebrity Endorser?", it can incorporate individuals from films, TV, sports, legislative issues, business, specialists, and people from the military. While in this advanced period of advertising, superstars may likewise be an energized character like Fred Flintstone, or a creature.

McCracken in his book *Culture and Consumption II: Markets, Meaning and Brand Management* gives an unmistakable definition depicting celebrity endorser as the one who "enjoys public recognition and who uses this recognition on behalf of a consumer good by appearing with it in an advertisement" (97). He further clarified celebrity endorsement as a "pervasive component of present-day advertising" (97). Friedman and Friedman portray celebrity endorser as a person who is known to open for their accomplishments in territories other than that of the item endorsed. Celebrity endorsements are a ubiquitous element of present-day marketing business.

Celebrities are involved in endorsing activities since the late nineteenth century. According to Katyal, one of the first sports endorsements in India was when Farokh Engineer became the first Indian cricketer to model for Bryl cream. Probably Lux, the soap brand has managed to realize and made it synonymous with celebrity endorsement in India till date.

Some of the early instances of a celebrity endorsing brands can be Tabassum (Prestige Pressure Cookers), Jalal Agha (Pan Parag), Kapil Dev (Palmolive shaving cream), and Sunil Gavaskar (Dinesh Suitings). This clearly indicated the growth and acceptance of celebrity endorsements on Indian television. In fact, celebrity endorsement is growing at six times in volume terms between 2003 and 2007. An example of Coke illustrates this claim. The Coke advertisement featured Indian film star Aamir Khan endorsing the brand. The result was a universally appealing Aamir cheekily stating *Thanda matlab Coca Cola*. The Parker pen brand, which by itself commands equity, used Amitabh Bachchan to revitalize the brand in India and it was observed that post-Bachchan, Parker's sales had increased by about 30%.

Today, India is one of the fast-developing economies and celebrity endorsement has turned out to be an enormous business. India is one nation, which has constantly venerated the stars of the celluloid world; along these lines, it bodes well for a brand to acquire a big name for its endorsement. Publicists are offering stars like Shahrukh Khan, Aamir Khan, Amitabh Bachchan and numerous others colossal compensation bundles to get them energetic about a specific brand. In India, there is an exponential probability for a celebrity endorsement to be seen as really applicable, in this manner propelling purchasers to go in for the product (Kulkarni and Gaulkar).

Consumer Buying Behaviour

In today's dynamic and competitive environment, customers are continuously exposed to various different brands through different marketing strategies. Consumer behaviour is an important and complex area for marketers as different people have different needs and satisfaction of consumer needs is the ultimate goal for a business. Thus, the marketer's job is to accurately identify the customer needs and accordingly develop a product that satisfies their wants.

Perner defined consumer behaviour as "the study of individuals, groups, or organizations and the processes they use to select, secure, use, and dispose of products, services, experiences, or ideas to satisfy needs and the impacts that these processes have on the consumer and society" (n.pag.). According to Perner, knowledge of consumer buying behaviour helps marketers in developing their marketing strategies by understanding the psychology of the consumers as to how:

a) They think, feel, differentiate, and select between different brands or products.

b) How the consumer is influenced by his or her environment (e.g., culture, family, signs, media);

c) The behaviour of consumers while shopping or making purchase decisions;

d) How consumer motivation and decision-making strategies differ between products that differ in their levels of importance; and

e) How marketers can adapt and improve their marketing campaigns and strategies to reach the consumer more effectively. (n.pag.)

Furthermore, it is not only important to identify and satisfy the customer's need, but also critical to know as to why a customer needs that. It gives marketers a better understanding of consumer behaviour which ultimately helps them in satisfying customer needs efficiently and increasing customer loyalty towards their products and services (Zeithaml, Parasuraman, and Berry).

Types of Consumer Buying Behaviour

According to Assael, there are four types of consumer buying behaviours that can affect the purchase decision making of a consumer based on the level of consumer-product involvement, interest in a product, situation, and difference between the products available. The four types of models are explained as under (Assael):

1) **Complex Buying Behaviour:** It more often than not happens when the purchaser is profoundly associated with the product purchase decision. The high product involvement happens when the product to be purchased is costly, rarely purchased, and profoundly expressive. Since these kinds of items are not purchased as often as possible, the purchaser doesn't think a lot about the items and tends to notice more contrasts among the brands accessible for example, purchasing an expensive car. Purchasers settle on this kind of purchasing choices cautiously after gathering a great deal of information about the item's key features, and quality.

As indicated by Assael, buyers' will in general experience psychological disharmony while settling on such complex item choices because of expanded hazard discernment in this kind of purchasing conduct. There are sure risks likewise included while settling on such choices for instance, high cost may bring about financial misfortune, profoundly expressive nature of the item may prompt psycho-social misfortune, and absence of proper knowledge about the item may bring about expanded vulnerability.

From a marketing point of view, advertisers need to ensure that they utilize the powerful methodologies to make their item stand apart from different other accessible brands. Furthermore, they also attempt to teach the clients about the significance, application and highlights of the item advertised.

2) **Dissonance-Reducing Buying Behaviour:** It happens when the purchaser is exceptionally associated with the product purchase and notices little contrast among the choices accessible. Subsequent to purchasing the item, the customer will, in general, accumulate more information about the obtained product that guarantees and approves his product purchase choice. By doing this, the customer attempts to diminish the disharmony or

misfortune associated with the purchase. This sort of purchasing conduct includes a foundation of trust, and conviction towards a brand.

3) **Habitual Buying Behaviour:** It occurs when the buyers purchase a similar item on ordinary premises over a given stretch of time. Under habitual buying behavior, purchaser – product association is low and there is little contrast between the brands accessible, for example, purchasing salt, sugar and so on. The purchasers purchase these items because of their trust or brand devotion. As indicated by Scott, customers don't experience the procedure of conviction, frame of mind. Customers purchase the brands they have utilized and are aware of. Be that as it may, it is fascinating to see advertisers continually attempting to move this sort of item particularly (FMCG items) from a low inclusion to a higher contribution status by separating them on different bases like wellbeing, security, and so forth. For example, advertisers are engaged with growing low-calorie sugar, cholesterol-free oil and so forth and selling them at more expensive rates.

4) **Variety Seeking Behaviour:** This sort of shopper conduct starts if the customer isn't content with its prior purchased item or out of the fatigue. It uncommonly occurs with the buyers who like to search around and give a shot with various sorts of items. In this kind of purchasing conduct, purchaser item inclusion is low, yet the distinctions among the brands are important. These sorts of buyers change their brand much of the time, not because of disappointment, however, out of weariness. Assortment looking for conduct is recognized as a key determinant factor for brand exchanging in shopper product class (Lee, Kyle, and Scott). As indicated by Assael, customers looking for a purchaser's conduct buy the brands which have higher degrees of seen hazard related to them and are commonly not seen as brand loyal.

Celebrity Endorsement as a Marketing Communication Tool

From an advertising communication point of view, it has turned out to be progressively significant for firms to plan techniques that give a competitive differential bit of leeway to its products and services. It endeavours to make beneficial outcomes in the psyches of purchasers. So as to accomplish this, the celebrity endorsement is a normally utilized marketing communication technique. Organizations spend huge measure of money to endorse their brands through these famous people. Numerous specialists accept that a promotion including a celebrity conveys a higher level of bid, consideration, review rate and potentially buy contrasted with the advertisements without big names and in this way contributing significant positive effect on monetary returns for the organizations.

Reasons for Using Celebrity Endorsers

Scientific research writing is bottomless in dialogues about the purposes behind utilizing celebrities in advertising. Belch and Belch express the reasons why organizations spend colossal measures of cash to have celebrities show up in their promotions and endorse their products are that superstars have halting force. They attract consideration regarding promoting messages and upgrade message review. Famous names help in acknowledgment of brand names, make uplifting frames of mind toward the brand and make a character for the endorsed brand. In addition, it is accepted that celebrities could positively impact shoppers' emotions, a frame of mind and buy conduct. Investigation of logical examinations permits recognizing three fundamental theories that base the explanations behind utilizing VIPs in publicizing:

Celebrity Endorsement Effectiveness

Models for explaining celebrity endorsement effectiveness are as under

1. Source Credibility Model

The source credibility model was first proposed by Hovland and his partners. Credibility in a wide sense alludes to a communicator's positive attributes that influence the beneficiary's acknowledgment of a message, in view of the exploration in social brain science. The model proposes that the adequacy of a message relies upon the apparent degree of aptitude and dependability of an endorser (Hovland, Janis, and Kelley). As per Kelman's research study, the exchange of information through a believable source (for example celebrity) can possibly impact convictions, assessments, and dispositions as well as to conduct through a procedure called disguise. Disguise happens when the source impacts the beneficiary and is acknowledged by regarding their own frames of mind and worth structures.

Source Credibility Scale

Ohanian characterized trustworthiness as the listener's degree of confidence in, and level of acceptance of the speaker and the message. The trustworthiness of an endorser is perceptual and relies upon the intended interest group. It alludes to the trustworthiness, uprightness, and acceptability of an endorser. Advertisers exploit these arrangements of qualities by utilizing celebrities who are most viewed as reliable, legit trustworthy and reliable among their fans and individuals (Ohanian, "Construction and Validation").

Expertise can be characterized as the apparent capacity of an endorser to make or give substantial statements. It incorporates the information, experience, and abilities created by the endorser while working in a similar field. A few authors propose that it isn't significant for an endorser to be a specialist; however, everything relies upon how the crowd sees him (Hovland, Janis, and Kelley). Ohanian contended that the apparent skill of superstar endorsers could easily compare to their allure and reliability in affecting purchase expectations. Master superstars are observed to be increasingly convincing and may impact the shopper purchasing choice (Ohanian, "Construction and Validation"). Speck, Schumann, and Thompson found that expert celebrities produce a higher pace of review of product information than non-expert celebrities (Erdogan).

The findings in the source credibility research are vague. It alludes to the endorsement process as uni-dimensional on the grounds that it is as yet unsure to state what elements develop the model and what elements could easily compare to others in various circumstances. Despite the fact that the investigation has demonstrated to have a significant and direct impact on frames of mind and social expectations, it might help advertisers in choosing the right endorsers anyway it isn't the main factor that ought to be considered in choosing celebrity endorsers (Erdogan).

2. Source Attractiveness Model

Patzer expressed that physical attractiveness is an informational cue that involves effects that are subtle, pervasive, and inescapable. He supported the utilization of alluring endorsers than normal looking endorsers. As indicated by him, individuals attempt to build their appeal and respond decidedly to the endorsers who appear as though them. Here and there individuals will in general feel that appealing individuals are a lot more astute and subsequently exceed expectations in different territories also. This is additionally called the halo effect. Attractiveness model is viewed as a segment of the source valance model, in light of the exploration in social brain research (McCracken, "Who is the Celebrity Endorser?"). The source allure model essentially focuses on four key zones to be specific.

a. Credibility

Credibility is the degree to which the beneficiary considers to be as having significant learning, aptitudes, or experience and trusts the source to give unprejudiced, target information (Belch and Belch). The two most significant parts of credibility are expertise and trust (Hovland, Janis, and Kelley).

Celebrities are viewed as dependable wellsprings of information and the credibility of a celebrity is portrayed as the aggregate sum of positive highlights that make and increment the acknowledgment of the message (Erdogan). Credibility is one of the most significant determinants of superstar endorsement. Credibility is especially significant when individuals have a negative demeanor towards the brand and ground-breaking contentions are expected to hinder the counter contending and decidedly impact the frame of mind towards the brand. Thus, when celebrities are trustworthy, it influences the acknowledgment of the message and the influence (Belch and Belch).

b. Expertise

The expertise of celebrity endorsement is being characterized as "the degree to which an endorser is seen to be a wellspring of substantial declarations" (Erdogan 298). With respect to mastery, it isn't significant that the celebrity is extremely a specialist in the field. It is significant that customers think and accept a celebrity has the capability.

To outline, in a selling setting a specialist sales rep made a fundamentally higher number of clients buy an item than the non-master sales rep did (Woodside and Davenport). Master sources likewise impact the impression of the item's quality. The source or celebrity that is an authority has been observed to be progressively influential (Aaker and Fournier) and creates more buy expectations (Ohanian, "Construction and Validation"). Besides, Speck, Schumann, and Thompson expressed that celebrities, who are viewed as a specialist in a particular region, induce higher brand acknowledgment than celebrities who are viewed as non-specialists (Speck, Schumann, and Thompson). The expertise of a celebrity will decide its credibility (Amos, Holmes, and Strutton). The more ability a big name has, the more compelling it will be. The mastery of a celebrity won't be changed by negative exposure, yet the trustworthiness and credibility will be contrarily affected.

c. Trustworthiness

Trustworthiness alludes to the honesty, integrity, and believability of an endorser (Erdogan). Organizations attempt to discover endorsers who are generally observed as trustful and who are viewed as fair, acceptable and reliable (Shimp). Trustworthiness is the most significant factor as to the source credibility and impacts believability Moreover, likeability is referenced as the most significant quality of trust (Friedman and Friedman). Promoters can make the most elevated impact by taking these two variables, liking, and trustworthiness, into the record. Since it is expressed when shoppers like a superstar, they will consequently confide in a celebrity (Friedman and Friedman).

Ohanian in his paper "Construction and Validation" argued that the trustworthiness of a superstar endorser had no association with the buy goals of the related brand by the buyer. This end had to do with the degree of contribution, which will be portrayed in the accompanying part. The trustworthiness is vital for powerful endorsers. On the off chance that customers accept what the endorser is telling and they trust the person in question, the acceptability of the promotion is higher and demeanor of the purchasers will be great. At the point when a superstar comes adversely into the news, this can influence the authenticity and the dependability of the endorser. Likewise, it will adversely impact the brand picture and offers of the related item.

d. Attractiveness

The idea of attractiveness doesn't just involve the physical allure. Attractiveness additionally involves ideas, for example, scholarly aptitudes, character properties, a method for living, athletic exhibitions and abilities of endorsers (Erdogan). Celebrities can be alluring on the grounds that they built up, for instance, incredible game exhibitions and individuals have extraordinary regard for their accomplishment and along these lines are pulled in to them. Physical appeal proposes that a superstar decides the efficiency of influence because of that shopper needing to resemble the endorser and needing to recognize themselves with that endorser. Then again, there are instances of a celebrity who are viewed as less alluring, however, speak to the picture the organization needs to make and have.

At the point when the match-up between brand and celebrity is available, engaging quality turns out to be less significant and, in this way, the organization may pick a less appealing celebrity. There are immense quantities of physically appealing celebrities who endorse an item. An example is David Beckham for the Armani brand. Most of the individuals are pulled in by David Beckham. Men need to be related to the soccer player and fashion man David Beckham, while the ladies are pulled in by his appearance as David Beckham consistently looks elegant and has extraordinary athletic exhibitions. He is amazingly believable and appealing and has a high level of likeness; individuals want to resemble him.

e. Similarity

The similarity is portrayed as a supposed resemblance between the source and the receiver of the message. At the end of the day: if a customer can distinguish him/herself with the endorser. Individuals can be impacted all the more effectively by an endorser who is like them. If the celebrity and the buyer have common features like basic interests or ways of life, a superior cohesiveness is made (Erdogan). That is the reason superstars are chosen upon their qualities that match well with buyers. Organizations additionally attempt to make compassion utilizing celebrity (Belch and Belch). Utilizing compassion, organizations attempt to make a bond between the superstar and the customer. Likewise, the degree of convincingness is expanded by utilizing similarity. Organizations may pick an ordinary-looking individual who isn't a superstar since purchasers can recognize themselves all the more effectively.

f. Liking

Likeability is the affection for the source as a result of the source's physical appearance and behaviour. It is observed that when individuals like the superstar they will likewise like going with the brand and in this way, celebrities are utilized in plugs and promotions. Celebrity endorsement will impact the buyer conduct and demeanor (Belch and Belch) and sponsors accept that a celebrity can impact the purchaser's vision of the organization's picture. In Kahle and Homer, the procedure of the disdained superstar is clarified in a study that contained an aggregate of 200 people taking an interest in the investigation. The test contains the case of celebrity endorsement utilized with expendable razors by methods for John McEnroe has been the celebrity endorser for this specific brand. John McEnroe is a tennis player who can bother individuals; his extraordinary unpleasant language on the tennis court is generally known. It tends to be expressed that he isn't the perfect endorser of a brand and that John McEnroe can be appointed to the despised celebrity gathering. The organization holds him since his picture suggests worry for insurance of personal circumstance; two factors the organization needs shoppers to be related with in regard to the utilization of expendable razors. In spite of McEnroe being a loathed celebrity, the organization utilizes him as an endorser.

g. Familiarity

Familiarity is the alleged likeness as information that a superstar endorser has through presentation (Erdogan; Belch and Belch). At the point when organizations pick a famous face, it is important to what degree buyers know about the celebrity. The more comfortable the customer is with the celebrity, the more positive the impact will be. It is additionally notable that shoppers, who are increasingly acquainted with a superstar and are progressively presented to a big name, will consequently like a big name more; this is known as the mere exposure effect. The impact of commonality on demeanor increments when there are brief exposures of the celebrity and when there are long delays between the exposures. The impact diminishes when there are long exposures of the superstar and when there are shorter deferrals between the exposures.

Advertisers pick superstar endorsers based on their physical allure to exploit their both qualities, i.e. superstar status and physical intrigue. Print ads depict the significance of physical appeal. Numerous specialists have discovered that alluring individuals are progressively powerful than ugly individuals at influence, evolving convictions (Baker and Churchill, Jr) and activating buyers expectations (Friedman and Friedman).

Similarity can be characterized as the apparent resemblance between the source and the respondent, nature as knowness of/about the source through understanding, and likeability as the degree of affection, care, and friendship for the source in the respondent because of the source's physical qualities and conduct. The attractiveness of the source doesn't emerge because of just physical characteristics. It might likewise incorporate the different attributes like scholarly expertise, way of life and so forth. (Erdogan). Cohen and Golden applied this model in publicising proposed that the physical attractiveness of the source chooses the effectiveness of persuasive communication through a process called identification. It happens when the receiver acknowledges the information from an alluring source as a desire to be related to the endorser.

3. Product Match-up model

The match-up hypothesis proposes that the effectiveness of a commercial relies upon the presence of an apparent 'fit' between the endorsing celebrity and the brand endorsed by him (Till and Busler). The Product Match-up model recommends that celebrity and product features should supplement each other for effective advertising (Kamins). The match between the product and celebrity relies upon the normal traits between product features and celebrity image. Advertising through a celebrity with moderately high product similarity prompts compelling publicizing when contrasted with a commercial highlighting less perfect celebrity (Kamins and Gupta; Erdogan). On the off chance that the characteristics of a superstar match-up with the brand endorsed by him, it might likewise build the celebrity authenticity and attractiveness among the focused group of spectators (Kamins and Gupta). Ohanian study ("The Impact of Celebrity Spokespersons") upheld the contention by expressing that it is basic to utilize celebrity who legitimately resembles with the brand and are specialists in their field.

Research by Bertrand and Todd argued that if an organization can effectively interface a connection between its item and celebrity image or the field celebrity represents considerable authority in, at that point, it can carry distinction and accomplishment to both. Past research regarding the matter expresses that clients additionally expect the similarity between the endorsed product and the celebrity. At the end of the day, clients make an apparent image of the product by contrasting the characteristics of the product and celebrity (Ohanian, "The Impact of Celebrity Spokespersons"; Callcoat and Phillips). Then again if there is no harmoniousness between the endorsed product and the celebrity, it may lead individuals to an end that the superstar is faking it since he is pleasantly paid to endorse the brand (Erdogan). From the above opinions, it can be secondary that resemblance between the celebrity and brand is required for effective advertising.

The product match-up model suggests that attractive celebrities especially attractive female celebrities are more effective at endorsing beauty products, the products used to enhance one's attractiveness (Kamins). For instance, Aishwarya Rai Bachchan is a renowned celebrity endorsing L'Oréal beauty products and Sachin Tendulkar, the famous cricketer endorsing Adidas products in India. Friedman and Friedman and Atkin and Block in their research argued that that the uses of celebrity endorsers are suitable where product purchases involve high social and psychological risk. Supporting the argument, Packard proposed that celebrity endorsement strategy is more effective for luxury products positioned and sold in the niche market segment because the featured celebrities are people from the high status and therefore it becomes easy for marketers to attract consumers to buy their products. Callcoat and Phillips opposed the argument by saying that consumers are generally influenced by celebrities if products are inexpensive and low involving.

After considering the findings and opinions, it becomes obvious that the match-up between the celebrity and the endorsed brand is important in order to attract the target audience and to make the message more effective.

4. Meaning Transfer Model

As indicated by McCraken's study, the past source models discussed above are not equipped with catching the achievement elements of the endorsement process. Desarbo and Harshman upheld the contention by expressing that neither of the source credibility, attractiveness or match-up hypothesis models gives a base to proper celebrity endorser choice. He expressed three issues identified with these models (Erdogan):

a) These models do not provide measures to cope up with multi-dimensionality of source effects.
b) These approaches ignore overtone-meaning-interactions between a celebrity and the endorsed product.
c) There is a lack of quantified empirical basis for proposed dimensions.

Hence, McCracken in "Who is the Celebrity Endorser?" proposed the meaning transfer model; the main idea of this model is to prove that celebrities possess unique sets of meanings which might be transferable to the products endorsed by them.

The meaning transfer model proposes that the viability of a celebrity endorser relies upon his/her quality to carry the implications to the endorsement process (McCraken). A celebrity has a bigger number of particular implications. Qualifications of status, class, sexual orientation, and age, just as character and way of life types, are spoken to in the pool of accessible superstars, putting an exceptionally different and inconspicuous bed of implications at the transfer of the showcasing framework (McCraken). For example, in India, Sonia Gandhi as a great lady, Amitabh Bachchan as a high-class individual, Aishwarya Rai for her stylish way of life and so on. Advertisers utilize superstars in ads accepting that since individuals pursue big names and attempt to appear like them, they may likewise devour items related to them (Fowles).

Celebrity endorsements are an interesting case of, an increasingly broad procedure of meaning transfer (McCracken, "Who is the Celebrity Endorser?"). As per McCraken, there is a methodical way for the exchange of cultural meaning in the purchaser's social orders. As per McCraken, meaning starts as something inhabitant in the culturally comprised world, in the physical and social world established by the classifications and standards of the predominant culture.

The meaning transfer model shows a three-phase process. It begins when the sponsor recognizes the cultural meaning expected for the product and chooses what he/she needs the product to express. From that point forward, the advertiser searches for the substances, people, and settings that can offer a voice to these meaning, for example celebrities. As such, in the primary stage, the meanings related to the celebrities move from the endorser to the product or the brand, and this importance is drawn out of the celebrity's public image. In the subsequent stage, this importance is moved from the endorser to the product and the way toward making a product personality happens. This procedure depends on the emblematic properties passed on by the endorser. When meanings have been moved into products, they should likewise be moved to purchasers. At long last in the last stage called the consumption process, the brand meaning is accomplished by the purchaser. Buyers perceive the representative properties of items and move them into meanings for themselves by giving them something to do in the development of their mental self-portrait. At the point when this is done, the development of the meaning-making is completed. The third and the last phase of the model exhibit the significance of purchaser in the endorsement process. (McCraken).

McCracken's meaning transfer model first only appeared to be a hypothetical idea; however, its genuineness was demonstrated in two studies by Langmeyer, Lynn and Walker. In "A First Step to Identify the Meaning in Celebrity Endorsers" they utilized a reaction elicitation position with a superstar endorser - Cher embracing Scandinavian health spas. In "Assessing the Effects of Celebrity Endorsers: Preliminary Findings" they utilized celebrity endorsers - Madonna and Christie Brinkley and products shower towels, VCRs, and pants. The investigation results uncovered that when big names joined with a product, these apparent contrasts influenced implications saw in items. Langmeyer, Lynn and Walker's studies exactly upheld the argument by McCracken in "Who is the Celebrity Endorser?" that celebrities represent different meanings and these meanings are passed on to products through endorsements (Erdogan).

5. The Elaboration Likelihood Model (ELM) was created to clarify the procedure by which persuasive communication (advertising) leads to influence by affecting dispositions. According to this model, the mentality arrangement relies upon the sum and nature of the elaboration of pertinent information that happens in light of a powerful message. In this manner, the effectiveness of a celebrity endorser in an advertisement relies upon the receiver's association level. There are observational confirmations, that the utilization of a celebrity endorser is increasingly prudent when the recipient's contribution is low, on the grounds that for this situation the celebrity's impact on frames of mind is progressively noteworthy.

6. The Three-order Hierarchy Model recognizes three response hierarchy stages dependent on perceived product separation and product association. These elective response hierarchy systems are the standard learning, disharmony/attribution and low-contribution models (Floyd). Learning about hierarchies and about the determining factors brings the valuable information about how the customers see and procedure information.

McCraken found that the utilization of celebrity endorsers represent a successful method for transferring meaning to brands as it is accepted that celebrity endorsers carry their very own symbolic significance to the endorsement process and that this cultural meaning attached to the celebrity is passed on to an item that is passed on to the customer. McCraken argued there lays a distinction among celebrities and an individual as it is accepted by him that famous people have the capacity of conveying the message of additional profundity, power and nuance and furthermore, offer a scope of the way of life and the character which can't be coordinated by unknown individuals. In the comparable vein, he keeps on demonstrating that most vigorously stereotyped celebrity produces single meanings as well as interconnected various meanings showing that superstar endorsers are definitely more viable than non-celebrity endorsers. In the light of organization reports and scholastic composition, it is protected to contend that celebrity endorsers are more successful than non-celebrity endorsers in producing alluring pay (Erdogan).

Celebrity Attributes Influencing Consumer Purchase

Celebrity attributes here imply the various characteristics and traits of celebrities that captivate the youths and force them to buy the products. Some respondents admitted that celebrity attributes play an important part in compelling them to buy the products endorsed by them, while most of them believed that the attributes have nothing to do with the product. Most of the respondents felt that the association of a celebrity with a product adds credibility to the product. The research also revealed that males are more likely to be influenced by celebrity attributes than females. According to respondents, Virat Kohli and Shahrukh Khan are the two most popular celebrities involved in the advertisement.

The marketers are always involved in changing the brand ambassadors for the product who are wooed by the public. Hence, it becomes imperative to analyse whether the change in celebrity changes the product image. The research discovered that the youths do not change the product often as the celebrity endorsing the product changes. Youths are rational thinkers and have a clear perception that celebrity does not use the product which they endorse. However, some of the respondents admit that the association of celebrities to a product lends values to the product. A few respondents admitted that the trustworthiness of the celebrity positively influences the purchase intention of the consumers. But the crux of the study based on data reflects that product image is mainly formed by the product quality and it is not changed with the change in celebrity.

Conclusion

Celebrity endorsement has changed the way advertising used to be a few decades ago. It has been accepted to be a ubiquitous feature of modern-day marketing. This research explored the current state of the youth's perception of celebrity endorsements. In accordance with the study objectives, the following conclusions are drawn. There is no doubt that the association of celebrity with a product amplifies the recall rate of the advertisement. But in order to transfer this recall rate into sales, the marketers must work on the product quality. Easy availability of the product is one of the important factors that should be taken into account in order to influence the consumer purchasing decision. As most of the youth consumers prefer the products which are easily available. Celebrity attributes add value to the product but switching the celebrity on a regular basis would not be as effective. It is because the youth does not change the product so often and at least not after getting influenced by the presence of a celebrity.

The selection of celebrity endorsers with the right attributes is crucial to the success of celebrity endorsement. It is because celebrity endorsements can help to create and reinforce the value of the product. Thus, the markets must carefully evaluate the celebrities and make sure the image perceived by the target customers is positive. According to the study conducted by Debiprasad Mukherjee on the impact of celebrity endorsements on brand image, it was recommended that the company must have thorough consideration and sufficient research before opting for endorsement by any celebrity. They must understand the preference and purchase behavior of their target customers so that the marketers can react to customer expectations. There was a strong belief among the respondents that the celebrities did not use the endorsed products themselves. To avoid this perception, product companies may wish to select celebrities who are using their products. Otherwise, advertising and media strategies should be developed to ensure that celebrities are using the same brands that they are endorsing.

Bibliography

Aaker, Jennifer L, and Susan Fournier. "A Brand as a Character, a Partner, and a Person: Three Perspectives on the Question of Brand Personality." *Advances in Consumer Research* 22.1 (1995): 391-95. Print.

Amos, Clinton, Gary Holmes, and David Strutton. "Exploring the Relationship Between Celebrity Endorser Effects and Advertising Effectiveness: A Quantitative Synthesis of Effect Size." *International Journal of Advertising* 27.2. (2008): 209-234. Print.

Assael, M. *Consumer Behaviour and Marketing Action.* Boston MA: Kent Publishing Co., 1981. Print.

"At $144-mn net worth, Kohli replaces SRK as most valuable celebrity brand" *Business- standard.com.* N.p., 20 Dec. 2017. Web. 1 Dec. 2018. <https://www.business-standard.com/article/current-affairs/at-144-mn-net-worth-kohli-replaces-srk-as-most-valuable-celebrity-brand-117122001036/>

Atkin, C., and M Block. "Effectiveness of Celebrity Endorsers." *Journal of Advertising Research* 23.1(1983): 57-61. Print.

Baker, Michael J., and Gillbert A. Churchill, Jr, "The Impact of Physically Attractive Models on Advertising Evaluations." *Journal of Marketing Research* 14.4 (1977): 538-555. Print.

Belch, George E., and Michael A. Belch. Advertising and Promotion: An Integrated Marketing Communications Perspective. New York: McGraw-Hill/Irwin, 2007. Print.

Bertrand, K., and S. Todd. "Celebrity Marketing: The Power of Personality; Golf Legends Drive Marketing Campaigns." *Business Marketing* 77.8 (1992): 24-28. Print.

Callcoat, Margaret F., and B. J. Philips. "Observations: Elves Make Good Cookies." *Journal of Advertising Research* 36 (1996): 73-79. Print.

Cohen, Joel B., and Ellen Golden. "Informational Social Influence and Product Evaluation." *Journal of Applied Psychology* 56.1 (1972): 54-59. Print.

DeSarbo, Wayne S., and Richard A. Harshman. "Celebrity-Brand Congruence Analysis." *Current Issues & Research in Advertising* 8.2(1985):17-53. Print.

Erdogan, B. Zafer. "Celebrity Endorsement: A Literature Review." *Journal of Marketing Management* 15.4 (1999): 291-314. Print.

Floyd, A.G, "An Examination of the Three-Order Hierarchy Model: Theories of Persuasive Communication." *Consumer Decision Making* 4.1 (1991): 20-32. Print.

Fowles, Jib. *Advertising and Popular Culture*. Thousand Oaks: Sage, 1996. Print.

Friedman, Hershey H., and Linda Friedman. "Endorser Effectiveness by Product Type." *Journal of Advertising Research* 19.5 (1979): 63-71. Print.

Hovland, Carl I., Irving L. Janis, and Harold H. Kelley. *Communication and Persuasion: Psychological Studies of Opinion Change*. New Haven: Yale University Press, 1966. Print.

Jain, Aviral. "Embracing the Change: A Concise Report on India's Most Valuable Celebrity Brands2016" *Duffandphelps.com*. N.p., 2 Nov. 2016. Web.15 Jan. 2018 <www.duffandphelps.com/insights/publications/valuation/celebrity-brand-valuation-2016/>

Kahle, L. R., and P M Homer. "Physical Attractiveness of the Celebrity Endorser: ASocial Adaptation Perspective" *Journal of Consumer Research* 11.4(1985): 954-961. Print.

Kamins, Michael A. "An Investigation into the Match-Up-Hypothesis in Celebrity Advertising When Beauty Be Only Skin Deep." *Journal of Advertising* 19.1 (1990): 4-13. Print.

Kamins, Michael A., and Kamal Gupta. "Congruence between Spokesperson and Product Type: A Matchup Hypothesis Perspective." *Psychology and Marketing* 11.6 (1994): 569-86. Print.

Katyal, S. "Impact of Celebrity Endorsement on a Brand." *Chillibreeze*. N.p., 30 Jul. 2007. Web. 20 Aug. 2017.

Kelman, H. C. "Process of Opinion Change" *Public Opinion Quarterly* 25(1961): 57-78. Print.

Kulkarni, A. Sanyukta, and U Sahir Gaulkar. "Impact of Celebrity Endorsement on Overall Brand." *Indianmba.com*. N.p., 2005. Web. 1 Dec. 2017. <www.indianmba.com/Occasional_Papers/>

Langmeyer, Lynn, and Mary Walker. "A First Step to Identify the Meaning in Celebrity Endorsers." *Advances in Consumer Research*. Ed. Rebecca, R. Holman, and Michael R, Solomon. Provo, Utah: Association for Consumer Research, 1991. 364-371. Print.

Langmeyer, Lynn, and Mary Walker. "Assessing the Effects of Celebrity Endorsers: Preliminary Findings." *American Academy of Advertising Proceedings*. Ed. Rebecca R. Holman. Dallas, TX: American Academy of Advertising Proceedings, 1991. 32-42. Print.

Lee, Jenny J., G Kyle, and D Scott. "The Mediating Effect of Place Attachment on the Relationship Between the Festival Satisfaction and Loyalty to the Festival Hosting Destination." *Journal of Travel Research* 51.6(2012): 754-767. Print.

McCracken, Grant. *Culture and Consumption II: Markets, Meaning, and Brand Management*.Bloomington: Indiana University Press, 2005. Press. Print.

McCracken, Grant. "Who is the Celebrity Endorser? Cultural Foundations of the Endorsement Process." *Journal of Consumer Research* 16.3 (1989): 310-321. Print.

Mukherjee, Debiprasad. "Impact of Celebrity Endorsements on Brand Image." *Ssrn.com*. N.p., n.d. Web. 6 Jan. 2018. <http://ssrn.com/abstract=1444814/>

Ohanian, Roobina. "Construction and Validation of a Scale to Measure Celebrity Endorsers' Perceived Expertise, Trustworthiness, and Attractiveness." *Journal of Advertising* 19.3 (1990): 39-52. Print.

Ohanian, Roobina. "The Impact of Celebrity Spokespersons: Perceived Image on Consumers Intention to Purchase." *Journal of Advertising Research* 31.1 (1991): 46-54. Print.

Packard, V. *The Hidden Persuaders*. London: Penguin, 1991. Print.

Patzer, G. L. "Source Credibility as a Function of Communicator Physical Attractiveness." *Journal of Business Research* 11.2(1983): 229-241. Print.

Perner, L. *Consumer Price Response*. Los Angeles (LA): Department of Marketing, Marshall School of Business, 2009. Print.

Shambhavi, Anand. "Bollywood steals show on celeb ambassadors' list" *Economictimes. indiatimes.com*. N.p, 1 Nov. 2016. Web. 25 Dec. 2017. <economictimes.indiatimes.com/industry/services/advertising/bollywood-steals-show-on-celeb-ambassadors-list/articleshow/55167789/>

Shimp, Terrence A. *Advertising, Promotion, and Other Aspects of Integrated Marketing Communications*. Mason, Ohio: South Western Cengage Learning, 2008. Print.

Silvera, D. H., and Austad, B. "Factors Predicting the Effectiveness of Celebrity Endorsement Advertisements" *European Journal of Marketing* 38.11/12 (2004): 1509-1526. Print.

Speck, Paul S., David W. Schumann, and Craig Thompson. "Celebrity Endorsements - Scripts, Schema and Roles: Theoretical Framework and Preliminary Tests." *Advances in Consumer Research* 15.1 (1988): 69-76. Print.

"Synopsis of Celebrity Endorsement during Jan - Jun 2013" *tamindia.com* N.p.,2013. Web. 1 Jan. 2018. <www.tamindia.com/tamindia/Adex_News_TV.htm/>

Till, Brian D., and Michael Busler. "Matching Products with Endorsers: Attractiveness versus Expertise." *Dictionary of Marketing Communications* 15.6 (1998): 576-86. Print.

Woodside, Arch G., and J. William Davenport. "The Effect of Salesman Similarity and Expertise on Consumer Purchasing Behavior."*Journal of Marketing Research* 11.2 (1974): 198-202. Print.

Zeithaml, A., Valarie A. Parasuraman, and Leonard L. Berry. "Problems and Strategies in Services Marketing." *Journal of Marketing* 52.2 (July 1985): 2-22. Print.

8.

Bewitching Bombay: A Reflection on the Fandom of an Urban Space

Shipra Tholia

Banaras Hindu University, India

> Not to find one's way in a city may well be uninteresting and banal, it requires ignorance nothing more. But to lose oneself in a city as one loses oneself in a forest- that calls for quite a different schooling. Then sign-boards and street names, passers-by, roofs kiosks, or bars must speak to the wanderer like a cracking twig under his feet in the forest.

> - Benjamin (*A Berlin Chronicle* 8-9)

To understand a city and especially a metropolitan city such as Bombay, one has to love it. Movements such as 'reclaim your city,' 'a late night walk through the city' may suggest at first glance of some feminist activity for reclaiming the city but it is the 'fans of the city' who want to have the authoritative right on the city, who share a common identity, a common taste, a common love and fascination for no other than the city Bombay, even though they represent different ethnic groups, different religious sects, different nationalities etc. This paper will undertake an attempt to comprehend how the fandom of urban space is to be understood in the complex scenario of interwoven identities with the examples taken from Bollywood films based on the city Bombay. This paper will also contemplate on the notion of 'elective belonging' and 'experiencing the location where a particular film was filmed,' 'virtual travelling or travelling without moving from the easy chair' by the fans of Bombay. Further, this paper will explore how this travelling helps in realizing the connectivity of fans and their interwoven identities.

Bombay – a dreamland for many is a city that enjoys the status of being the most popular city of India. Bombay (now called Mumbai) is loved not just by its inhabitants but also by the 'outsiders'. Before unwrapping the complex nature of fandom of a place, this paper will try to understand the very phenomena called 'fandom' in the Indian context. What is fandom? What does it mean to be categorized as fan of a personality, of a culture, or of a place? According to the general understanding of the concept, fans share a common interest, common understanding and fascination for an object, thus creating a subculture. Fans are deeply involved in knowing the smallest details of their object of fascination. In Hindi, the word 'Anuragi' may convey the same meaning. Talking about common interest and sharing common (sub)cultural identity leads us to our main topic i.e. fandom of urban space. When it comes to the fandom of a space, the things that immediately occur to our mind are 'mass consumerism,' 'new ways of marketing', 'commodification of urban leisure' and fans as part of 'an undifferentiated, easily manipulated mass,' etc (Jenson). Well, the urban space or city is a place where people from different linguistic background, different cultural and economic background gather. In spite of their different 'roots' there is something that connects them with the city. The elite class cannot do without the labour/working class and vice versa. Seeing closely Indian cities especially Bombay is a hub of different ethnic groups, though some may like to qualify them as migrants. These migrants supply the very engine of the city i.e. the workforce. Although using the term 'migrant' or 'refugee' may be misleading for this work as a migrant is someone who is forced by his economic and political conditions to move to a new place, whereas the term 'fan of a city' conveys the natural love and admiration for the same. Their love and fascination for Bombay are of course conditioned by their experiences of particular localities, everyday interaction with the city in its various forms, constitution, and reconstitution of identity and affinity in everyday life. Hence creating a sense of 'nearness'. However, this sense of nearness does not dissolve the hierarchies that exist in society. Thornton argues that "fans are not to be seen as a counterforce to existing social hierarchies and structures but, in sharp contrast, as agents of maintaining social and cultural systems of classification and thus existing hierarchies" (255).

To analyze the concept of urban fandom we shall dwell upon the influence that works on people while developing certain likes and dislikes about a place. Longhurst, Bagnall, and Mike Savage in their essay "Place, Elective Belonging and the Diffused Audience", talk about the 'elective belonging' to examine attachment of people to places where they have decided to live:

> Such attachments to place should move debate around issues of globalization and attachment away from dichotomies like locals/incomers to consider how people locate themselves in places through parenting, shopping, working, and engaging with media and so on. Their project considered audience experiences against the backdrop of 'elective belonging' to show how media processes contribute to subtle processes of ordinary living in places, with due attention to identity, imagination, and performance. (126)

Elaborating their ideas further, they contend that

> We took four contrasting locations near Manchester, in the Northwest of England, as the site for between forty and fifty in-depth interviews. In each location we took the electoral register as our sampling frame, took a one-in-three sample of particular streets, and arranged interviews. Our research was based in Particular locales but not predicated on the existence of bounded living. Rather, the places were sites to investigate people's connectivity and its relationship to everyday life and experience. (137)

The choices of places or 'elective belonging' to a place is influenced as mentioned above by many factors such as economic, geographical, political and of course, social. But apart from these, there is one more factor that plays a vital role in helping people falling in love with the places. It is called the media. The way a city is depicted in a film also casts a spell on people. We, the fan, create a kind of image of a city just by seeing and experiencing in films without even having been to that place. Couldry calls it the place of media power, where the image of a city is stoked up by media. The place of media power is important, as is the way in which association is fueled and fed by media to become increasingly audienced.

They further illustrate the concept of elective belonging by saying people make choices about where they live. Belonging to an area is not simply about being born there, or a matter of conforming to local tradition. Not all people can afford to live in the places depicted in films. According to Longhurst, Bagnall, and Savage, "elective belonging takes place in unequal and divided societies. Such divisions are not only structural, but cultural through and through" (137).

Fans of Bombay have their own reasons of fascination for the city, which is not to be confused by the concept of 'son of the soil' or misleading concept of patriotism. Fans of Bombay are not just the people who live or have relatives in Bombay, but there is a whole crowd of fans out there who have never been to Bombay but have experienced it only through films. Nick Couldry in his article "On the Set of the Sopranos" talks about media tourism. In his words:

> Everyone is familiar with the experience of tourism, and most people are fairly familiar also with the experience of media tourism, visiting sites specifically and only because they have featured in a media narrative. It is a commonplace now for the second type of journey to be used to market the first. We are familiar, also as part of the second type of tourism, with being taken "inside" the fiction, even if many media tourist sites offer this only minimally, with that experience being limited to a basic moment of recognition ("oh, that's where it was filmed"). (143)

Brooker also substantiates this with the argument of a fan claiming, "if a movie is like a dream, then standing in an actual location is like stepping into the dream, there is a weird kind of energy to it" (168).

The Virtual Travel of Fans

In contrary to visiting sites where a particular film or TV soap has been filmed, there is another kind of tourism that we as 'fans' enjoy. That is 'virtual tourism'. No one can deny the pleasure we derive while visiting London in SRK's films, Berlin in *Run Lola Run or Berlin Calling,* New York in Woody Allen's films, California in *La La Land* and of course Bombay featuring in films and songs. Will Brooker calls it 'travelling without moving' whereas Aden defines it as 'symbolic pilgrimage.' Aden in his *Popular Stories and Promised Lands: Fan Cultures and Symbolic Pilgrimages* compares watching *The X-files* as a "symbolic pilgrimage-a trip without drugs, a journey and return without leaving the easy chair. According to him, Fans leave their structured, everyday environment to enter Agents Fox Mulder and Dana Scully's diegesis – a fictional world that echoes the panoptic control of normal working life yet allows a playful exploration of these structures and always includes, at the end of the episode, the reassurance of an exit" (149-50).

He further elaborates: "Each trip to the funhouse is a new yet ritualistic experience for both the agents (Mulder and Scully) and their vicarious partners, the fans. In fact, the show's recurring forms mirrors the pilgrim's journey as described by Edith Turner ... 1. Separation (the start of the journey), 2. The liminal stage (the journey itself, the sojourn at the shrine, and the encounter with the sacred) and 3. Re-aggregation (the homecoming)" (Aden 152).

This ecstatic feeling of visiting your favorite city with the perspective of a film camera is something that this paper strives to explore with the fans of Bombay. The very feeling of visiting slums and garbage-filled places in films like *Salaam Bombay, Slum-dog Millionaire, Chandnibar, Chameli,* etc. gives a kind of aesthetic pleasure to fans. Fans are not ashamed by watching slums or dirty sites of Bombay but on the contrary, they derive the joy by having recognized the place. That feeling of 'Hey! This is from Dharavi' or 'Hey! It was Chatrapati Shivaji road.'

Will Brooker qualifies such viewers as 'pilgrims', entering a different state that qualifies as a journey, albeit 'symbolic'. He illustrates it by citing examples of *Lord of the Rings* fan. In his own words: "When we consider a *Lord of the Rings* fan making the trip from Britain to the New Zealand film locations, the word 'pilgrim' comes more easily, but does a fan sitting in his or her own domestic environment, watching a screen – even though we readily grant the fan the status of an active viewer rather than a passive receiver- really deserve such associations of adventure?" (Brooker 158-59).

The films like *Ghar* (1978) by Manik Chatterjee, *City Lights* (2014) by Hansal Mehta, *Chandni Bar* (2001) by Madhur Bhandarkar, etc. are some of the films, which take the fan through the city life and its concerns. The city becomes the place where innocents from a small town or village come to be corrupted, to be drawn into a world of shady deal-making and cold concrete skyscrapers. Bombay is characterized by the continuing presence of a large countryside where the majority of the population lives. The countryside supplies a constant flow of migrants and labor. By the twentieth century, the urban had become the typical form of experience in the West, something that is not true in India even in the early twenty-first century. The city in Hindi films displays the contrast shown between city and village. While the city is characterized through noise, disappointment, depression and false illusions, the village offers peace and calm, nature and of course friendly relations. For instance, *Gaon Hamara Shaher Tumhara* (1972) by Naresh Kumar, *Coolie* (1983) by Manmohan Desai, and *Do Bigha Zamin* (1953) by Bimal Roy portray migration from villages to cities in a dramatic way. In India, the city constantly acknowledges its rural other, a point that is very much explicit in the history of cinematic representation. Apart from this city films, especially those that take fans to a 'pilgrimage' of Bombay have a wide range of cinematic aesthetic at their disposal. The city becomes a metaphor for misery, poverty, struggle, deprivation and of course, squalor. For instance, besides capturing the truth and audacity of urban poverty, *Salaam Bombay* and *Slum-dog millionaire* cover an important aspect of the city films, i.e. hope intact in squalor, dreams embedded in the garbage, hunger for power, money, and fame. The depiction of children selling tea, collecting garbage, robbing old people and stealing at railway stations, selling drugs and sex trading/human trafficking are strikingly realistic. The film *Salaam Bombay* which is one of the most celebrated Indian films on Bombay street children covers the city with its camera running through the slums and garbage. Mira Nair made great use of the streets in depicting the story which actually emerged while working with the actual street kids.

When we talk about the virtual travelling of Bombay in the city films, not just streets but railway stations, crowd, local festivals, etc. become major sites of action in these films. It is obvious that the fans experience the city through the eye of the camera. But I would like to understand the camera as a painting brush, which fills colors in the virtual city experience. It is this aesthetic journey that every fan makes while watching city-films. In such films, the city is not merely a site of action but becomes the main protagonist. In *Salaam Bombay*, a village kid Krishna abandoned by his family comes to Bombay to earn 500 bucks. He works at a small tea stall near Grant Road railway station.

He gets a new name *Chaipau* (the tea boy). His job makes him take a regular round through the railway station and red-light area of Falkland road, which is also known as the harem of prostitutes. With the *Chaipau* fans travel red light streets of Bombay. In the red-light area, Krishna meets *Sola Saal* (sweet sixteen) - a young girl brought from Nepal to Bombay to be dragged into prostitution. She is kept in a room to be prepared for her highest bidding client. Another character in the film is named *Chillum* (a Hindi expression for opium) - is a drug-selling bumpkin. The conversation between Krishna and Chillum reveals their longing for *desh*, i.e. village. Whereas scenes such as stampede in a local *Ganpati Rally* during *Ganpati Puja* portray the urban crowd with religious fervor, something that fans can easily associate themselves with. The use of two-wheelers and auto-rickshaws highlights an important aspect of Indian urban culture. Through the use of streets in films, the director takes us to the real locations in Bombay. In this virtual urban space, Bombay may emerge as a city of contradictions and instability, rotting, chocked and clustered but the plot makes it clear that it is not without hopes and dreams.

Jean Baudrillard once said, that "to grasp its secret, you should not then begin with the city & move inwards towards a screen, you should begin with a screen & move outwards towards the city" (56). This explains the journey of a fan from reel to real. In order to experience this Bombay fans begin with the cinematic Bombay and move towards the real cities. Having virtually visited Paris through Woody Allen's film *Midnight in Paris*, Vikash Bahl's *Queen*, etc. when I finally visited Paris and the iconic tourist sites, the blissful feeling that was crossing my mind was, 'Oh! I know this site, this is where Owen Wilson filmed that scene.' The fascination and love that I have gathered over the years for Paris through Paris-films was finally realized. The very site of Eiffel tower gave me as much pleasure as I derive by watching it on the screen. Roaming on the streets of Paris made me feel like one of the characters in city-films.

Well, coming back to Bombay, in Bombay-films positive and negative images of the city are inextricably intertwined. On one side we get a glimpse of flashy hotels, expensive cars, airports and monumental streets, and on another side, we have 'ugly slums,' cycle rickshaws, stalls, cheap red light areas, and sweatshops. Another set of films like *Dil Toh Pagal Hai* (*The Heart is Crazy*, 1997) and *Dil Chahta Hai* (*The Heart Desires*, 2001) traverse the glittering lifestyle in Bombay. When we watch these films, we travel through a different Bombay.

The different Bombays of these films can be understood by using Rahul Mehrotra's understanding of kinetic city. In his "Bazaar City: A Metaphor for South Asian Urbanism", he elaborates the concept of 'kinetic city'. According to him, most of the South Asian cities comprise two elements in the same space. The first is a static city or permanent city, which is immovable. Made of concrete, brick, and steel, this static city is monumental and can be traced on maps. The other city is the kinetic city, which is a city in motion- "a three-dimensional construct of a fragmented ground reality" (Mehrotra 97). Further, "built of recycled waste, plastic sheets, scrap metal, canvas, waste wood- all juxtaposed with dish antennas, webs of electric wire, cable, etc. – it is a kaleidoscope of the past, present and future, compressed into an organic fabric of alleys, dead ends and a labyrinth-like, mysterious streetscape that, like any organism, constantly modifies and reinvents itself" (97).

The kinetic city cannot be understood through its architectural design. In the kinetic city, space is marked by its relationship to people. Large processions, festivals, hawkers, street vendors and dwellers are all part of this streetscape that is in constant motion. The kinetic city is energetic and dense; space and the urban crowd converge here, creating a unique site of tension that is both productive and unproductive. The association with the kinetic city makes the fan feel as part of the city and his connectivity with the rest of the fans. Apart from this, there is one image of the city that is created in a particular film and there is another image of the city that a fan cherishes through watching several city-films.

Ranjani Mazumdar in *Bombay Cinema* highlighting the cinematic narration in Gangster films, writes, "the conscious use of an aesthetic of decay, we are in many ways provided with a metaphor of the city as garbage dump, a metaphor that treats the bodies as unwashed, unruly and irrational, walking through a space of abundant waste" (179). She elaborates further:

> In 'Satya' (a gangster film of the year 1998), Bombay is a disenchanted city where the gang becomes part of an everyday violence that can help them escape the boredom of their existence, the banality of their situation, and the degradation befalling each one of them. By philosophically approaching death as the cinematic theatrical performance of urban violence, Satya constantly thwarts the desire for a healing touch that can help provide closure. (179)

The city is being understood in relation to late capitalism, globalization, migration, and postmodern culture, and the challenges these pose to classic modernity. Whereas the emergence of *Shiv Sena*, emergence of Dalit politics, movement of slum dwellers, the presence of crowded and dirty places and the growth of the NGOs are some of the remarkable features of urban space which are evident in Bombay films. Thomas Blom Hansen's recent study provides a fascinating account of the rise of the *Shiv Sena* as an expression of 'vernacular modernity.' Hansen shows that the *Shiv Sena's* emergence was made possible by the erosion of the older elitist political culture that underwrote 'classical

Bombay'. The *Shiv Sena* utilised this space to press its claims aggressively and violently combining nativism with anti-Muslim propaganda. For example, the films like *Black Friday* (2004) by Anurag Kashyap and *Bombay* (1995) by Mani Ratnam depict the atrocities and terror present in the city Bombay. The fans through their background knowledge can not only associate themselves but also become the very part of the terror and atrocities.

Conclusion

While experiencing the city through the cinematic narration in Hindi films based in Bombay, the fact that cannot be ignored is, the identity and friendship is based on an association within the city. This association is realized in true sense by its fans. According to Benjamin, the city is a complex site of 'perception and memory'. The meaning of urban spaces is bound up in 'individual and cultural memory'. He didn't see urban meanings as simply contained in the physical forms of the city. Rather, these forms gave themselves to the subject at different moments; the sense of material space was derived through experience. The fan travels the difficult terrain, feels the speed of running cars and smoke, and suffocating crowd at railway stations of Bombay in the city-films. It's a kind of journey in the favorite city that a true fan can go on while sitting in his comfort zone.

Bibliography

Aden, Roger C. *Popular Stories and Promised Lands: Fan Cultures and Symbolic Pilgrimages.* Tuscaloosa: University of Alabama Press, 1999. Print.

Baudrillard, Jean. *America.* London: Verso, 1988. Print.

Benjamin, Walter. "A Berlin Chronicle." *Reflections: Essays, Aphorisms, Autobiographical Writings.* New York: Schocken, 1986. 3-60. Print.

Brooker, Will. "A Sort of Homecoming: Fan Viewing and Symbolic Pilgrimage." *Fandom: Identities and Communities in a Mediated World.* Ed. Jonathan Gray, Cornel Sandvoss, and C. Lee Harrington. New York: New York University Press, 2007. 157-173. Print.

Couldry, Nick. "On the Set of the Sopranos: "Inside" a Fan's Construction of Nearness." *Fandom: Identities and Communities in a Mediated World.* Ed. Jonathan Gray, Cornel Sandvoss, and C. Lee Harrington. New York: New York University Press, 2007. 139-148. Print.

Hansen, Thomas Blom. *Wages of Violence: Naming and Identity in Postcolonial Bombay.* Princeton: Princeton University Press, 2001. Print.

Jenson, Joli. "Fandom as Pathology: The Consequences of Characterization." *The Adoring Audience: Fan Culture and Popular Media.* Ed. Lisa A. Lewis. New York: Routledge, 1992. 9-29. Print.

Longhurst, Brian, Gaynor Bagnall, and Mike Savage. "Place, Elective Belonging and the Diffused Audience." *Fandom: Identities and Communities in a Mediated*

World. Ed. Jonathan Gray, Cornel Sandvoss, and C. Lee Harrington. New York: New York University Press, 2007. 125-138. Print.

Mazumdar, Ranjani. *Bombay Cinema: An Archive of the City.* Ranikhet: Permanent Black, 2007. Print.

Mehrotra, Rahul. "Bazaar City: A Metaphor for South Asian Urbanism." *Kapital & Karma.* Ed. Angelika Fitz. Wien: Kunsthalle, 2002. 95-110. Print.

Thronton, S. *Club Cultures: Music, Media and Subcultural Capital.* Cambridge: Polity Press, 1995. Print.

Further Reading

Benjamin, Walter. *The Arcades Project.* Cambridge: Harvard University Press, 1999. Print.

Couldry, Nick. *The Place of Media Power: Pilgrims and Witnesses of the Media Age.* New York: Routledge, 2000. Print.

9.

Fandom of Banaras:
Beats' Guiding Star of East

Ashima Bhardwaj

Naropa University, Boulder, Colorado, USA

...the embankments, red temples spires, toy mosques, trees and squat white shrines walling in the bend of the river upstream to the long red train bridge at Raj Ghat an inch high.

- Allen Ginsberg (130)

Banaras' fandom is a kaleidoscopic phenomenon. The space of Banaras differs with different perspective shifts thus generating diversiform fandom. To the seers, Banaras represents the exact cosmos settled on the trident prongs of *Shiva*. Whereas, to a commoner, it can appear like a maze interspersed with *lingams* (an iconic image of Shiva) and deities. Since ages, Banaras has been consolidated as a sacred space where various spiritual lineages converge. The spiritual nucleus of Banaras thus attained, exerts a centripetal force that convokes fandom.

The universal fandom of city space can be measured by the core attributes that have created it. The steady current of its fans has flowed unabated through the alleys of Banaras since times immemorial. The cornerstone of the fan worship is the fact that the site has been attributed to having primordial origins preceding the advent of Gods themselves. The city's choreography has been consistently shaped by mythology leading to the idolization of the city. The fame of Banaras has been centralized through spiritual narratology about a region and then disseminated among larger communities. In the process, Banaras has generated powerful discourses that have touched the foreign shores as well. In the *Kashi Khand* (a division of *Purana* dealing with Kashi) of *Skanda Purana* (a Hindu religious text), it is mentioned that Banaras was a zone between two god-created rivers—the one was *Asi* representing the sword, and the other was the Averter-*Varana*. In the *Vamana Purana* (another Hindu religious text), it is mentioned that the *Vamana Purusha* or primordial man issued *Varana* from the left foot and *Asi* from the right (Singh). The city has thus been personified as a living being with the head at the river *Asi*, the feet at the river *Varana* and loins at

Manikarnika Ghat, a riverfront at the Ganges where bodies are cremated (Parry). One can observe how the topography, climatic changes, and natural forces have been defined in a spiritual syntax. The city projects a belief system that is supposed to be based on metaphysical reality. Banaras is said to be free from earthly connections as it nestles on Shiva's trident. The three points of the tridents are the three lingams- *Omkareshvar* in the north, *Vishveshvar* at the center and *Kedareshvar* in the south. Placed on the three points, Banaras is believed to be a city suspended in space untouched by the laws of spatial and temporal reality. It is the city of *Shiva* (a Hindu God), where his elixir *Ganga* (river personified as a goddess) purifies mortals and helps them to transcend the cycle of life and death. It is believed that once the consciousness awakens, Banaras would appear in its aura, pulsating with Shiva's energy.

The primordial origins and continuity of the space inhabitance to date have imparted unique stardom to the city space. As a cynosure of spirituality Banaras has projected innumerable facets of worship and belief systems since times immemorial. Banaras, also famous as 'Varanasi,' 'Kashi,' and 'Benares,' has been one of the oldest living cities of India, dated since 1000 ca. BCE. The reference to Kashi is perhaps the oldest as it appears in *Atharvaveda,* the fourth ancient scripture of Vedic collection composed around 1200-1000 BCE. The *Mahabharata* also has a reference to *Kashikshetra,* the territory of Kashi. In the *Puranic* treatise, ancient Indian scriptures, the name Varanasi has been used. The Buddhist *Jatakakatha,* tales of Buddha's rebirths, call the land as Banaras (Singh). The *ghats* (riverfront steps leading to the river), temples, *akharas* (compounds), deities and lingams have an authorial presence in the scriptures. Understanding this polysemy of Banaras is crucial for perceiving the fandom of the city. From the centre to its outermost orb, the city is a prototype of cosmic cartography. Banaras is presented as a microcosm of the universal reality. Its geography has been equated to a *mandala* (a pattern representing cosmic energy) formation complete with eight directions (Gesler and Pierce). Banaras' fandom generates from the fact that it is a compact pilgrimage in itself. It constitutes replicas of the holy places and water bodies spread all over the country.

Banaras as space has become a revered entity. It has achieved stardom and has a massive fandom. From the streets of Banaras arises the sanctity that has enthralled its fans all over the world. Pilgrims from different cultures and communities arrive in Banaras to have a glimpse of the revered space. The attachment of its pilgrims germinates with the after-life merit earned from visiting Banaras. The historiography of Banaras shows how the city gains wider attention in the Mughal Period. Though orthodox Brahmanism had its foothold in the city, yet it became an experimental ground for *bhakti* (theistic devotion) revolutionaries, south Indian and western Brahmanical orders, *tantric* (an esoteric tradition of Hinduism) traditions from the east, Sikh, and

Sufi cults along with Christian missionaries. Various philosophical schools flourished in the city. Christopher Bayly suggests that the city was situated at the crossroads of different linguistic territories (Malik). This locale proved to be a competitive site for discussions and debates on rationale and logic. Various philosophies were discussed in the public sphere that encouraged the critique of native and western arguments. It was not only an ancient sacred site but also a place of empowerment through knowledge, training, and logic. The city was ravaged four times by Muslim invaders, but its inherent richness was also enhanced by some Mughal emperors. Akbar and later Dara Shikoh's interest in Banaras added to mutual cooperation between the Hindu and Muslim traditions. It was only after the revolt of 1857 that the British Raj started to put religious practices under the scanner. Banaras with its *ghats*, boasting of representative aristocracies from all over the nation subsisting peacefully on the Ganges, was a matter of concern for the state.

Imperial narratives always used the politics of space to augment the heathen aspects, in order to justify the civilization propaganda. The fandom of Banaras in the colonial period differed than that in the post-independence period. To gauge the full impact of the spread of Banaras' contemporary fame, it is essential to locate the independent upsurge of the city in the West, rather than situating it only within the European colonial ken. Indian spirituality, when transported to America, not only seeped into prevalent religious practices but also made forays into the areas of health care, psychology, fashion, and lifestyle. The access to Indian philosophy initiated neoteric lineage where one could practice eastern *mantras* (sacred utterance of sound or hymn), meditations and adopt Indian deities without deserting the prevailing American religious traditions. It was a progressive and positive appropriation that conflated the Western religiosity with Indian spirituality. Philip Goldberg comments that this transformation could be equated to "a Great Awakening" for "the practices we've imported from India are changing the way we understand ourselves and our place in the universe...a much-needed antidote to religious extremism" (6).

Inroads to India were persistently traversed in somatic and psychic terms by the Americans. The encounters between America and India generated massive cultural, social and spiritual accounts apart from the political and economic dossiers. The 'Tranquilized Fifties' (Lowell) and annihilation fear, after the nuclear bomb, instilled doubt among the masses. Xenophobia was encouraged through the state machinery. Amidst the rising capitalism and McCarthy witch hunts, the East offered a respite from the growing dissatisfaction. The flux of imported *gurus* (spiritual teachers) in New-Age America was on the rise. The influence of India was strong, and even some metropolitans such as Los Angeles were named as the "Benares of America" (Goldberg 115), and San Francisco was termed as the 'New Jagganath Puri.'

The *avant-garde* American Beat writers were among the first post-war iconoclasts who opened the doors towards the East. The Beat movement reared its head, offering spirituality to the beaten-down masses. In conversation with Jack Kerouac, Herbert Huncke gave the term 'Beat' to their generation. The Beat writers appreciated the beatific aspects of the downtrodden and marginalized communities. They offered spiritual solace for junkies, prostitutes, drug peddlers, bohemians, jailbirds, and hobos. What was at stake was the spirit of man. Some Beat writers came to India for exploring spiritual possibilities. While others imbibed India through translated texts and practices prevalent in America.

Beat writers' sojourn to India was a progressive step as it led to a unique cultural syncretism. Allen Ginsberg along with his partner Peter Orlovsky came to India in 1962. They were supposed to travel together in India with Gary Snyder and his wife Joanne Kyger, who had already reached India from Japan. The meeting of the Beats in India had generated a lot of curiosity. In a letter, dated 5 January 1962, from the editor Lawrence Ferlinghetti of City Lights Bookshop to Allen Ginsberg in transit to India, it is stated, "Your meeting seems to be known all over the U.S., in the bookstore circuit, that is. Everybody saying Allen got to India to meet Gary yet? Like some kind of international sorcerer swamis' conjunction…" (Morgan, *I Greet You* 135). This message somewhat shows the anticipations of an American intellectual circle keenly awaiting the consequences of the meeting, as if the two writers would attain voodoo-swamihood on a sacred terrain. In their travel, these Beat fans became more than tourists and globe trotters. They became participants of the rising global fandom of sacred Indian spaces.

Allen Ginsberg and Peter Orlovsky felt the full thrust of India on touching the Bombay shore at the Gateway of India. The enormity of India and its mammoth diversity were visible on the first train ride from Bombay to Delhi. On this train journey, they witnessed an accident where a man was cut to pieces by the train. What amazed them was how death was dealt with in this country. The death imagery hovered around Ginsberg as he saw the ultimate celebration of death at the ghats of Manikarnika. Usually, the crematory grounds are kept at the margins of a city. But in Banaras, the cremation grounds were at the centre, and the rest of the city lay at the periphery. For Ginsberg, there was always an obsession with death. Banaras gave him an unprecedented way of dealing with death. Banaras was formed out of the ashes of the dead corpses, a city that sent its dead to the other world.

Banaras has been the spiritual vortex of India, where death redeemed mankind. For the Beats, Banaras became the guiding star of the East. They were seekers of wisdom and were in search of a luminary that could impart them a holistic understanding of the fellahin culture. Banaras became the star, and they were its fervent fans. Bill Morgan, Allen's biographer, states that for

Allen Ginsberg "India was a world unto itself; the customs and rules of the West were non-existent here. If he had spiritual and visionary questions and new doubts about faith, they would certainly be answered" (*I Celebrate Myself* 345). For the beatific fans, Banaras was a star in all its glory. It had its stardom reflected through its practices, cultural traditions, and spiritual richness. The Beats were its ardent fans who wanted to explore every aspect of this celebrity city. They found new experiences and cultural traditions at every nook and corner of Banaras. The non-interference of foreign entities in Banaras, as compared to other metropolitans, had preserved an ancient touch in the city. For Ginsberg and Orlovsky, it was rare and unique to behold five thousand years old practices of praying on the Ganges.

Banaras, with its divine cartography, provided the visionary moment to Ginsberg. This visionary flash was a celebrated phenomenon in Beat writings. Such transcendence was a route to escape from the materialism and mundane routines. Before Ginsberg had set his foot in India, he had already reached the place through his dreams. In his dream entry, dated 7 November 1961, he writes: "I wonder what city I'm in, I'm deliriously happy, it's my promised land . . .I'm wandering in India, it's like a new earth-I'm happy-I wake...." (*Indian Journals* 5). In his dream state, he imagined being in India roaming in the state of bliss and happiness.

The Beats found it unique how the ancient, contemporary and modern amalgamated in Banaras. Ginsberg was also keen to find a spiritual guru in India. But instead of a persona, he was advised by holy men that "Poetry is your sadhana (sadhana is path, disciple, yoga) and 'Take Blake for your Guru'" (Morgan, *I Greet You* 175). This message deeply affected Ginsberg and he realized that "I never read Blake thru, studied him, I'm getting interested in doing it finally" (Morgan, *I Greet You* 175). Banaras provided a space for the Beats to deal with one's fears and questions. Instead of a guru, Ginsberg found that the city had much to teach through its lifestyle and culture. There was ample room for discussion, argument, and debate in the lanes of Banaras. Being a cradle of a varied religious stream, it became a perfect space for its Beat fans to experiment and evolve. Beats got an opportunity to witness a plethora of spiritual lineages and then appropriate them.

With perturbed mind and multiple pieces of advice from various saints across India, Ginsberg had entered the fandom of Banaras, a city that was spirituality incarnate. As the Beat writers reached it, after their travels across the Indian terrain, they found a condensed space that reflected various traditions. There were no specific altars to become holy, rather the city and its pilgrimage were considered sacred. On the burning ghats, the Beat writer must have witnessed the ego dispersion as the body was cremated in ultimate union with the five elements. They had become ardent lovers of the city and stayed here, filing extensions for visas. Banaras with its culture had captivated the Beat imagination. The ghats of Dashavamedha and Manikarnika offered everything that was unheard of in America.

In Banaras, various legends evoked the cultural memory of a class and strengthened the fandom of the place. Banaras' *Dasashwamedha* ghat had the lore that *Brahma* sacrificed ten (*das*) horses (*ashvas*) here and invited Shiva. Several epic narratives have contributed to the sanctity of Manikarnika ghat. The word '*Manikarnika*' in Sanskrit refers to an ear jewel-ornament. It is believed that Goddess *Sati's* ornament fell here. In order to avenge the insult of her husband Shiva, she had thrown herself into the sacrificial fire at her father's house. The earring fell at the ghat when her charred body was being carried by her consort, Shiva. Another narrative maintains that Shiva's earring fell as he performed *tandav* (the dance of destruction). The fandom of an entity is directly proportional to the regenerative capacity of the cultural memory. Every age renegotiates with the cultural memory of a revered space and generates narratives to bind the fandom together. Post-Independence Banaras acquired an independent existence in the cultural recollection and evolved its own semantics based on the legends. The prevalent narratives consolidated and strengthened the position of the space. Thus, the sacred space's fame transmitted to the global audience. Beats acknowledged how the signifiers and symbols gained potency and became the dominant force in shaping the economic, socio-cultural, political and spiritual procedures.

Ginsberg watched the *doms* (the priests who cremate the dead bodies) burning the corpses, a practice perhaps as old as humanity itself. The burning bodies, charred remains, and the ceremonial recitals were intense images that consolidated later in his works and writings. The city was intriguing for the Beats. Thousands of years old practices and cremation ceremonies had remained intact at Banaras. It offered a plethora of tastes, smells, sights, sounds, and sensuality.

Ginsberg's first expression of the city in his journal reverberates with the enthusiasm of a fan, as he wonders: "Kashi oldest in the world/ continuously inhabited city" (*Indian Journals* 118). Banaras also became a testing ground for many of the core beliefs espoused by the Beats. The indulgence in spiritual experimentation, creativity through drug-intake and intoxication, homosexuality had altogether different connotations in India. The fandom of Banaras augmented due to the experiential possibilities that it offered.

In Banaras, the Beats did not comply with the earlier Western outlook of 'saving' India from its squalor and heathen practices. They deconstructed the colonial narratives about the city being squalid, impoverished and deformed thus gaining a spiritual understanding of an ancient landscape. Banaras, for them, was a star entity that was pulsating with raw primeval energy. Each day was a spiritual feast for its zealous Beat devotees. Ginsberg wanted some solace from his overburdened lifestyle and was in search of a newfangled approach in Banaras for his literary documentation. He felt a "need for some basic change in composition as violent as cut-ups" and for this, he took on the journey to accomplish his "postgraduate course in the world-scene...to improve my (his) education" (Morgan, *I Greet You* 145). For Ginsberg, Banaras was a luminary of spirituality. With its sensibilities, experiences, and mysteries, Banaras had an enduring impact on the poetics of the Beat writer.

The first place rented by Ginsberg and Orlovsky was out in the cantonment area. It was too far from the ghats. Both of them were deprived of viewing the famous ghats and activities on the Ganges and so soon shifted to a room on the third floor right above Dasashwamedha ghat. They took a great room with nine French doors overlooking the market and Ganges bank, bathing ghat, balconies where the cows constantly contrived to steal vegetables from the women. The window of the room opening onto the *ghat* provided them with a slice of the Banaras life. Every morning the room gave them a view of the star attractions of Banaras. The *pandas* (priests) on the stone-steps offering water to the Sun, Hindus bathing into the Ganges to wash away their sins, beggars lining up the banks, and the holy cows straying at the *ghats* all day long presented the theatricals of *Banarasi* (related to Banaras) life. Ginsberg gives a colorful account of the tussle between women selling vegetables and cows in the lanes of Banaras that engages its residents. From his window, he loved to capture the market scenes that went on as: "same cows and same ladies morning after morning like a repeated comedy- nobody gets mad for more than a minute-cows put heads together and plan new attack on baskets every ten minutes" (Morgan, *I Greet You* 166).

On his first day in Banaras, Ginsberg watched the burning piers at the Manikarnika ghat and roamed the riverfront all night. The entry in the *Indian Journal* about his first night-walk captures the awe that Banaras inspired as he saw "Cows (11) wandering in *Manikarnika ghat* at midnite under a full moon, eating the rush ropes of the corpse-litters left behind on the sand near the woodpile on which corpses wrapped in white cloth are burning" (Ginsberg, *Indian Journals* 118). Banaras on the full moon with burning piers was enchanting. Ginsberg used to take a walk up to Manikarnika and watch the burning pyres. Ginsberg also came in contact with *sadhus* (saints), with whom he smoked *ganja* (opium) from clay pipes. It was a retreat into ancient wisdom that was sought after by Ginsberg and Orlovsky. Coming from the land of plenty, Banaras offered an alternative way of life. The simple household items such as straw mats on the floor and water in clay pots initiated a lifestyle unadulterated by consumerism. A hundred-watt bulb dangling from the roof, a cooking stove purchased with a dollar, a red-bellied

Ganesha (elephant-headed God), and wooden *Chaitanya* (spiritual leader of Gaudiya Vaishvanism) statue in the alcove completed the home décor. In the chill of winter, Ginsberg lay on "a charpoy (rope bed on wooden frame), plenty blankets for cool winter in Benaras -a desk and shelf to hold accumalatedness. And notebooks-feel at home & happy" (Ginsberg, *Indian Journals* 125).

The stardom of Banaras played a decisive role in the life of Ginsberg's partner Peter Orlovsky. It constructed and devastated him at the same time. The drug habit that Peter had cultivated in France grew worse in India as there was easy access to opium in Banaras. He fell in love with a woman Manjula and also learned to play *sarod* (string instrument) in Banaras. The music and love stayed with him for a long time and often helped him seek refuge from his depression and suffering. Peter Orlovsky had inherited mental illness, led a poverty-stricken childhood and in his youth was constantly worried about his siblings who also shared the psychological problems. He was discharged as a psychological misfit in the Army and was relieved of his duties at nineteen. With Ginsberg, Peter shared a life-long relationship though interspersed with several fights and partings. Ginsberg and Orlovsky had reconciled after a fight in Europe and thenceforth traveled together towards India. Here they wanted to escape the growing media attention. India held a particular charm for Orlovsky. His excitement can be seen in his journal entry dated 20 May 1961, where he says that the narratives of Indian food and politics as told by Jacques Stern (a friend) would want all of them running to the place. Banaras' burning pyres had captured Orlovsky's imagination. As an ecstatic fan in his anxiety to be united with his star, he wrote: "Hooray ... we come and you will now know we passed through your belly and sniffed your funeral pyres and seen arms cracking and eyes popping like sparks and fingernails turning black and crisp like twigs" (Orlovsky 139). Peter Orlovsky engrossed himself in the rich musical traditions of Banaras. It was an attempt on part of a devotee to indulge in all possible aspects of his beloved star. The city has been a hub of cultural activities, folk music in *biraha* (separation from beloved) tradition and music *gharanas* (schools of classical music). Peter Orlovsky described in a letter (dated 22 March 1963) to his family the rich musical heritage that he was accessing in Banaras, saying "I want to get a small size harmonium (a small piano) to use in my singing lessons I am now taking and I also have a *sarod* teacher here. In fact, I got a whole bunch of new music friends..." (Orlovsky 200). In another letter dated 17 May 1963, to Ginsberg in Calcutta, Orlovsky shares that he constantly practiced his *sargam* exercises and then took a bath at *Goranga ghat* excited at, "lots of happy happenings to do here" (Orlovsky 201).

The Beats were fascinated with varied images that captivated Banaras' fandom, such as its musical heritage, couture, gods, and cremation grounds and mentioned them in their accounts. These images became immensely popular and generated radical offshoots during countercultural protests in America. Through the efforts of the Beats in post-war America, the stardom of Banaras expanded and received an international fan following. Indian forms of music, mantra- chants and non-violence *satyagraha* (insistence for the truth) methodology were incorporated in the cultural dissents. Julie Stephens has mentioned that "India was novel, and 'things Indian' were fresh, original and innovative in a way which had as much to do with a particular capitalist expression of modernity (very familiar to participants in Sixties movements) as with a metaphysical pursuit of the eternal" (60-61).

The majority of the strict ritual-based Indian philosophies could never appeal to the American palette. Banaras' philosophical schools followed rigid codes involving *yoga* (art of meditation) postures, strictly vegetarian diet, and abstinence from sex and drugs. After the popularity of Indian spirituality through the Beats-initiated efforts, a commixture of Orthodox Church, Buddhist practices along with mantra-chants developed. The Beats became mascots encouraging an inter-religious dialogue.

The fandom of Banaras gained momentum as Ginsberg transposed Banaras' alleys, Hindu deities, and mythologies on another reality. As a result, he was able to create a community space that transformed into a site of cultural revolt. Ginsberg and Orlovsky actively participated in rallies, demonstrations, and sit-ins. In one of his letters to Gary Snyder, Ginsberg wrote that the Government was becoming uneasy at his presence. This was, in fact, the sought-after goal, in which, activism on the part of people, was becoming potent in disrupting the totalitarianism. The practices of *mantra* chanting, cymbal-driven ecstasies, *kirtans* (devotional singing) and circumambulations discovered on the ghats of Banaras were incorporated by Ginsberg and Orlovsky's in social protests by Rocky Flats Truth Force and at Human Be-in event and Vietnam protests.

What made Ginsberg and Orlovsky experience the fandom of Banaras was their willingness to blend in the Banarasi culture. They wanted to be one in the crowds and then understand the mysteries of Banaras. They preferred to adopt the Indian manners and respect the traditions rather than protesting against the dirt, filth, and poverty around. This attitude separated them from the touristy crowds who came only for easy junk access. One can observe the affinity that the Beats created with Indian living style as they roamed the streets of Banaras, "walking (in dhoti & lumberjack shirt) thru Benares alleyways, turning corners past toy stands, thru red gates up Vishwanath alley past the temple- thru a grate seeing crowd round the lingam chanting slow-beat of drum vary-voiced tuneless mass- beautiful harmonies, ending as I passed out the back courtyard past the huge stone cow, with acceleration of drums- past the square where in daytime sell red and blue & yellow bright colored powders displayed in cones of dust" (Ginsberg, *Indian Journals* 137).

The ease with which they mingled among the crowds was enough to put them under suspicion. No foreigner was seen happily hanging around beggars and lepers, meditating later on the *Manikarnika ghat*. The police authorities could not understand what was the need to come from America and settle in the by lanes of Banaras. For the state authorities, the growing popularity of Banaras on the world arena was difficult to gauge. This ignorance can also be seen as the effect of seething Indo-China turmoil. As if it was not sufficient, CID also suspected the need for the Beats' stay in India. A spy was put on duty to gather information about the two writers. It was only after interviews with neighbours and the poets that they left them in peace. Ginsberg later realized that the entire suspicion had brewed at the campus of Banaras Hindu University.

Ginsberg was invited by the students to deliver a lecture at the Benares Hindu University. He used the four-letter word which proved to be much ahead of its times in India. Allen Ginsberg was a progressive poet and projected a daredevilry in his vocabulary and ideas. The terminology in his poems offended the students as they considered it to be a derogatory usage of language. For Ginsberg, it was a weird incident. After all, it was his signature style that had influenced millions of young minds in America. His texts like "Howl" had empowered and challenged the authority, becoming an iconoclastic literary masterpiece. Banaras was not ready for this liberation yet. The students underlined the obscene language and sent a copy to the CID. It was suggested that the poets must be Chinese spies (Morgan, *I Celebrate Myself* 368). This incident later created trouble for Ginsberg as his visa was not being extended to February. But no one could throw him out from Banaras, a city that he loved. He ruminated, "I can go out there to Benares Hindu Univ. to visit this pie-shaped church front stairs- behind which a statue of Buddha-anytime-whether invited or not" (Ginsberg, *Indian Journals* 170). He went to Delhi and used political links through Pupul Jayakar, finally getting an extension till June.

Ginsberg stood up to his beliefs. He believed in his star- the city of Banaras. As an avid fan, he knew that this small incident, in fact, was the cornerstone of mutual acknowledgment of what lies at the core of two different cultural streams. The American freedom of expression and its headlong collision with Indian modesty through poetics had larger ramifications. It was also a relevant episode for Banaras' academia. It showed the Indian audience, the need to open up and have a freedom of expression. Poetry is a potent tool to destruct conservatism. The very fact that the students were offended showed that Ginsberg had done his job. He had shaken people through his sounds and made them aware of what lied beyond the so-called ethics of language. The unethical was loud and clear in expressing freedom. Ginsberg though felt sad at his boldness and reconsidered his stance. Ginsberg, in fact, provided an insight into post-war American poetic traditions that were rebelling against the state measures. He also introduced a break from British colonial languages that had dominated the Indian academia.

At this juncture, Ginsberg perceived the challenging side of Banaras' fandom. The city through its ways had taught Ginsberg to control his outbursts. As a devotee of Banaras, Ginsberg was prepared to accept the challenges of its idol. He started *pranayama* (breathing exercises) and yoga to control his anxiety. Bill Morgan points out to a more transformed Ginsberg of this period, who wrote calmer and less critical letters to his father. He was altering and vowed to cut down his smoking and temper. Ginsberg later acknowledged that his temper control was an outcome of his stay in India. Banaras the star had altered its admirer. With its million experiences, the city had infused patience and acceptance in the author. Ginsberg sat under the *Bodhi* tree [the tree under which Gautama attained wisdom or 'bodh' and became Buddha] at Sarnath along with his visits to Nalanda and Rajgriha. The places gave him a yardstick to span the present Buddhism with its past glory in the ruins of Kashikshetra. Ginsberg also travelled to *Stupa* (a mound-like structure where the relics of Buddha have been placed) where he saw the three fish sign that became his life-long logo. In America, Buddhism was a modulated philosophy, but his trip to India was the one that made him "realize(d) the role that the body plays in Buddhism" (Mortenson 79). Ginsberg used to sit at the ghats every day and watch the dead bodies being cremated. The insanity, madness, and transit attained another dimension at Banaras. Bill Morgan writes that "treating a corpse as a treasure, as was done in the West, led to all sorts of unconscious misunderstandings and fantasies about heaven and hell. Thinking of himself as a piece of meat sometimes came in handy to Allen in the years to come. It was a good way to lose one's ego, and a large ego was one of Allen's biggest traits" (Morgan, *I Celebrate Myself* 364). Observing the death at Banaras was a contemplative exercise for Ginsberg. It offered a rare somatic insight into the final consumption of the body and focused on the futility of life's struggles.

A strange chemistry ensued between the star and the fans. Ginsberg and Orlovsky adhered to the ways of their idol city and incorporated the teachings in their life. Banaras transformed them. Under the tutelage of Banaras, the Beats observed that the fandom of Banaras had a stronger appeal in the afterlife. People came to Banaras to die and attain *Moksha* (freedom from the cycles of birth and death), the ultimate aim of the soul. The relatives of a dead person have also been mentioned in Ginsberg's accounts. He could see them, saying prayers and offering burning charcoal to the lips. In a moment the fire would flare up and "he would receive his real education...where he found no social hierarchy" (Morgan, *I Celebrate Myself* 364). In a journal entry on Sunday, 18 December 1962, he penned his, "long walk at dusk from the orange Raj Ghat bridge-finally to Manikarnika" (Ginsberg, *Indian Journals* 125) as if the answers to existence lay buried in the ashes at Banaras.

Ginsberg was a conscious poet who understood that what was at stake was humanity. Both Orlovsky and Ginsberg participated in Peking Peace March being already under the scanner of officials. Amidst the rising Indo- China war crisis they believed that sanity lay with protestors who were calling for peace. He wrote an entry on 20 March 1963, that said "...Give China your Wheat and Machine America. But however, recreate India? Bang Bang Bang continues the bronze gong of Kali [Hindu Goddess of tantric pantheon] downstairs" (Ginsberg, *Indian Journals* 193). Through this entry, he also indicates to the upcoming destruction and Kali's role in ending evil. The goddess played a compelling role in Ginsberg's poesy. Images of Kali fired Ginsberg's imagination. The subterranean aspects of the city of Banaras held the secret to the cosmic knowledge. Banaras in its illustriousness was an epicenter of a subterranean faculty of fandom as well. The transcendental reality and metaphysical dimensions were at the core of Banaras' stardom. The Beats acknowledged the esoteric aspects and immersed themselves in the sub-cultural facets of stardom.

Banaras' subterranean life deals with *tantra*, school of esoteric practices. The popular belief says that there is an underground city of Banaras, kept intact by the seers and *tantrics* (practitioner of tantra). Ginsberg associated with many sadhus in his quest for meaning. His obsession with Kali bespeaks of his interest in the most tantalizing aspects of Indian spirituality. Smoking ganja with sadhus in cremation grounds of Nimtala and Manikarnika must have initiated conversations on tantra and *aghoori* (ascetic Shaivism) traditions. Hugh B. Urban in his work *Tantra* says that "...for Ginsberg and other voices of the American counterculture, Tantric imagery is turned into a powerful weapon to criticize the dominant sociopolitical order, which is perceived as repulsive, bankrupt and corrupt. With its emphasis on the terrible, erotic Mother Kali, *tantra* seemed to offer a much-needed antidote to a hypercerebral Western world that had lost touch with the powers of sex, femininity, and darkness" (Urban 225).

By 1970s American tantra took a center stage. Banaras' Tantra traditions and Calcutta's Kali rituals had created distinct trajectories from the city's existing fandom. The levitation ceremony of Pentagon, performed in 1967 amidst the *mantra* chanting and exorcising of demons gave an all-new level of protest language to America. It was a Beat led demonstration that evolved an untapped lexicon of protest. The imagery of ancient landscapes like Banaras was efficient in challenging the dominant conceptions of spatiality. For instance, the image of *Kali*, roaming in the *samsaans* (cremation grounds) became an innovative medium to express discontent over American politics. Ginsberg transfixed the figure of *Kali* on the Statue of Liberty. He evolved the image in "Strotras to Kali" as "the skulls that hang on Kali's neck, Geo Washington with eyes rolled up & tongue hanging out of his mouth like a fish, N. Lenin upside down...Roosevelt with grey eyeballs; Stalin grinning, Mussolini with a broken Jaw,...an empty space for Truman...jingled in the Cosmic Dance" (Ginsberg, *Indian Journals* 13).

The Beats utilized Banaras' paraphernalia in social activism. An interfaith development also initiated with the efforts of the Beat fandom. Specific religious Western traditions' encounters with Eastern spirituality engendered appropriated religious offshoots. For instance, Christian meditation, bhakti attitude for Christ, and Buddha's Four Noble truths for Christ, Torah yoga, Bhaktifest, green yoga, ganja yoga earmarked a new territory in American religiosity (Goldberg). For Ginsberg and Orlovsky, a human to a human relationship was the requirement for a new consciousness that was essential in the aftermath of the nuclear bomb and Cold war. Insistence on lived experience and movement through Indian spiritual spaces proved to be an intellective exercise to break free from the existing modes of thought. Mobility through Indian pilgrimage proved to be a destabilizing force:

> Engaging with India in the Sixties was primarily a sign of rebellion... 'exotic' had come to stand for a rejection of the constraints of both industrialized society and 'straight' politics...India came to be seen as a particular embodiment of specific countercultural tenets....To imbibe India was, in one dramatic gesture, both to demolish the prison of technical Western rationality and to destroy the constraints of nationality. (Stephens 51)

A subtle change in American syntax also became visible in the Sixties. The concepts of *karma* (deeds), yoga, mantra, *mudra* (yogic postures), moksha dominant in Banaras' semantics seeped into American slang. American skyscrapers saw an architectural metamorphosis. The skylines were dotted with temple shrines and *yoga* centers. American markets saw an influx of Indian artefacts, accessories, and handicrafts. Ginsberg and Orlovsky also popularized *khadi* (handspun cloth) among the counterculture hippies. Like rhapsodic fans, the Beats were bent on disseminating the tokens of their star, Banaras.

Peter Orlovsky chose Banarasi attire on leaving India via Pakistan, Iran, and Turkey. In a letter to Allen Ginsberg, dated 7 October 1963, from Tehran, Peter Orlovsky mentioned, "...I went walking, sightseeing mosques and tombs and graveyards and went through markets and store streets saying hello to ten thousand Persians dressed in (my) orange Varanasi lungi [sarong] and orange sadhu shirt tradition Calcutta...Young student on crowded street came alongside me asking what religion are you?... I said I love all religions..." (Orlovsky 209). On his transit route, he walked through the streets of London flaunting his "Banaras Gandhi pajamas [pants]" (Orlovsky 212). India in general and Banaras, in particular, had provided a palette of religious traditions and beliefs. Banaras had refreshed Peter Orlovsky as he declared that he hoped "to walk into New York with my orange happy clothes' passing on the message, 'help America to help the World'" (Orlovsky 210). Ginsberg's in his loose khadi shirt, pajamas, *chappals* (slippers) with cymbals in hand depicted a persona drenched in the ways of Banaras. Chanting poems in American protests he became the revered authority for millions of hippies celebrating freedom on the streets of America. According to Ken Kesey's description, as cited by Jackson, while confronting police force Ginsberg went "right into the lion's mouth with his cymbals. Ching, ching, ching" (Jackson 249). Fandom of Banaras left an indelible mark on the Beat poets who in turn left their imprints on the ashes of the burning ghats.

Bibliography

Ginsberg, Allen. *Indian Journals: March 1962-May 1963 Notebooks Diary Blank Pages Writings.* New York: Grove Press, 1996. Print.

Gesler, M. Wilbert, and Margaret Pierce. "Hindu Varanasi." *Geographical Review* 90.2 (2000): 222-237. Web. 13 Apr. 2015. <http://www.jstor.org/stable/216120/>.

Goldberg, Philip. *American Veda: From Emerson and the Beatles to Yoga and Meditation-How Indian Spirituality Changed the West.* New York: Harmony Books, 2010. Print.

Jackson, Andrew Grant. *1965: The Most Revolutionary Year in Music.* New York: St. Martin's Press, 2015. Print.

Malik, Jamal, ed. *Perspectives of Mutual Encounters in South Asian History:1760-1860.* Boston: Brill, 2000. Print.

Morgan, Bill. *I Celebrate Myself: The Somewhat Private Life of Allen Ginsberg.* New York: Viking, 2006. Print.

Morgan, Bill, ed. *I Greet You at the Beginning of a Great Career. The Selected Correspondence of Lawrence Ferlinghetti and Allen Ginsberg 1955-1997.* San Francisco: City Lights Book, 2015. Print.

Morgan, Bill, ed. *The Selected Letters of Allen Ginsberg and Gary Snyder.* Berkeley: Counter Point, 2009. Print.

Mortenson, Erik. *Capturing the Beat Moment: Cultural Politics and the Politics of Presence.* Carbondale: South Illinois University Press, 2011. Print.

Orlovsky, Peter. *Peter Orlovsky, A Life in Words: Intimate Chronicles of a Beat Writer.* Ed. Bill Morgan. Boulder: Paradigm Publishers, 2014. Print.

Parry, Jonathan P. *Death in Banaras.* New York: CUP, 1994. Print.

Singh, Rana P.B. *Banaras: Making of India's Heritage*. Newcastle: Cambridge Scholars, 2009. Print.

Stephens, Julie. *Anti-Disciplinary Protest: Sixties Radicalism and Postmodernism*. Cambridge: Cambridge University Press, 1998. Print.

Urban, Hugh B. *Tantra: Sex, Secrecy, Politics, and Power in the Study of Religion*. Berkeley: University of California Press, 2003. Print.

Further Reading

Baker, Deborah. *A Blue Hand: The Beats in India*. New York: Penguin, 2008. Print.

Bell, Daniel. "Religion in the Sixties." *Social Research* 38.3 (1971): 447-497. Web. 7 Apr. 2013.<http://www.jstor.org/stable/40970070/>.

Eck, Diana L. *Encountering God: A Spiritual Journey from Bozeman to Banaras*. New Delhi: Penguin Books, 1993. Print.

Fell, Rachel, and Jeffrey J. Kripal, eds. *Encountering Kali: In the Margins, at the Center, in the West*. Berkeley: University of California Press, 2003. Print.

Ginsberg, Allen. "Howl." *poetryfoundation.org*. N.p., n.d. Web. 15 Feb 2013. <https://www.poetryfoundation.org/poems/49303/howl />.

---. "Interviewed by Thomas Clark." *Theparisreview.org*. 8. Web. 16 Feb. 2013. <http://www.theparisreview.org/interviews/4389/the-art-of-poetry-no-8allen-ginsberg/>.

Foley, Jack."Same Multiple Identity: An Interview with Allen Ginsberg." *Discourse* 20.1/2 (1998):158-181. Web.

Gold, Herbert. "Hip, Cool, Beat—and Frantic." *The Nation* 185.16 (1957): 349-55. Print.

Gupta, Raj Kumar. *The Great Encounter: A Study of Indo-American Literary and Cultural Relations*. Maryland: The Riverdale Company, 1987. Print.

Gutschow, Niels. "Benares: The Centre of Hinduism? A Discussion of the Meaning of "Place" and Space." *Erdkunde* 48.3 (1994): 194-209. Web. 13 Apr. 2015. <http://www.jstor.org/stable/25646593/>.

Harding, S. John, and Hillary Rodrigues. *Introducing to the Study of Religion*.London: Routledge, 2009. Print.

Hertel, Bradley R, and Cynthia Ann Humes, eds. *Living Banaras: Hindu religion in Cultural Context*.Albany: State University of New York Press, 1993. Print.

Jackson, Carl T. "The Influence of Asia upon American Thought: A Bibliography Essay." *American Studies International* 22.1 (1984): 3-31. Web. 11 Feb. 2013. <http://www.jstor.org/stable/41280625/>.

Kern, Louis J. "The Beat Apocalypse: The Religious Visions of Kerouac, Ginsberg, and Burroughs by John Lardas." *Utopian Studies*1.2 (2002):162-165. Print.

King, Winston L. "Eastern Religions: A New Interest and Influence." *Annals of American Academy of Political and Social Science*. 387.1 (1970): 66-76. Web. 25 Oct. 2013. <http://www.jstor.org/stable/1036739/>.

Lowell, Robert. "Memories of West Street and Lepke." *poetryfoundation.org*. N.p., n.d. Web. 12 Feb. 2013. <www.poetryfoundation.org/poems/48338/memories-of-west-street-and-lepke />.

Oldmeadow, Harry. *Journeys East: 20ᵗʰ Century Western Encounters with Eastern Religious Traditions.* Canada: World Wisdom, 2000. Print.

Paglia, Camille. "Cults and Cosmic Consciousness: Religious Vision in the American 1960's." *Arion*10.3 (2003): 57-111. Print.

Prothero, Stephen. "On the Holy Road: The Beat Movement as Spiritual Protest." *The Harvard Theological Review* 84.2 (April 1991): 205-222. Web. 2 Jul. 2012.

Singh, Rana P.B. "Water Symbolism and Sacred Landscape in Hinduism: A Study of Benares." *Erdkunde* 48.3 (July-Sep.1994): 210-227. Web.13 Apr. 2015. <http://www.jstor.org/stable/25646594/>.

Tweed, Thomas A., and Stephen Prothero. *Asian Religions in America: A Documentary History.*New York: OUP, 1999. Print.

Urban, Hugh B. "The Counterculture Looks East: Beat Writers and Asian Religion." *American Studies*29.1 (1988): 51-70. Web. 27 Dec. 2012.<http://www.jstor.org/stable/4062254/>.

Cultural Politics of War-heroes:
Revisiting the Soldier Bio-icons of Jammu

Jamiel Ahmad

University of Kashmir, India

This essay proposes to explore the cultural politics of representation of some war-hero statues situated in the region of Jammu, Jammu and Kashmir, India. It engages with the iconographic study of hero and hero worship via some bio-iconic war memorial sites. It debates such activities as not simply literal ways of commemorating but also discusses them as visual spins through the politics of iconography. The main essence of this essay lies in its inter-relational dialogue between various theoretical frames and the images dealt in it. Nicholas Mirzoeff is quite instrumental in this subject as he traces the emergence of visual culture developing from W. J. T. Mitchell's 'picture theory' and has questioned the Western supremacy of the logos as the privileged, preferred and the highest form of intellectual practice. Visual culture as an academic field is primarily rooted in the concept of image, which, according to W. J. T. Mitchell, is "not just a particular kind of sign, but something like an actor on the historical stage, a presence or character endowed with legendary status, a history that parallels and participates in the stories we tell ourselves about our own evolution from creatures 'made in the image' of a creator to creatures who make themselves and their world in their own image" (Mitchell 504). The bio-iconic statues of soldiers dealt in this paper are images, concrete stories, and texts which have multiple issues latent in them. Stuart Hall argues about a process called 'encoding-decoding', which seems to be quite pertinent in representing the politics, and the poetics of such signs of masculine valor and heroism. These masculine bio-iconic visuals are not mere signs of some innocent cultural commemorating activities but are rooted in a complex dynamics of power. Martyrdom as a 'spectacle'[1] is quite basic to these visual creations, which paints masculine valour in the shades of patriarchy and nationalism. Placing these visuals in the midst of the life of a community has an 'affect'[2] on their life and thinking processes; such signs become emblems of male bravery, of masculine somatic markers, of nationalism and/or of various sub-nationalisms (appendix Fig. 1 & 2). Starting with Carlyle's description of a hero, this image-essay represents these bio-iconic statues via a theoretical intervention based on Roland Barthes, Stuart Hall, Benedict Anderson, 'Spectacle' and a bit of 'affect theory.'

I am preparing this essay against the backdrop of watching an event a few days ago. On 10th January, 2016 while coming back from my campus, I saw people celebrating the 'martyrdom-anniversary' of a soldier in a village where they have erected his statue. They had organised a celebration, like a festival, and people were participating in it like any other cultural event (appendix Fig. 3 & 4). This is an event of 'hero' worship, which has its roots in the cultural categories and discourses loaded with power. Heroes and icons are people who grow out of the communities we live in. A particular act/event underlies the process of hero-making and icon-formation, and that act/event itself is a superstructure of many other cultural norms.

Thomas Carlyle debates the 'heroic qualities/attributes' of some historic global personages. Carlyle states:

> We have undertaken to discourse here for a little on Great Men, their manner of appearance in our world's business, how they have shaped themselves in the world's history, what ideas men formed of them, what work they did; --on Heroes, namely, and on their reception and performance; what I call Hero-worship and the Heroic in human affairs. (Carlyle 5)

What Carlyle seems to be focusing upon is the criterion of 'greatness', as the measuring scale to baptize heroes within a cultural framework. His 'Great Men' are human beings with a record of transforming individual and collective lives within different historical epochs. Taking on such heroic souls, Carlyle says, "they were the leaders of men, these great ones; the modelers, patterns, and in a wide sense creators, of whatsoever the general mass of men contrived to do or to attain" (6).

The cultural monuments of a place can retell history, make a revision of the past, and keep it vibrant in the present times and the era to come. Commenting upon the recent happenings in Bangladesh, Nandini Bhattacharya[4] writes:

> Dismantling of Lady Justice Statue in Dacca at the behest of Islamic fundamentalists reminds me of a Bengali proverb "cow dung laughs in derision as cow dung cakes burn". In the 17TH century, these very *kattar* [radical] European Christians had initiated a systemic destruction of icons and iconography at the behest of Puritan Protestantism. Our dear old cultural sacred cow John Milton even wrote a pamphlet called ICONOKLASTES, even though he was primarily targeting the iconizing of the king. (n.pag.)

Basically, she is pointing towards the fundamentalism of religions, which at times turns up to engulf the concretized icons of a culture, or forbids the practice of iconisation. But, some of the Semitic texts, like the *Bible*, reveal the iconic reincarnation of God in human images, and thereby a religious context of iconisation. We can also examine the complex and tortured relationship between the need to glorify 'martyrs' and icons and its ideological objections in the Abrahamic set of religions such as Islam, Zionism, and Protestant Christianity. These very instincts point towards the practice of iconisation, or objection to icon-worship, with its base in religion; but it is to be kept in mind that icon-making is not simply a religious activity as it has its roots in the community one lives in and the education system we live in. The point of discussion is to debate the process of iconisation as an old and complex cultural process, which has taken new routes in contemporary times; which is our main focus. Most recently, we have been watching 'digital-icons' like M S Dhoni's[5] and Sachin Tendulkar's[6] Bollywood pieces. Narendra Modi, the current Prime Minister of India, is emerging as an ideal-icon, and also there are icons who are made out of 'ordinary' masses like soldiers as 'martyrs', rebels as 'martyrs', politicians as reincarnated historic figures, sports 'stars', and most importantly the icons made out of mass media. This new trend of iconisation via audio-visual mediums, the virtual world, the operations of non-verbal emoticons, and the tendency to culturally iconise sports, political figures, and cinema rock stars undercut the orthodox religio-ideological impediments but do not erase them entirely. It is like these new tendencies render the old beliefs to a state of radical and unresolved tension.

This image-essay is an attempt to put forth a theoretical intervention of some iconic and (micro) historic heroes by exploring the monumental statues and sites commemorated in their honour. Jammu has a good number of statues and sites, which have been raised as heroic tokens in the honour of some prominent men. The level of hero-making and hero-worship and the ideological impact of this cultural exercise on the minds of the masses is evident in the following statement: "Jammu is the land of warriors, without a doubt. These warriors, in their own way, have brought immense pride and prestige to the state. The installations of their statues at the main roundabouts and naming of roads after their names, is truly what we can do in their respect" (Rasgotra n.pag.).

However, in contemporary times, the reflection of these heroic figures is quite clear when we enter the arena of visual culture,[7] wherein image, as an ideology takes the central position and the processes of visualism[8] serve as the base. Discussing the field of visual culture, Pramod K. Nayar[9] writes, "Mirzoeff (1998) argues that the modern age is characterised by its visualising tendencies. Recently, Tasveer Ghar[10] launched a project entitled, *Manly Matters*, which focused on the 'pictorial analysis to representations of maleness – both spectacular and mundane – as it proliferates in South Asian popular visual practice, especially in printed images produced for the mass market'" ("Tasveer Ghar" n.pag.). Like this, heroic human figures take the form of icons, which in the words of Bishnupriya Ghosh[11] are taken as 'bio-icons.' Defining this iconic category of persons, Bishnupriya Ghosh means, "Bio-icons are lives that have become the focus of visual and media saturation as social demands are placed on them" ("Tasveer Ghar" n.pag.). In her book, *Global Icons: Apertures to the Popular*, Bishnupriya Ghosh revealing the corporate set-up of heroic figures writes, "such widely iterated public images of our bio-icons, accruing capital through their equivalence with other bio-icons, often function as intermedial templates for a range of expressive reassemblages that directly address the original" (Ghosh 149). The process of bio-iconisation is exemplified by the blurb of Bishnupriya Ghosh's work as:

> A widely disseminated photograph of Phoolan Devi, India's famous bandit queen, surrendering to police forces in 1983 became an emotional touchstone for Indians who saw the outlaw as a lower-caste folk hero. That affective response was reignited in 1994 with the release of a feature film based on Phoolan Devi's life. Despite charges of murder, arson, and looting pending against her, the bandit queen was elected to India's parliament in 1996. Bishnupriya Ghosh considers Phoolan Devi, as well as Mother Teresa and Arundhati Roy, the prize-winning author turned environmental activist, to be global icons: highly visible public figures capable of galvanizing intense affect and sometimes even catalyzing social change. (Blurb)

Furthermore, Bishnupriya Ghosh's 'bio-icons' (as mediated images) are rooted in a corporate and consumeristic market with quite an apparent economic impetus, but apart from this market-game the figures that have been revisited in this work have a connection with the hidden capital and power discourses of a state. It is not purely an open market business but a cultural/governmental/social commemoration that is embedded in their basic norms. The thing that is similar for both the categories of bio-icons is that these are image – images mediated by the capitalist market or the 'sovereign states/communities.' Though, Bishnupriya Ghosh's 'bio-icons' are – 'highly visible public figures' – who have had a considerable affect on the masses at national as well as global level but the ones represented in this essay are not publically visible at a global level; they are the local/regional/community heroes. In an edited volume, entitled *Revolutionary Egypt* by Reem Abou-El-Fadi, Walter Armbrust represents an episode depicting a lady as:

. . . Sally Zahran, a young woman who had been briefly prominent in a revolutionary mobilization energy when she appeared in a newspaper feature depicting fourteen 'socially representative' martyrs in the early days of the uprising against the Mubarak regime. Initially the story was that she died in the Revolution on 28th January, the 'Friday of Rage', killed by the Mubarak regime's thugs on her way to Tahrir square . . . . The story led quickly to her being called 'the icon of the revolution', but it just as quickly fell apart. (84)

Sally Zahran turns out to be quite an interesting image in such an atmosphere, whose activity leads to her iconisation. An 'image' is an interesting ideological trope that has been talked about by various theorists. Like Roland Barthes in his work, *Image Music Text*, tries to investigate and understand the information that is encoded in images, and the role they perform in creating and shaping an ideological worldview. Barthes questions the notion of how ideologically charged images are, and how these transmit 'affective' messages to the society. Though, Barthes focuses on commercials as they put forth a dense image that attempts to carry forward the encoded message in the most efficient manner. In his book, *Image Music Text*, Barthes writes:

According to an ancient etymology, the word image should be linked to the root *imitari*. Thus we find ourselves immediately at the heart of the most important problem facing the semiology of images: can analogical representation (the 'copy') produce true systems of signs and not merely simple agglutinations of symbols? [...] Thus from both sides the image is felt to be weak in respect of meaning: there are those who think that the image is an extremely rudimentary system in comparison with language and those who think that signification cannot exhaust the image's ineffable richness. Now even - and above all if- the image is in a certain manner the limit of meaning, it permits the consideration of a veritable ontology of the process of signification. How does meaning get into the image? Where does it end? (32)

Many such men of honour have been represented via the figures included in this study, and a pictorial analysis of these statues reveals the multiple levels of discursive processes latent within them. The statues that figure in this essay are images which share public space, and which concretize their individual history/life within the public domain as encoded 'symbols' thereby enriching the layers of the 'greater' national/community history. This very 'original' nature of an image has also been debated by Stuart Hall in his essay "Encoding/Decoding", wherein he writes:

The 'object' of these practices is meanings and messages in the form of sign-vehicles of a specific kind organized, like any form of communication or language, through the operation of codes within the syntagmatic chain of a discourse. The apparatuses, relations and practices of production thus issue, at a certain moment (the moment of 'production/circulation') in the form of symbolic vehicles constituted within the rules of 'language'. It is in this discursive form that the circulation of the 'product' takes place. The process thus requires, at the production end, its material instruments - its 'means' - as well as its own sets of social (production) relations - the organization and combination of practices within media apparatuses. ... Once accomplished, the discourse must then be translated - transformed, again - into social practices if the circuit is to be both completed and effective. If no 'meaning' is taken, there can be no 'consumption'. If the meaning is not articulated in practice, it has no effect. (137)

So taking insights from Stuart Hall, I propose to read these bio-iconic statues as a sort of visual texts which make history and historical events 'real' and quite accessible. Another proposition is to align them with the visual cultures of 'affect', which circulate, inform, and immerse the masses. The main query which represents the cultural politics underlying these statues is to untangle the affect of these icons on the minds of the people. It is to be addressed why would people celebrate the martyrdom anniversaries of persons on whose death the same date some years back they have mourned the loss? Why will be the youth of a particular region/community/sub-nationality attach themselves to the valour of the iconic figure and join the defence services? Why should people name streets and *chowks* (squares) after the names of such brave heroes, and what makes the community sanction a specific space for commemorating the valiant acts of such men of honour? Why do we usually find them with culturally sanctioned hard and fast masculine somatic markers like moustache, guns, swords, sticks, etc., in statues and pictures?

The pivot to the success of such personages in turning to worshipped-icons lies in the discourse of nationalism, which is associated with the patriarchal 'bravery' and 'valour' of a soldier. The somatic markers in these images also point towards the politics involved in the practice of iconisation. All of these statues have been portrayed as brave men with broad chests, moustaches, guns, or sticks, which are the masculine markers of hard-core valour and commitment. In the Introduction to his book, *Imagined Communities*, Benedict Anderson cautions the reader

my point of departure is that nationality, or, as one might prefer to put it in view of that word's multiple significations, nation-ness, as well as nationalism, are cultural artifacts of a particular kind. To understand them properly we need to consider carefully how they have come into historical being, in what ways their meanings have changed over time, and why, today, they command such profound emotional legitimacy. (4)

The culturally constructed love-for-the-nation discourse is the basic impulse that gives 'courage' to soldiers for achieving martyrdom. Martyrdom as a spectacle is quite instrumental to make the nation-discourse operate successfully. To understand the whole process, let's move back to Sally Zahran, who according to Armbrust

> instantiates a common process of popular iconization that originates in a corporate media site, a newspaper in this case, but becomes, for a brief eye-catching time, something far greater as people outside or on the margins of corporate and state-controlled media appropriate it. . . . Such 'bio-icons', as Bishnupriya Ghosh calls them, 'bear an indexical charge for collectives that place social demands through them' (Ghosh 2011:12). In these circumstances, the process of martyrology works by making claims through the idiom of the martyr. Claims are predicated on the fact that the martyr paid the ultimate price for a cause. (84)

Martyrology as a process is associated with the emotions of human beings, like Pramod K. Nayar situates scar culture to the "suffering which is tied to 'spectacles' of bodily injury and 'vulnerability'" (Nayar 147). The discourses of suffering that he refers to in his essay, according to him, deploy 'a trauma-aesthetic.' The discourse of nation and the spectacle of 'martyrdom' are the encoded 'mantras' which cater to the demands of the state/culture from installing these statues/commemorating these bio-icons. The decoding part is a sort of 'affect', wherein masses become fans of these heroic figures and let them enter into their public as well as private spaces/lives. This very collective emotion leads to the activities of hero-manufacturing within a community, wherein such icons are displayed as the 'norm' against the bigger population. They are given the form of statues, decorated, garlanded, and their birthdays and martyrdom anniversaries carve out space in the calendars of the place. Their photos and portraits come up in the mass media, like newspapers, news, advertisements, cultural shows, as 'images of bravery' and 'patriotism.' So, in a way, these statues perform a role on the part of the 'heroes' in whose memory these have been commemorated. Another thing to be mentioned is that generally there are titles of an army regiment,[12] which serve as a sort of sub-national identity instrumental in 'affecting' that particular cult of the community. Not only this, but various other aspects also come up to the foreground, like, mostly these bio-icons are of males (no female statues were found) and it depicts the prevalent patriarchal notion/nation of the culture. In other words, it can be put as, "masculinity is intuitively associated with muscular power and virile strength, but there are also contexts in which men appear vulnerable and fragile? Beauty has generally been associated with the female figure" ("Tasveer Ghar" n.pag.). Such factors are quite effective in generating an 'affect' among the masses, who may also be attracted towards the somatic markers of a particular bio-icon, leading to a sort of fan following.

To conclude, I argue that the exercise of hero-making and hero-worship in the context of such statues and various other bio-iconic sites needs to be revisited so as to make attempts to investigate, find out, and debate about various other aspects regarding such heroic emblems. This essay is a starting impulse to kick on a new debate in the study of our cultural icons.

Notes

1. The spectacle is a central notion in the Situationist theory, developed by Guy Debord in his 1967 book, *The Society of the Spectacle*. In its limited sense, *spectacle* means the mass media, which are "its most glaring superficial manifestation." Debord said that the society of the spectacle came into existence in the late 1920s.

2. Affect theory studies human emotions/subjective feelings as distinct categories which are connected to associated responses. Such responses may be physical as well as ideological.

3. Prof. Nandini Bhattacharya is a senior professor at University of Burdwan, West Bengal, India. She is a writer, has taught at CU Hyderabad, CU Jammu, and many other universities. Her facebook posts can be viewed on www.facebook.com /nandini.bhattacharya.39.

4. M S Dhoni is a cricket player of the Indian Cricket team. He has captained the team in all formats of the game and won laurels for the country as a player and as a captain.

5. Sachin Tendulkar is considered as the 'god of cricket' in India. He is the batsman with the highest number of centuries to his credit and the highest number of runs in international cricket.

6. Visual culture is an emerging aspect of the technological human society which has turned out to be an interesting study area in humanities and social sciences. It often intersects with the disciplines of Film Studies, Psychoanalytic theory, Sex Studies, the study of television, etc. It includes comics, video game studies, advertising, and various other media which have crucial visual importance.

7. As a term, visualism came from Johannes Fabian, a German anthropologist, who developed it to criticize the dominant/preferential role of vision in scientific discourses and procedures, like 'observation' is pivotal to scientific studies.

8. Pramod K. Nayar is a professor at University of Hyderabad (India), who in an expert in teaching, and writing, of Cultural Studies.

9. It is 'a trans-national virtual "home" for collecting, digitizing, and documenting various materials produced by South Asia's exciting popular visual sphere including posters, calendar art, pilgrimage maps and paraphernalia, cinema hoardings, advertisements, and other forms of street and bazaar art'. (tasveerghar.net)

10. With a doctorate from Northwestern University, Bishnupriya Ghosh is Professor of English at the University of California, Santa Barbara, where she teaches postcolonial theory and global media studies. Much of her scholarly work interrogates the relations between the global and the postcolonial; area studies and transnational cultural studies; popular, mass, and elite cultures.

11. In the Indian army there are various army units technically called regiments, like Dogra Regiment, Jat Regiment, Garhwal Regiment, Jak Li, etc.

Bibliography

Anderson, Benedict. *Imagined Communities: Reflections on the Origin and Spread of Nationalism.* London: Verso Publications, 1996. Print.

Armbrust, Walter. "The Iconic Stage: Martyrologies and Performance Frames in the 25 January Revolt." *Revolutionary Egypt.* Ed. Reem Abou-El-Fadi. London: Routledge, 2015. 83-111. Print.

Barthes, Roland. *Image Music Text.* Trans. Stephen Heath. London: Fontana Press, 1977. Print.

Bhattacharya, Nandini. "Dismantling the Lady Justice." N.p., n.d. Web. 15 Jul. 2018 <www.facebook.com,/nandini.bhattacharya.39/>.

Carlyle, Thomas. *On Heroes, Hero-worship, and the Heroic in History.* Philadelphia: Henry Altemus, 1899. Print.

Ghosh, Bishnupriya. *Global Icons: Apertures to the Popular.* Durham: Duke University Press, 2011. Print.

Hall, Stuart. "Encoding/ Decoding." *Media and Culture Studies: KeyWorks.* Ed. Meenakshi G. Durham, and Douglas M. Kellner. Malden: Wiley-Blackwell, 2012. 137-44. Print.

Mirzoeff, Nicholas, ed. "Invisible Empire: Visual Culture, Embodied Spectacle and Abu Gharaib." *Radical History Review* 95 (2006): 21-44. Print.

Mirzoeff, Nicholas, ed. *The Visual Culture Reader.* London: Routledge, 2009. Print.

Mitchell, William John Thomas. "What is an Image?" *New Literary History—A Journal of Theory and Interpretation* 15.3 (1984): 503-537. Print.

Nayar, Pramod K. "Scar Cutures: Media, Spectacles, Suffering." *Journal of Creative Communications* 4.3 (2009):147-162. Print.

Rasgotra, Sahil. "Roundabouts in Jammu: What Do They Tell About Us?" *thenewsnow.* N.p., 21 Aug. 2016. Web. 20 Sep. 2018. <www.thenewsnow.co.in/newsdet.aspx?q=10296 />.

"Tasveer Ghar: Digital Archive of South Asian Popular Visual Culture." *tasveerghar.* N.p., 20 May 2017. Web. 20 Nov. 2018. <tasveerghar.net/cmsdesk/essay/133/>.

Further Reading

Resser, Todd W. *Masculinities in Theory: An Introduction.* Chichester: Wiley Blackwell, 2010. Print.

Appendix

Figure 10.1: Statue of N.K Rifleman Kuldeep Raj who died while fighting against the enemies in Baramulla, Kashmir. His martyrdom turned out to be the hero-making factor for him and he is an iconic figure for his villagers, his cult, and for the nation.

Figure 10.2: This figure represents NK Rifleman Kuldeep Raj's war-statue at his native village in Samba, Jammu and his prominence as a regional war bio-icon. We can see the title 'shaheed' given to him, which means a 'martyr'.

Figure 10.3: People visiting the statue-site of Kuldeep Raj on his martyrdom anniversary. It seems to be a festival organised by his village people. This very event has turned Kuldeep Raj's existence to a sort of bio-icon, who has a specific space in the cult of male valour and sacrifice.

Figure 10.4: People relishing meals served in the compound of Kuldeep Raj's statue-site.

11.

Indigenous Heroes of Nature and Culture: Fashioning Environmental Fandom in *Hodesum*

Rajanikant Pandey

Central University of Jharkhand, India

This chapter narrates the unsung saga of indigenous heroes of *Hodesum*. Hodesum is the land of one of the bravest *Ho* tribals, also called *Larka Kol* (fighting Kols) of Jharkhand, India. This area is now administratively identified as West Singhbhum districts of Jharkhand and is known for its rich iron ore resources and mining activities. The distinctive ethnic identity of Ho indigenes in this undulating, impenetrable land of hills and forests of the southern extension of Chotanagpur plateau characterize the imagination of indigenous homeland. British encroachment in 1837 led to the formation of separate 'Kolhan Government Estate' for Ho indigenes. Then the process of "ethnogenesis" (Streamer 20) rooted in a symbolic identity of a common brotherhood and self-governance of land and resources took place. During the colonial period, this place remained a site of the clash of identities between Ho and mainstream Hindu *Rajas, Bhuiyans* and *dikus* (outsiders). This sentiment has continued till date and is sometimes reflected in the claims of the separate ethnic nation for Ho and is submerged within the struggle for nature and culture. This has given birth to local leaders and fighters like Poto Pingua, Nara Ho, Gono Ho, and Lako Bodra, etc. who have sacrificed their lives to protect their natural and cultural resources. The recent surge of indigenous environmentalism coupled with territorial identity and self-determination has created a set of contemporary indigenous heroes and their followers. This local fandom is born out of struggles for survival. The present paper tries to locate a specific kind of heroism and fandom emerging due to challenges posed to the environmental and economic existence of local Ho owing to rampant mining based industrial interventions in the Hodesum.

There are two types of environmental heroism in Hodesum namely the civil society actors and local indigenous people. However, there are critical differences and overlaps in their method and purpose of achieving environmental justice.

Ethnographic analyses of the social forces of environmentalism point to civil society as an important protagonist in every part of the world. However, there is no colossal model of universal civil society, activists and non-government organisations (NGOs) practices. The role of these actors varies according to the given regional context. The civil society actors, spread across spaces, have continuously engaged with issues of local environmental and social concerns in Singhbhum to create a sense of urgency to look into what is actually going on in the name of sustainable mining of resources. Sociologist Nancy Lee Peluso has theorized that community resistance is embedded within "specific historical and environmental circumstances" (13). Peluso taking a cue from James Scott asserts that the nature of resistance shapes the kind of social, political or technological weapons available to indigenous communities at the time. Saleem Ali based on this concludes that the weapons at the disposal of indigenous communities are quite different from NGOs. Planning and organizing a protest validate NGOs' existence in any given area. NGOs capable of popularizing the protests are more engrossed in the process of protests than the possible results. Community, on the other hand, solely depends on positive outcomes of any protest; local people gain nothing if a movement fails. Therefore, activists are sometimes questioned as self-proclaimed spokesperson of community and at the other time lauded for sincere and genuine efforts visible on their part. That is why it deems necessary to critically examine the role of environmental heroism coming from community and NGOs distinctively. In this pursuit, this ethnographic inquiry was conducted in a mining frontier named *Noamundi* town of West Singhbhum district of Jharkhand state to grasp the making of environmental heroes in the tribal heartland of India.

This study describes the role of civil society, activists, and NGOs in shaping the mining-related environmental and social hero-dom in Noamundi and how it creates community fan following of a specific kind. By focusing on social-environmental concerns shaped over the years, I have tried to reflect upon how resistances against mining-induced disruptions have influenced the emergence of environmental concerns at the fore of community life providing space for the emergence of environmental heroism in the indigenous communities. This paper initially discusses a case of community contesting the dominant ideas about sustainable mining having conceived, organized and deployed by corporates in furthering the cause of the extractive industry. By outlining the contributions of activists and prominent community members and underlining their lifelong commitments to ecological justice, they have been identified as unsung heroes of the environment. The attempt is to offer comprehensible insights into the fashioning of environmental heroism and fandom in indigenous India.

A Century of Conflict

This section talks about a particular case of resistance and conflict associated with a displaced village named *Korta* to assess the historicity of challenges in an iron resource frontier. What mining corporations glorify as "history of giving" (Rajak 266) is differently conceived by the indigenes. People have experienced a different set of struggles and challenges living in a resource-rich zone. The historical narratives collected from people and activists help in analyzing the emergent realities in the mining town of Noamundi in hodesum. This specific case will reflect the way local environmental heroism is nurtured through the indigenous struggle for land, water, and forest.

On the 26th of February 2016, in *Gitillor* village people were gathered for a scheduled procession. The people were assembled in more than five hundred numbers near village Gitillor from where they were planning to walk around six kilometres to reach their original village Korta which now falls within the mining plant of Tata Steel. People who celebrate their *Maghe* (major religious festival of Ho) during this season believe in offering prayers to *sasandiri* (Stone structures at burial ground) and *desauli* (Sacred Grove and place for worship). They have planned to go to their traditional village and pay worship to their ancestors. This whole event is being organized to protest the continuous injustice being meted to them since they have been displaced from their traditional village when mining began in the year 1925. People marched in a group from Gitillor to Korta amidst several attempts on the part of the company and local police to stop such a kind of procession. The people in Noamundi town market area were simply looking from their terrace and windows at tribal crowd marching towards the Tata Steel premises to worship their spirits.

The people, firstly, gathered at the village market or *haat* (though the weather was cloudy and it was raining slowly), all dressed in the best of traditional and modern clothes and were enjoying the festivities around. When the number of villagers increased to good strength, they had a small meeting to discuss the plan. They were carrying their musical instruments and celebrating, dancing and enjoying *Maghe*. They walked a large distance without any expression of tiredness and reached the venue amidst protest and negotiation with company guards about a number of issues. After reaching the venue, they offered prayers according to Ho beliefs and rituals. The village priest Murlung Hembrom presided over rituals assisted by Sukhram Hembrom and Junu Hembrom. The usual rituals of *Maghe* were organized. People were dancing in a circular formation and having all other rites going on during prayers. They offered sacrifice and remembered their *Bongas* (Gods) and *Desauli Bonga* (God of Village Sacred Grove) to help them in such a crisis. The procession was completely under the surveillance of the Tata Company's guards and officials along with local police. The activists like Mangal Singh Bobonga, Ramesh Jarai, Jairam Barjo, and Jairam Hembrom were leading the people. Sukhram, Guira, Rependa, Hurdus, Manjari, Sukhmay Hembrom were actively looking after the arrangements and discipline.

The police personnel were keeping a close watch on the entire procession starting from village to the *Maghe* rituals in the Korta. It was overheard that policemen were in plain clothes here and there to keep vigilance. It was planned that the villagers must behave properly and there should be no hooliganism and shouting against the company. The Tata Steel, as per some news reports, officially avoided accepting that any such event was organized in Noamundi. They did not give any official statements in the local news daily as they usually do about the smallest of incidents in Tata company areas. Initially, the management was hesitant to allow villagers to do worship in the mining area. They kept citing the safety norms for entering into mining areas. Even before the event, the police station tried to intervene and pressurize villagers to stop such procession or make it unsuccessful. The villagers were told by the police station that only twenty people could go at a time because the mining area is not safe for the crowd. Later, the company agreed to allow only village residents in small numbers to the place. They tried to impose a strict prohibition on the participation of any outsider other than village people in the procession. However, villagers were adamant about bringing everyone who wanted to join the celebration. The tribals were told that for security reasons, they shall be provided with safety gear and helmet after identification as local residents. One day before police asked them to turn up to the police station and tell the exact number of people attending the procession next day, the local Ho women present in the station got agitated and clearly said that their number would be in thousands and they cannot stop them from celebrating their rituals. The camera and photography were strictly prohibited by the company and the administration. The company and local police station, however, had planted several closed-circuit television cameras and photographers at quite a few places in mining areas, Tata Township, and the roadside. They wanted to keep outsiders or unknown activists under surveillance who could be identified in case of any mishap.

Contextualization of Event

The case depicts how the indigenous villagers through such confrontation and protests are fighting this battle against the giant mining company for a century, and some of the ordinary Ho people depict extraordinary characters. Mangal Singh Bobonga being an older member of Ho community feels a responsibility towards this historical injustice. He has signs of the ageing on his face but carries a resolute look. He along with his Ho brothers has started this protest against Tata Steel. He told that people have their own *desauli* and *sasan* (graveyard) in Korta. He clearly articulated that this protest is an attempt to reassert the ownership of villagers over the land and forest. When he repeats it, people welcome his statement with sounds of drums getting louder and dance. He articulates the details in a personal conversation with the researcher:

> The villagers of Korta along with some other small hamlets were displaced from their actual settlement in 1927, without any legal agreements between people and the miners. There was no rehabilitation policy, and they were not compensated for their land and house. They were not even rehabilitated and resettled by the Tata Company. For ninety years, the mining is going on, and millions of tons of iron ore have been extracted, and crores of rupees have been made by the Tatas, but we have got nothing. No job and no infrastructural facility were provided to the people since then. It was British period, and we were common village folks and were not aware of any displacement rule or agreements. Our ancestors left the village because of fear of blasting for extraction. They moved to different places like Masuligarha, Murga, and Gundijora. Five families which were granted permission of Munda of Gundijora have today converted into around 47 households of Gitillor Village. Around 120 families are now actually affected by that displacement. Some of them are now settled in distant places including the neighbouring state of Odisha. These people have kinship ties with those displaced families, and they have also come to join the procession today to show solidarity with us. (Bobonga)

The Tata steel has always proclaimed through media and public communication that land was acquired by the British government from the villagers and it was handed over to them through the due legal process. Even officials believe that there must be compensation/ payment by the British government for acquiring land from Ho people in Korta. Therefore, mining company officials always consider it a non-issue, which does not warrant any merit. The corporation believes that it is a matter of land acquisition in 1925-26 and the lease was acquired through lease number 221/32 in September 1926. Later complaints were raised, but issues were amicably resolved when the state was with Bihar. The villagers totally deny such claims that they were ever compensated and laugh at legal arguments given by the company. Jairam has taken this issue to Jagannathpur court and he fights the court case with the help of funds generated by the villagers. They have been appearing in every court hearing for these many years. They want their land rights to be recognised and ask to be compensated for their land and historical injustice done to them for generations. Bobonga Ji informs that "in 1985, the cases were filed against the Tata Steel. We have gone to the court many times but nothing happened. So far six lakh rupees have been spent in the court." He further adds "when the job is not given to the landholders then the land should be returned to the rightful owners. The company never thought of us. The officials gave the same answers again and again that go to court, go here, and go there" (Bobonga). The people wish that the government and politicians should come forward to help them get back their land and ancestral places. However, the court and officials of the district administration are not even aware of any such case. The local administration is unable to tell anything about this case with clarity. Raising money to fight the case for the ordinary Hos would not have been easy. Another villager, Jairam Barjo explained to me:

> We have the land of ancestors. We sold the woods, timber and collected money, deposited our wages and spent it in fighting the case. By which, we made one rupee, two rupees, ten rupees. Until the government accepts our demands, we will continue to fight the case. We will not leave our demand for ancestral land in any circumstances. (Barjo)

Chaibasa based NGO activist Ramesh Jarai also articulates the same concern:

> Apart from 7 displaced families of Korta, 50 families of Balijhor and Masuribera have been affected too. The identity of these villages was eroded because there is neither the graveyard of these villagers nor the desauli, which symbolizes the existence of the village. However, for identification there is a tamarind tree and the tamarind doesn't grow in the natural forests. (Jarai)

The displaced families describing their wretched situation wrote an application in the name of Noamundi Iron Mines, Tata Steel Company's General Management. In the subject matter of the application, villagers wrote, "being displaced by the Tata Company from Korta village" ("Newswing Reports"). In relation to the miserable situation in the absence of any employment, they refer to the land details "We are native to Noamundi, West Singhbhum. We have land of people whose account number 20; plot no 94, 97, 104, 105, 115, 168, 174, 175, 191, 192, 203, 208, 264, 117, 187, 206, 207, and 211" ("Newswing Reports"). These numbers come under Korta *Mauza* (village), which was taken by Tata Company in 1927-28 for the purpose of mining. They have requested in this application that the local landowners should be given jobs on the basis of land ownership and monetary compensation should be given in lieu of cutting mango and jackfruit trees and also for the houses which were destroyed in the process. Similar applications have been written by the other villagers as well, but they know that proper hearing on such applications is less likely to happen. Even if the hearing takes place, the results do not go further than hollow assurances.

In the court of sub-divisional officer (SDO) Jagannathpur block of West Singhbhum through SAR Case No. 01/1998, Jairam Hembram and others have petitioned against Tata Steel Ltd. and others. Responding to the show cause, the state government has clarified that, according to the current accounting the land under question has been in the possession of the Tata Iron and Steel Company (TISCO) since 1926. The state government has told the court in its reply that according to the current survey, the Korta village *khatiyan* (Record of Land Rights) was released on 11 September 1963. Now 35 years have passed since the petitioner took no action under Section 83, 87 or 90 of Chota Nagpur Tenancy Act (CNTA). Therefore, in this lawsuit, the defendant Tata Steel (Then TISCO) has a legal lease from 1926. In such a case under the said section of CNTA, there is no case of illegal eviction from the land. It was also highlighted by the company that Tata Steel Ltd. regularly is paying off its taxes and surface rent to the mining officer of Chaibasa. Therefore, the claimant and their ancestors, stating their interests have lost their rights. The argument placed by lawyers from the company says that the applicant has not placed the entries in the *khatiyan* in the appropriate manner. The powerful lawyers of company meticulously articulate that the genealogy of the families of tribals presented by the applicants is not correct. Therefore, there is no evidence in government records to support the ownership claimed by tribal people. Land, on which questions have been raised, according to the survey report, is 'old non-agricultural' land hence it is not tenant land (*raiyat*). In case of such absence of it being '*raiyat*' Section 71-A will not be effective. So it cannot be established that applicants have been removed from illegal means. The company lawyers were also able to establish that applicants are as current residents of Gitillor village (where they are actually living after displacements), their relationship with the Korta village (ongoing mining project area) was not stated.

Former MLA Mangal Singh Bobonga, advisor of the *Jameen Bachao Samanyava Samiti* (JBSS) a Coordination Committee for Protection of Land in West Singhbhum has been in front of the villagers in this fight with Tata Company. He tells that "the fight is not easy, but the truth will win." When I met him for interviews about Korta case, Bobongaji drove me in his Bolero car to the village immediately and collected around ten elder men from the village and asked me to interview in front of people. He said that "it is their plight and better if we talk in front of them"(Bobonga). He, during the conversation, got emotional and said: "with the help of the administration, the company wants to wipe out our existence. But I will not let it happen till my last breath" (Bobonga). Bobonga further describes the matter in following words:

TISCO as it was named then took the land of people of Korta village wilfully in the year 1927-28 but in return, not a single family got jobs and compensation. The villagers were evicted from the village. They have been completely removed from the mining area of TISCO. The people of Balijor's village are too being evicted by the company in such a way that their existences will completely vanish. Right now, Korta village has become mining projects, there is a sasan, a desauli, a pond, planted trees which prove that it has certainly been a village. (Bobonga)

Bobonga ji clearly articulates in a strong voice that "TISCO has no proof" and the company simply says that "TISCO has taken a lease from the government" (Bobonga). He explains:

Tata Steel has been refusing to show any document. The villagers have all the documents, circumcisions and maps etc. They totally have their claim. We are resorting to the mass movement along with the court to strengthen the fight to pressurize government on this matter. And people will definitely get their rights. Together with the capitalists, governments have been violating the constitutional and fundamental rights of tribals. As far as the religious place and transit land are concerned the government cannot acquire it even if it wanted to. Such land cannot be given on lease to the company. It is a matter of deep concern that the religious sites, transit land and the entire village of the tribals have been evacuated. Where is justice? We want to know that after all this on what basis these indigenous village sites, agricultural lands, graveyards; religious places have been given to TISCO? Or how TISCO has acquired it? (Bobonga)

Explaining the need to perform worship after so many years in the mining area, Bobonga Ji asserts that

we organized this program to save our culture. There is the soul of our ancestors in the sacred forests or in the graveyard or in the village. This is our faith. Our *Singbonga* (supreme deity) resides in the village. We could not leave it. Considering the place as our own, we organized the program in a traditional way. TISCO officials tried to stop the program by telling that the area is prohibited. The administrative officer of the government says that since the Tata Company has taken it on the lease, in such situation, there should neither be any kind of program organized nor outsiders can trespass there. The police tried to cancel this program. Forcefully an attempt was made to stop this program. It is a direct attack on our faith and religious belief as well as our culture and environment. (Bobonga)

Jairam further drops in to add that

> There is an attempt being made to erase that place. Inside the mining area near the graveyard and cemetery, pumping work has been started. In some places, a large amount of garbage was dumped. We protested against it. After that, some places have been cleaned. The area is being surrounded by the barbed wire. TISCO Company wants to erase the existence of the place by resorting help from the administration. After the verdict comes from SAR case, we will go to the court's shelter. Through conspiracy, the corporate house and the administration are suppressing the tribals demand. (Barjo)

To validate his criticisms against the company, Barjo brings examples from other places to show the inhuman approach of the company: "The way the villages in *Kalinga Nagar* were being shot to grab land, by adopting the same measure, such situation is being created here too. This is a violation of the constitution and we justice seekers are being treated like terrorists. The government, administration, and people of TISCO are adopting the path of exploitation" (Barjo).

Contesting Natural Resources

The indigenous people in Noamundi who have been displaced for mining a century before have survived the consequences of industrialism and self-sustained themselves adhering to their traditional modes of existence. They have learned, from their fighting heroes, the ways to safeguard their territory, place, and people by maintaining relative independence. The making of resource frontier has been so overpowering for them that they have been unable to conceptualize the brutal consequences of mining-based transformation in the area. The discourse and language of industrial development was so promising that people got trapped in vision and failed expectations of modernity. Over a period of time, they have learned that fruits of mining go somewhere else and all they have is broken dreams. The people have claimed their rights over natural resources like the land, forest and water bodies through various means. They have pleaded, protested, and fought in court and negotiated their rights over natural resources. These demands have always been articulated in terms of Water (*Jal*), Forest (*Jungle*), and Land (*Jameen*). Indigenous people have never been interested in resources that are hidden below the earth. There is still no articulation of claims over mineral resource ownership in Ho communities. Though they have a deep historical understanding that area and place belongs to them and they are ruled by the *Munda-Manaki* system (traditional juro-political system) before any other law. These claims to land have no explicit demands for ownership of beneath the earth's resources. Sometimes people talk about their claims and the rights over mineral resources, still the community voices are shaped in terms of the discourse of *Jal, Jungle, and Jameen.*

The case of mining-induced displacement in Korta typically depicts the nature of contestation over land. There are other affected villagers of *Kutingta, Balijhorin* who routinely stage several dharnas under the banner of NGO *Jameen Bachao Samanvaya Samiti* before the SDO of Jagannathpur. They submitted a memorandum demanding rehabilitation and resettlement for families who have lost their lands. During one such event, the tribal leader John Miran Munda, according to local media outlet *Newswing,* asserted that during the protest "the General Manager of Tata Steel (locally still referred to as TISCO, its old name) had promised their rehabilitation during a public hearing. But till date, there is no response from the company side. Therefore, people will continue demanding compensation for their ancestral land" ("Newswing Reports").

There are several other instances of land alienation where people have not been properly compensated or rehabilitated. In the month of June 2016, under the leadership of local member of the Parliament, Shri Laxman Gilua, and *Zila Parishad* member, Laxmi Suren, around five hundred affected villagers blocked the railway loading point of Tata Steel Bottam Bin plant. The people holding banners and display cards were demanding employment for the affected villagers of Noamundi, Maudi, and Padapahar. People claim that they were promised a job during the public hearing in the year 2012. Police have to impose section 107 of the Indian Penal Code due to the agitated mood of the public to avoid any violent incident. The villagers were demanding at least one rack of loading manually instead of the machine at the loading point. This would provide temporary job opportunities to thousands of villagers. The local member of the Parliament warned of continuous agitation until the company furnishes people's demands. Seeing a stubborn approach from management, it was planned that an indefinite strike will be launched at the end of the month. The *Zila Parishad* member Laxmi Suren was also seen demanding that "Tata Steel must adhere to its commitments."

The Noamundi block is forested with an abundance of natural vegetation in and around mining areas and villages. The *Kolhan* has witnessed a famous forest movement called *Jangal Katai Andolan* to challenge the government's claim over the region's forests. Similarly, in Noamundi some young enthusiasts joined hands to protect adjoining degraded *sal* forests. In 1998, Laguri Ji united locals for preventing cattle from trespassing into the region. They convinced the villagers that the regeneration of the forests will ensure a regular and sufficient supply of firewood. They told people how it will also help in better rain and good crops. The regional NGOs organize plantation drives. However, there is no direct forest movement to counter mining-induced deforestations in the area. Recently the villagers of *Mundasai* have formed a forest committee to resist the extension of Tata mines in the village forest. The land was transferred in 2007. However, there is no mining in the leased forest area in the last five years and thus locals are demanding that such land should be returned to *gram sabha* as per provisions of Forest Act, 2006.

Iron mining requires a huge amount of water for its washeries for washing out impurities of ore bodies and for other production and cleaning purposes. The extraction of groundwater is strictly not allowed in this low groundwater zone of the state. There is only one water source in the company's lease area that is *Balijore Nallah*. So, Tata Company utilizes surface water from *Baitarani* river which is around twelve kilometers from the mining areas. The river is a perennial stream and acts as a natural boundary between the states of Odisha and Jharkhand. The Tatas have constructed a massive pumping station since 1962 at *Deogaon* village to fetch water from the river. The water from this river is since then being sent to the collieries and washeries situated at a distance of around twenty kilometers through the pipeline. The villagers are unable to use the water as promised because of irregular supply. They still have to depend upon natural streams and ponds which generally run dry during summer. A citizen's forum was formed to stop illegal use of water from Baitarini River. The Central Ground Water Board has allowed 81 companies to extract water from the basin of river Baitarani. A few other companies have been permitted to draw 8,600 kilolitres/hour from Baitarani. The forum brought to the fore the demand to protect river Baitarani. The water of the district is allocated to different industries and mining houses, without any consultation with the people here, who have the first right on the water. The residents of the area argue that owing to mining operations and dumping of mineral wastes by the industry owners near the river basin, Baitarani has become polluted. Soil erosion has taken place because of massive deforestation on both sides of the river. The riverbed is filled with pollutants decreasing the water carrying capacity. Due to the massive commercial use of underground and surface water by industries, the water table has declined by over fifty feet in the past couple of decades. A number of streams and rivers have also dried up in all these years. As a result, the nearby villages have to face drinking water problems throughout the year. The villagers believe that the big pond near the Noamundi market which used to cater to the need of people throughout the year has dried out because of mining explosions and deep mining crates.

Public hearings are important sites of voicing community protest and showing strength of the people. The first of its kind public hearing which was organized by Tata Steel mines at Noamundi at the Middle School building situated inside the company colony in September 2004. The villagers did not know about the public hearings and were not informed by the company beforehand. When the activists of the local *Johar* NGO came to know about Environmental Impact Assessment (EIA), they informed and mobilized villagers to participate in EIA meeting. The villagers from around seven villages surrounding mines (nearly 1500 people) went to participate in the public hearings on that day. Seeing them, the company authorities ordered to close the gate so that such a large number of people could not enter the venue. This made people very angry and resulted into the blocking of traffic at the main road (George). The chairman of Jharkhand State Pollution Control Board (JSPCB) started mediating between people and corporate, and they requested that people should be allowed to attend the meeting. The JSPCB person asked the villagers to send some representatives instead of the large crowd which clearly defies the basics of public hearings. The villagers demanded that this hearing should be announced illegal as there was no prior information given to the people. The locals were prevented from attending the hearings. At the end, people came to know the hearing was recorded valid by state administration and clearance was given to people. Public hearings are a mere formality, and the quality of the EIA assessments are reportedly very poor, yet they remain the only democratic space available for communities to voice their grievances. EIA which should guarantee environmental accountability is actually guaranteed in favour of mining activity. In fact, all the instruments to safeguard environmental concerns in mining have become corporate tools to win environmental certifications and good image of green corporate.

Ecological challenges to land, water and forest are the everyday affair in a resource frontier like Noamundi, but the tribals have to face socio-cultural backlash as well. The exploitation of tribal women labourers by contractors mostly goes unreported. The tribal social and cultural fabric in mining zones gets disturbed with the cultural dominance of outsiders. In 1991, in the festival of *Holi*, a rowdy group of TISCO employees molested a team of Adivasi women labourers on the construction site of the Company's sports stadium. The women protested the advances of drunken TISCO employees that they can not join in the Holi celebration as *Ba Parob* (a tribal festival associated with agricultural rituals) is yet to be performed in the village. The custom does not permit them any celebration outside the village till *Ba parob* worship has been completed by local *deuri* (priest). The angry drunken men molested these women and applied colour on their breasts and genitals. The women approached Munda (traditional chief) of their village Noamundi Basti who complained to the company demanding that a case be registered against the workers by the company. It was refused by TISCO, and the police station too declined to lodge a FIR (First Information Report). The Munda of Noamundi Basti using his customary jurisdiction ordered all the workers to vacate Jojo Hatting. TISCO has no place to accommodate around a hundred workers and their families. TISCO had to give up and allow the police to file a case against the workers. Meanwhile, the TISCO trade union threatened and gave an ultimatum that they will go on strike if the case is filed. The adivasis in the village started losing patience seeing no action against the workers. They were backed by All Jharkhand Student Union (AJSU) having strong political clout during those days.

The people of *Mahudi*, who were since long protesting, the TISCO Palletising Plant construction on grabbed lands of the villagers supported the plight of their kins of Noamundi Basti. They surrounded and locked the gate of P-Plant. On duty workers suddenly became the hostage and the next shift of workers were stopped from entering the plant. The agitating villagers kept its gates locked for days. TISCO security men (private security) in a highly illegal action opened fire on the villagers. To safeguard TISCO, local police admitted that administration fired the shots. Police and the railway station officers lodged criminal cases against the villagers and AJSU activists. Out of the fifteen accused, a few members, Xavier Dias, John Barjo, Moso Munda, and Rajaram Tanti are still alive. The rest have died leaving behind families to face the consequences. These activists have been on bail (after surrendering and going to jail then), and they have been attending all the court hearings for the last two decades. But in a surprise development, the lawyer handling their case joined another steel company without handing over the case to another lawyer. Thus, the court issued the arrest warrant again, but they could not get informed on time, resulting in a '*Kudkhi*' warrant or seizure of properties of the accused. The story was reported by Xavier Dias in the public domain before the activist surrendered before the Magistrate. They were sent to judicial custody. This is the price of their lifelong commitment to tribal service which required agitation against the unwarranted expansion of mines in Noamundi. But he believes that such repression only goes to strengthen their determination and efforts.

Unsung Heroes of the Indigenous Land

These local protesters and activists from the indigenous community and civil society organisations are the unsung heroes of mining frontiers in West Singhbhum of Jharkhand. Max Weber has identified three kinds of leadership authority—charismatic, traditional and legal-rational— in a society. Every society produces leaders with different leadership authority characteristics. The regional history of Hodesum is portrayed as a history of resistance where people have maintained and fought for territorial belongings to extend their claims over natural resources in the area. Paul Streumer strongly depicted the historicity of Ho's intentions to demarcate the boundaries of their place and culture in his recent work. The Ho people always came in conflict with varieties of external forces, but they always resisted them strongly. The history of Hodesum is characterized by resistance and rebellions. The land has produced charismatic leaders, from time to time, to strongly claim their territorial rights and cultural identity. The heroes like Poto Pingua, Nara Ho, and Gono Ho are well established in people's memory as examples of early saviours of land and territory. Similarly, people in this land have also resisted alien cultural dominance and revived their tradition to enrich cultural practices. Guru Lako Bodra and Dhanur Singh Purty are such 'enlightened and charismatic' individuals who emerged as local cultural heroes. The indigenous resistance has produced extraordinary leaders whose charisma transcended into traditional leadership and continues to operate in people's sentiments in the long run. In the contemporary time, the Hodesum has produced leaders like Machua Gagrai and Dibendar Majhi during *Jungal Katai Andolan* of 1978, where the events of conservation converted into rebellion. The so-called 'tree protectors' became 'tree cutters' to challenge the monocropping by forest departments. Similarly, Gangaram Kalundia showed extraordinary leadership in protest against *Itcha-Kharkai* dam construction. These were examples of early environmentalism and tribal heroism in Singhbhum.

This place has continuously produced its own heroes when and where the situation demanded it. The land has witnessed ordinary people filling the need of leadership as and when required. Mining in the region gave rise to the need for environmental heroes in frontiers like Noamundi as well. These people have fought the mighty corporations and challenged them when things have gone drastically wrong. The emergence of such a charismatic leadership is visible even in a small forest village like Gitillor. The life history of some of these leaders can depict the intent and content of individual efforts to raise the community voices and sentiments towards mining in the region. Who are these people in local situations like Noamundi who become Heroes? How do they command people's consent and support to protest, organize and fight their battles and what are the circumstances which make them champions of their cause?

Mangal Singh Bobonga, discussed earlier, is a short-statured man in his 50s with a very clear understanding of the local situation. He is a self-motivated political personality but different from other politicians in the area. Debram Tubid is a young man in his late 30s also very active with Bobongaji in fights of land and displacement in Noamundi. Debram was offered several backdoor bribes to stop raising land issues. He was even sent 'big offers', but he refused to give up for such easy money. Jairam Barjo is *Munda* (Chief) of Meralgarha village, a silent man who can very well articulate the resistance to the mining disruption in his own village and other villages of the area. Xavier Dias and Ajitha George, an aging couple, are examples of devoted civil society members. Ajitha started her work for women's health seeing the neglected situation of tribal women. She, with the help of five indigenous women, founded an NGO *'Oman Mahila Samiti'* in 1998. They started training local women about ethnomedicines which could provide easy health solutions for them. *Oman* means in Ho language 'the sprouts of seed,' and Ajitha attempted to sprout indigenous medicinal wisdom among tribal women. She has transformed herself into an articulate writer on mining issues in Noamundi. She has represented locals in several mining-related conflicts, land issues, health, and biodiversity concerns. The couple has always stood with local subalterns in their battles of various types. Xavier Dias, as discussed earlier, has been jailed for his activism against exploitation of local tribals.

Global environmentalism emerged since the 80s and has influenced the discourse of environmental conservation widely. Anguelovski and Martínez Alier have stressed that

> Environmental movements assert common values related to place, identity, and culture. Activists' concepts such as ecological debt, environmental justice, environmental liabilities, land grabbing, environmental gentrification, corporate accountability, climate justice, food sovereignty, or economic growth are the keywords of the networks of the global Environmental Justice movement. At the same time, such concepts support the rural and urban movements that remake place for marginalized groups, re-assert traditional practices, and protect the territory from contamination, land appropriation, and real estate speculation. (167)

The territorial claims to state ownership came into conflict with the rights of forest dwellers and marginalized indigenous communities. These communities protested for their rights to natural resources in terms of indirect protests utilizing what Scott has termed 'weapons of the weak'. Spanish economist Juan Martinez-Alier calls it "environmentalism of the poor" (100). Mining-related conflicts also started to center around the issue of environmental disruptions since enhanced consciousness towards environmental sustainability. Mining environmentalism has become commonplace globally. However, the resource frontiers in Noamundi, Jharkhand have not seen a very powerful effective and direct environmental justice movement imbibing the global discourse of environmentalism. The story of grassroots environmentalism in Noamundi has mostly focused upon the livelihood issues and sloganeering of *Jul, Jungal, Jameen*, carried forward by local people's concerns with their survival. These local heroes either from community or civil society have shown abilities to influence policy issues by mobilizing public protests.

Ho people have always conceptualized the mining influences in terms of loss of livelihood but, in anthropological understanding, the local activists in Noamundi are yet to take up and grasp the global environmental justice agenda. In Noamundi, the issue of indigenous people and their traditional land rights and the territorial claims is a major issue of contention than the actual environmental conservation and ecological pollution. The global idea of conservation in the era of extractive capitalism has not given birth to any dedicated environmental NGO which can carry out rigorous scientific research and action to create anti-politics of corporate environmental propaganda. The local heroes of nature and culture are the sole champions of the environmental cause. The 'local people's environmentalism' of such intensity is not very effective in Singhbhum, which can strongly counter the claims of 'corporate environmentalists' in the area. However, these limitations have created a set of indigenous heroism, trusted and followed by the indigenous people in their everyday negotiations with mighty corporations and state machinery.

Local Ho community understands the problems of displacement, the alienation of land, degradation of forest, contamination of water bodies, and pollution of air but they mostly articulate it in terms of failed promises of health and education, employment, modern infrastructure and other expectations of modernity. They have witnessed industrial development reaching to people who settled later in their land. They feel disillusioned and confused when asked why Hos are not living close to Noamaundi town and enjoying the benefits of the market and running shops etc. in the centre town. They chose forest as their destiny, and when they realized that they have been deceived in the process, it was too late by that time to respond and retaliate. Ho now understands that historical injustice has been done to their ancestors. Now they have lost their land to people who are *dikus* and smarter than them.

Indigenous claims to land are not based on any written document, but 'indigenous' claims to natural resources and territory. Ho people have an increased understanding of being first settlers in the area, and they assert their indigeneity now with the help of activists. They believe that they could defeat the Britishers but not the corporate as they have become weak over time. The *Ho-Larka Kol* unity is no more like traditional time. Because they have no more abundance in mother nature to feed and be strong like earlier days. They say the powers of Bongas are not enough to defeat guns and barrels. Indigeneity is one of the important ways in which peoples' sense of belonging and attachment to place continue to be important sources of cultural production (Escobar). Indigenous right as the discourse has emerged since the 90s, but activists at Jharkhand are still unsure of the legitimacy of such ideas when the Indian state does not recognize 'indigenous' as a constitutional category (Beteille; Xaxa). The constitutional and legal safeguards provided to Scheduled Tribes have not provided desired benefits to the community. The international laws for indigenous people outlined by James Anaya have no legal sanction in the Indian context. The discourse of indigeneity provides a worldview and symbolic capital to organize community by activists, but it does not augur well with the judicial process and legal battle in court. It provides a framework to exercise indigenous environmental rights to land and territory but does not guarantee substantial claims to counter corporate legal strategy. The Ho demand for the separate ethnic nation during the 1970s has been resolved by the government, and there is no future leadership that can raise such disputed issues at the international fora. It is observed by Gedicks as well as Kirsch that globally extractive industries have experienced the greatest threat from the discourse of indigeneity than the environment.

Conclusion

Saleem Ali challenges the conventional theories of conflict based on economic or environmental cost-benefit analysis, which does not fully capture the dynamics of resistance at the local level. He proposes that in these places the underlying issue has less to do with environmental concerns than with sovereignty, which often complicates relationships between tribes and environmental organizations. Activist groups, he observes, fail to understand actual tribal concerns and often have problems working with tribes on issues where they may presume a common environmental interest. Anthropologist William Fischer based on his *Kaypo* ethnography has concluded that unique feature of indigenous environmentalism is the indeterminate quality of environmental concerns as a social issue, supporting Ali to concur that environmentalism at any point needs to be analyzed as a social product. The environmentalism as a social product can provide a mechanism to look at structural links that environmental protests in mining areas have with politics of socio-cultural and economic relations (Ali). The environmental concerns in Noamundi are also interdependent upon the social and economic needs of people. The people want changes that can eradicate challenges of poverty, and this is coupled with their desires to protect, preserve and own the natural environment which they have done over the generations.

These local environmental heroes have largely been unrecognized in the democratic system of rewards and recognition. However, they have always been saluted, celebrated and remembered among the local fans. People have glorified them through folklores transmitted orally over generations. Youths are attracted to their contemporary community heroes, and there is social consciousness to revitalize such hero-fan relations at various youth forums and virtual platforms. There is a resurgence of fan following of community heroes and rejection of pan-Indian nationalist leaders. The state has also started to recognise local heroes and contextualizing them into the mainstream historical discourse of the nation. The local heroes of environments created due to mining-based perturbations have succeeded in raising their environmental sentiments in terms of local social and historical traditions and have garnered fandom for such charismatic leadership.

Bibliography

Ali, Saleem H. *Mining, the Environment, and Indigenous Development Conflicts.* Tuscon: University of Arizona Press, 2009. Print.

Anguelovski, Isabelle, and Joan Martínez Alier. "The 'Environmentalism of the Poor' Revisited: Territory and Place in Disconnected Glocal Struggles." *Ecological Economics* 102 (2014): 167-176. Print.

Barjo, Jairam. Personal Interview. 16 Sep. 2016.

Beteille, Andre. "The Idea of Indigenous People." *Current Anthropology* 39.2 (1998): 187-91. Print.

Bobonga, Mangal Singh. Personal Interview. 16 Sep. 2016.

Escobar, Arturo. "Culture Sits in Places: Reflections on Globalism and Subaltern Strategies of Localization." *Political Geography* 20.2 (2001): 139-74. Print.

Fischer, William. "Megadevelopment, Environmentalism and Resistance: The Institutional Context of Kayapo Indigenous Politics in Central Brazil." *Human Organisation* 53.3 (1994): 220-232. Print.

Gedicks, Al. *Resource Rebels: Native Challenges to Mining and Oil Corporations.* Boston: South End Press, 2001. Print.

George, A.S. *Status of Adivasis Series-2 – Jharkhand.* New Delhi: Akar Publication, 2015. Print.

Jarai, Ramesh. Personal Interview. 6 Dec. 2016.

Kirsch, Stuart. *Mining Capitalism: The Relationship between Corporations and their Critics.* Oakland, California: University of California Press, 2014. Print.

Martinez-Alier, Joan. *The Environmentalism of the Poor: A Study of Ecological Conflicts and Valuation.* Northampton, MA: Edward Elgar Publishing, 2003. Print.

"Newswing Reports." *newswing.com.* N.p., n.d. Web. 20 May 2017. <http://www.newswing.com/hi/node/8425. 2016 Publications/>.

Peluso, Nancy Lee. *Rich Forests, Poor People: Resource Control and Resistance in Java.* Berkeley: University of California Press, 1992. Print.

Rajak, Dinah. "Corporate Memory: Historical Revisionism, Legitimation and the Invention of Tradition in a Multinational Mining Company." *PoLAR: Political and Legal Anthropology Review* 37.2 (2014): 259-280. Print.

Scott, James C. *Weapons of the Weak: Everyday Forms of Peasant Resistance.* New Haven, CT: Yale Univ P, 1987. Print.

Streumer, Paul. *A Land of Their Own: Samuel Richard Tickell and the Formation of the Autonomous Ho Country in Jharkhand, 1818-1842.* Hauten, The Netherlands: Wakkaman, 2016. Print.

Weber, Max. *Economy and Society.* Totowa, NJ: Bedminster Press, 1921/1968. Print.

Xaxa, Virginius. "Tribes as Indigenous People of India." *Economic and Political Weekly* 34.51 (1999): 3589-3595. Print.

Further Reading

Anaya, S. James. *Indigenous Peoples in International Law.* Oxford: OUP, 2004. Print.

Ferguson, James. *Expectations of Modernity: Myth and Meanings of Urban Life on the Zambian Copperbelt.* Berkeley: University of California Press, 1999. Print.

Li, Fabiana. *Unearthing Conflict: Corporate Mining, Activism, and Expertise in Peru.* Manitoba: Duke University Press, 2015. Print.

Sawyer, S., and Terence Gomez, eds. *The Politics of Resources Extraction: Indigenous Peoples, Multinational Corporations, and the State.* London, UK: Palgrave Macmillan, 2012. Print.

12.

What My Hero Means to Me:
The Confession of a Batman Enthusiast

Amar Singh

Banaras Hindu University, India

"Simply put, Batman and Robin can't be allowed to fade into obscurity. Gotham needs us too much for us to allow that to happen. It needs someone to keep its dark half in check, someone to fight for impossible (....) **Because Batman cannot die. We can't let him."**
– Bruce Wayne, (Manning 1)

But I don't want to go among mad people,' Alice remarked.
'Oh, you can't help that,' said the Cat: 'We're all mad here. I'm mad, you're mad.'
'How do you know I'm mad?' said Alice.
'You must be,' said the Cat, 'or you wouldn't have come here.'
Lewis Carroll, (*Alice's Adventures in Wonderland* 90)

Grant Morrison began his celebrated graphic novel, *Arkham Asylum: A Serious House on Serious Earth*, with the above quote of Lewis Carroll as an epitaph to it. The purpose was clear: to represent the similarity of Batman with the inmates of Arkham Asylum. The difference lies in the fact that Batman has not crossed the line of insanity as that of the inmates. But has he not? This is the question that has made this character so lionized, obviously apart from his other skills as well, which is him being super-rich, world's best detective and a man devoid of superpowers. His fans over the years have pondered over this question much like Hamlet's examination of insanity and have found themselves being more intrigued and overwhelmed without any resolution. Here, however, I would like to shift the interest of this question from Batman towards his 'fans' (including myself). What is so enigmatic about this character that makes the readers care about him so much? Do they attend him while deliberating over his 'issues' or do they investigate themselves while doing the same? Anna-Maria Covich in her article "Heroes with Issues: Fan Identification with Batman," suggests a response to this:

Batman's responses to his emotional challenges are as important to many fans as his engagement with the villains that threaten Gotham. They give the reader a point of similarity to Batman, which they can use to immerse themselves in the story. These personal battles give Batman and his supporting cast extra depth while justifying the story in a way that is easily recognized and understood. Batman's psychological 'issues' make him an exaggerated version of other, ordinary people. He has been through real trials in life, lost loved ones, and found a way to cope with that. (*Fan Phenomena: Batman* 43)

To the same question, I would like to draw another observation that comes from Stephen Fry. In one of his promotional stand-ups for his book, *More Fool Me* on Netflix, Stephen Fry talks about his love and reverence for Oscar Wilde and his affinity with him. He remembers his younger days when he first encountered the words of Oscar Wilde through a movie on his play, *The Importance of Being Earnest*. From there, he spent days and weeks reading and memorizing the works of this wonderful writer. After being done with his complete works, he asked the librarian if he could read something on Oscar Wilde. He then was handed *The Trials of Oscar Wilde* by Montgomery Hyde, which was 'a kick in the teeth, in the gut, in the heart, in the balls, everywhere.' He realised that this 'extraordinary' and 'wise' and 'kind' man who was also 'loathed' and 'despised' shared in his words 'nature' and in our words 'sexuality' with him. He felt as if his life is going to be the same as that of his: "one of pain and exile and rejection and shame" (*More Fool Me*).

Further, as the years passed by, he explored more of this man not only knowing about him but also about the ones who either influenced him, or he did to them. He realised that he has a kinship with those writers, some of whose life has been tragic and of some extraordinarily open, which provided him with the conclusion that, "without being remote, without being to stuck miles away from lemon, without the feeling of otherness and difference...except through the printed words of dead men and women from years and years and thousands of miles away, I might have never been vindicated or solaced into the belief that my life was at all worth living" (*More Fool Me*). This resolution of his helps us to answer one of the questions that this paper aims to address: Why do we love Batman? Answer: Because we empathize with him on a personal and psychological level, as also suggested by Anna-Maria Covich. He strikes us on a personal level, making us emotionally investing in him, which is the utmost important feature of any character or work to become likeable. And once intertwined within his world psychologically, a 'fan' tries to find his footings with the other fans. Thus, creating a network where they believe their voice holds meaning. Their existence is not devoid of purpose. However, there comes a difference even in the intensity of being a fan. Stephen Fry's anecdote puts light on this minute facet of fandom, which if missed changes the whole trajectory of one's position within the same. For Stephen Fry, he discovered Oscar Wilde and then invested himself in his world to understand his existence in the flux of life. In a way, he can be termed as a 'nerd' (to whom I would like to term as absoluter) or 'geek' knowing the ins and outs of his idol. The nerds need not be confused with that of what we call as blind-follower or a student, more aptly termed in Hindi as *mureed.*

The difference can be located in the context that nerds or geeks carve out their idol in their image. No compromises, no compensation, no modification will work for them until approved and authorized by them. For them, the idea of the idol dominates over the idol itself. Another sets of a fan (within which I count myself) are that of admirers, or to use a Hindi term here, *anuragi.* Such are the ones who from a distance (but not detached) treasure their idol but also at the same time can critique it in aesthetic terms. Professor William Uricchio of MIT suggests his understanding of fans and non-fans as narrated by Roberta Pearson in her article "Bachies, Bardies, Trekkies, and Sherlockians," that non-fans can "engage in aesthetic reflection or are temporarily moved by cultural texts" but that fans "incorporate the cultural text as a part of their identity" (Pearson 102). Going by such classification, it can be extended upon the same that not only the non-fans are capable enough to do the aesthetic readings of a text in question but its admirers (*anuragi*) can do it as well. The admirers reside somewhere in between the nerd fans, culturally mediated fans, and non-fans. They enjoy the fruits of all.

The passage next follows with what can be categorized as culturally mediated fans. "A general appeal to shared humanity," says Slavoj Zizek, "can cover up any particular horror, it holds for the victim as well as for his/her executioner" (100). And Zizek rightly says so. In a world where nations have unchained themselves to the effects of market, forces have not only made them susceptible to greater changes (or doom) but have also made their denizens vulnerable to claim their identities. Asserting an identity, which now has become as Zygmunt Bauman terms "surrogate of community" (*Community* 15), comes with its false pretense of "collective insurance against individually confronted uncertainties" (16). Losing yourself within the race of defining and categorizing within a community gave the market an opportunity to exploit it for its benefits. Not only it is exploited but also accelerated by them with the assurances of making things all right again. As Don Drapper emphatically lays down the mantra of advertising in the pilot episode of *Mad Men* that, "advertising is based on one thing: happiness. And do you know what happiness is? Happiness is the smell of a new car. It's freedom from fear. It's a billboard on the side of a road that screams with reassurance that whatever you're doing is OK. You are OK" ("Smoke Gets in Your Eyes"). The market realised the huge potential that nests within the ignored section of the society, who to identify their grounds turn their attention to a 'text' (as in the case of Stephen Fry, he found that in Oscar Wilde). Its effects were realised when the original *Star Wars* came, and much later when Harry Potter mania swept the whole world. Since then being nerd started becoming 'cool.' Since the 1960s and 70s, marketing and advertising companies started relying upon their strategies to beguile generations in convincing that they have cracked the solutions to their mundane issues.

Homer exclaims in *The Simpsons*: "When will I learn? The answer to life's problems aren't at the bottom of a bottle. They are on TV" ("There's No Disgrace Like Home"). A euphoric response was given to what can be called as 'commercialization of fear' (Bauman). The greater problems of life were shrunken to the fictional trajectory of Luke Skywalker, Han Solo, Indiana Jones, Dr. Who, Harry Potter, etc., whose path, if one follows may derive all the solutions. The fear of 'I don't mean anything' and the struggle which then follows that 'I could be something' swelled the market forces to launch greater campaigns (even negative campaigns generating profits) to tell people where the answers reside. So one is now bound to choose an option, to give his loyalty to a brand, to be 'left' or 'right', to be of Obama's or Trump's or Modi's syndicate: "Marketing is dedicated to the discovery or invention of questions to which recently introduced products can be seen as providing the answers, and then to inducing the largest numbers of potential clients to ask those questions with ever growing frequency" (Bauman, *Moral Blindness* 103).

It does not matter whether they understand what they go for, what becomes necessary is to *choose* a side. It's not that such hypocrisy did not exist before, but it was never experienced in such urgency. Once even to have questioned Shakespeare or Dickens might have stigmatized anyone as foolhardy, lacking in taste, belonging to lower order. But now such labeling can be extended upon one if dared to put fingers on *Game of Thrones, Sherlock, Breaking Bad*, and so on. A culture has developed out there where identity exists only if you define yourself as a 'fan' of something/someone. One basically becomes what one chooses to follow. Or, if correctly said, one is known for what one successfully fakes to follow.

Can a Fan Response be Considered as Art?

Now, where do these meandering over fan discussions lead us? Obviously, apart from other things that this paper aims to discuss, one issue that first and foremost comes into the mind when talking about fans is, how much of a serious consideration shall be disposed to their responses that often results in the manner of fan fictions, paintings, cartoons, theories, songs, trolls etc.? To discuss them all would require another paper in continuation. So, considering the checks and limitations of this paper, I would like to engage in the deliberation of fan fictions (and on that of Batman), which in turn shall satisfy the queries of all.

Batman – The Art

Even with their noblest of intentions, Bob Kane and Bill Finger may not have fathomed the idea of the success that Batman would enjoy over the years. Yes, there were slumps and depression that he underwent with his farcical POW! ZAP! representation in the 60s and 70s, but once Frank Miller took the task of penning down the story of an old, retired Bruce Wayne to don himself again as Batman in *The Dark Knight Returns* (1986), followed by Michael Keaton's dark and brooding portrayal of the same in Tim Burton's 1989 Batman film, there was no looking back from there for this character (apart from a small glitch of George Clooney's stoic, expressionless, with nipple clad armored Batman that almost killed the franchise in 1997). It was Christopher Nolan's rendition though, of Bruce Wayne and his alter-ego in *Batman Begins* (2005) that satisfied not only the geeks but also brought under the rug a new set of audience who were unfamiliar with the adventures of this dark knight. With the coming of *The Dark Knight* (2008), the fans went berserk in their interpretation of not only of Batman but also of his relationship with Joker. Fans interpreted their story in every possible manner they could, ranging from Rachel being the love interest of Joker to consequently being his heartbreaker to homosexual innuendos within Batman-Joker relation.

The question then comes, which one to consider as artwork among all? Does *Batman* qualify as an art (as does the intrigue of Mona Lisa) or is it just a travesty in the name of it? If understood in terms of Terry Eagleton,[1] this character pertaining to popular culture would exercise upon us the need to suspend our faculties when oscillating between Hamlet(?)/ Don Juan(?)/ Faust(?)/ Batman. The decline in the alertness and seriousness of the academicians in the name of culture studies, which Eagleton assiduously points out, has become more apparent today than ever where in the name of artistic creativity anything goes by without any due consideration and moral responsibility to the society. For instance, after the 9/11 incident, the shower of movies that came, dystopian fictions and superhero movies, deriving their source materials and inspirations from the event, it made us only question: Are we celebrating the event itself by reincarnating them over and again, and if so, what in the name of art are we leaving for the society? If considering to what Leo Tolstoy[2] understood the art of future to be, the barrage of works that we have been exposed to, most of them do not qualify as artwork from even an inch of their flesh. Now, considering these artworks that Arthur C. Danto construes as "a material object, some of whose properties belong to the meaning, and some of which do not" (38).

It is in the viewers that he maintains resides the true power to interpret the meaning out of the meaning-bearing properties that the artwork intends to convey. So if taken into consideration what Eagleton to Tolstoy to Danto is establishing as art and artwork to be, the meaning becomes haywire because there are others like Mussolini as well who in *Popolo d' Italia* talks about how masses should be considered as raw materials to which a work of art is possible. All one needs is "a government, a man, a man who has a touch of the artist and the hard hand of the warrior" (Todorov 33). A belief which is only furthered by Hitler who being stimulated by Richard Wagner's idea of art and society considered art as "a sublime mission that demands fanaticism" (Todorov 41). So if the purpose of art is to move beyond the hands of few privileged to be understood and appreciated by all, to make people more susceptible towards its smouldering burns that are caused upon us unnoticed, then there seems to be no reason for scholars like Eagleton to cry over the failure of the political mating of theories that supposedly is being caused by the *leisure* of new academia that has emerged in the form of culture studies, which are now realised with *tour de force* in fan fiction.

If one hates the idea of not knowing where *Coriolanus* ended and *Coronation Street* began (where *Hamlet* ended and *Batman* came), then it is in a way asking to adhere to what Mussolini and Hitler gestured, art in the hands of few. When fans bring their own readings of a text in the manner of fan fiction, it serves only to art by means of interpretation. Art produces art; art extends art; art interprets art. The problem of interpretation refuges in translation. There ensues a conflict in-between the text and its process of normalization via translation. The job of a reader is to validate the text confirming it to his experiences and knowledge. If the job is well done, the text loses its charm, if not it continues the perpetual looping of stabilizing the entropy. The complication, if taken a cue from Wolfgang Iser,[3] dwells in the performative act of fans in interpreting the text. While translating, the emotive essence is overlooked for meanings that subdue the significance of the text under consideration as an inconsequential effort is made to normalize it rather extend the arch of its diversification. Rather choose to be one among the many voices (polysemy), it attempts to be *the* voice. That is why most of the fan fiction fails to establish itself as a work of art.

Now, if this analysis is to be imposed upon the multitude works of Batman, it can aid to analyze the readers as to which one to consider as a serious piece of art and which ones to be ignored. Considering Christopher Nolan as one of the fans of Batman, his authored *Batman Begins* (he grabbed the opportunity of directing it by convincing the executives of Warner Brothers by giving just a pitch, which shows his level of intimacy as a fan with the character) and *The Dark Knight* gallantly stand as artworks as not only they continue the saga of Bruce Wayne embracing his alter-ego, but also of the consequences that befall thereafter. More than assigning and imposing the meaning to what Batman is, they delved deep into what he stands for, enlarging the epic stature of this character. *The Dark Knight Rises*, however, fails in this regard (though not entirely) because, in the haste of giving a befitting ending to his trilogy, Nolan walked the boulevard of 'What Batman Means' to him. Nonetheless, more than the fact whether any interpretation qualifies itself worth as artwork, it cannot be ignored *en masse* that Batman is *the* art that is the genesis and inspiration behind every other artwork that follows its lead. It required the genius of the artists, Bob Kane and Bill Finger, the creators of Batman character, to introduce this character among its admirers but it is the very image that became, much like music or painting or opera, the reservoir of creative interaction, acceptance, and translations that succeeded henceforth. Howsoever catch-22 it may sound, it is not. It is the image of Batman drifting as an idea (like God maybe?), which is the Art behind all arts.

The Shadow of Batman and My *Weltanschauung*

As prisoners responded to the shadows on the walls of the cave in Plato's allegory of cave carving their world out of it, my response to the events of the world is governed by the shadow of Batman that is cast upon me through his fiction. Over the years my adulation of Batman has made me realise that a fan need not be judged only by the responses that he brings for the text but also by how he responds to the event outside of the text. Being an Indian fan of an American superhero does not blindside me of the wrongs that the writers try to garb out of his fictions to justify the wrongdoings of America neither it stops me to accolade him when it critiques its malpractices. Here is a response of an admirer (*anuragi*) to the event of 9/11, to which America not only responded on physical terms but also ideologically by calling upon the fictions of Superheroes. The examples that I am going to draw do not limit itself to Batman but is a response to the Superhero cinema that Hollywood has been using as an ideological weapon to win approval.

9/11: A Day when the Language Collapsed

September 11th, 2000 CE is marked as a day when the world changed. With the sequential events of the destruction of the twin towers of the World Trade Center and its horror being transmitted via satellite channels all over the world defined it as a day that displayed the "bankruptcy of all national frame of reference" (Fine 8-9). Ulrich Beck calls it a day of the collapse of language that brings forth the idea of changing the old order with the new; that is, the idea of moving from methodological nationalism to methodological cosmopolitanism. The event which was graphic and horrifying to watch, morbid, sad and a blot on humanity at the same time, if we see the iteration of the same event prior to the event itself, it may come as a shock that the event was very much ritualized. What it means is, since the day the foundation of WTC was laid down, America was preparing itself for its death. Its destruction became a part of the popular culture through movies and graphic novels:

> King Kong was the first to climb them in Dino Delaurentis's pointless 1976 remake of the giant gorilla classic. They'd been smashed by tidal waves, blasted by aliens, shattered by meteor strikes, and pulverized by rogue asteroids. The terrible fall of the World Trade Center towers on September 11 has the curious inevitability of an answered prayer or the successful result of a black magic ritual. (Morrison Loc 6189)

Months before the event there released a series of comics with "images of plane and ruined towers" – Garth Ennis's *Punisher, Adventures of Superman* (No. 596), Grant Morrison's *X-Men* (No. 115) are among the few that got published before the event and projected the event itself or similar events like that as if like the time loop got distracted and the future started influencing the past (Morrison Loc 6189).

How America responded to 9/11, the world knows it. The war, the killings, the hunt, the xenophobia – their fear and hatred came out almost in every possible manner. It was a wound that America was not willing to heal very much like the hole in Iron Man's chest. The most interesting response came from Hollywood, which has always come to rescue the American pride whenever they bleed deep, whether during Vietnam war or Watergate Scandal or Gulf War or the Economic Depression, so why not for the 9/11 when they needed to cover their mistakes to justify the wrongs they did and were about to commit. Besides producing few movies upon the real 9/11 incidents in which some fared well, and some did not, Hollywood hit the bull's-eye with the genre of superhero movies. It was an instant connect with the global audience. The potential of these movies lies in the fact that the American policies which the world vehemently criticises, they receive approvals when we cheer for the acts that these heroes do to 'protect' their people. When Batman surveillances over the cell phones of Gotham to catch Joker, it brings relief to the audience to know that a guy like Batman is there who is 'watching us.'

Amidst the celebrations of this superheroism, the antithesis of it also surfaces itself latently. These days a new trend has begun – the ensemble superhero movies. It is a Disney spectacle where people get to see all their favourite characters at once. One of the reasons if it has to be reasoned here as to why these movies are treated like an event is that people are scared. We do not want a hero to save us but only heroes. We rejoice in their power, but it scares us subconsciously to think of someone to have such power as they possess. What if one goes rogue? Or, what if you pick the wrong cause to fight it right? What if saving us becomes an addiction on the part of such hero like Iron Man whom we saw being healed at the end of the third instalment of the *Iron Man* movies, but in *Captain America: Civil War* we see him being suited in his armour again where he claims that he just cannot stop? What if like Ozymandias in *Watchmen*, the hero himself is the cause of the massacre, killing millions as collateral damage to bring world peace? What if the grieving mother in *Civil War* is correct that Tony Stark is fighting for himself and not for the others? So, behind all the spectacle of the ensemble casting, one of the reasons that people crave for them is that we cannot put our trust in just one hero. We have our likings; we pick sides; thus, if one's action does not cater to our taste, we wish for the others to intervene and set him right.

Hollywood started its campaign of superhero movies strategically with the motif to avenge the wrongs done to America. The catastrophe was portrayed as Biblical in nature. The falling off of the twin towers was akin to the dismantling of the tower of Babel. America painted the towers as an illustration of the towering efforts of humans to unite the world. The cosmopolitan vision that America brought onto the table was to unite the world with them being in charge of the world state. The destruction of WTC was a blow to that idea, destruction that came in the form of the *death of language* – meanings lost their values and were postponed indefinitely. The only thing that could characterize the event was the term Horror! Horror! And Hollywood capitalized on that horror. The public sentiments were swayed by (re)framing America as the saviour. If divided into the phases since the outburst of superhero movies since 2000 CE, the first phase can be seen as the 'denial' of the risks that America itself has created. The heroes are fighting the terrorists, saving their utopia by keeping the aliens out. The second is that of the 'passive acceptance' that they might be in the wrong, and the "dinner time utopia is now an empty incantation. The idea that one can lock the aliens out, send them back, localize them, or confine them so that the rest of society won't need to worry about them is simply untenable. The aliens are here. They are already integrated into our lives, even if they have not yet been integrated into our national political societies or our consciousness" (Beck and Willms 42). Thus enters Superman with a reboot of *Man of Steel* where he is the alien fighting for the American cause and if needed, he will kill his own people to save them. Not only he fights for America, but also, he becomes the state embracing the S of the USA in his chest, which to him stands as hope. The third phase which recently has commenced is that of 'complete acceptance' where they recognize the fact that they may be the cause of the damages in the form of life and property around the world.

Thus, they in themselves may be the monsters they are fighting with, and all this time they were blaming their mistakes on the others. In the *Civil War*, the Secretary of the States shows the Avengers the footages of the destruction that they have caused while fighting terrorists around the world. They just cannot deny it and have to be liable for that. The conversation that later ensues in between Tony Stark and Steve Roger as to whether work under the leadership of the UN or to be independent, splits the audience to pick sides. A laudable strategy is to let the audience choose what kind of heroes they want to fight for their cause. A recent inclination towards the R-Rated superhero movies like *Deadpool* where the hero does not need to act as an institution but candidly displays that he can be mean-tempered, diabolic and heroic at the same time, or the box-office success of a movie like *Suicide Squad* shows that they accept that they might be the monsters, but if so, still they will fight for the just cause.

Conclusion: What My Hero Means to Me

Why do I care about Batman? Well, the answer to it certainly befalls upon the realm of autobiography. However, not to pester anyone with the biographical detailing, I would like to answer this by going through a query that Bill Moyers put up to Joseph Campbell as how the writer Thomas Berry felt that we are in between the tales - the old tales are not working anymore and we have not learned a new one. Campbell partially agrees with this statement and retorts that not all the old tales have gone obsolete. Batman, to me, stands for the same: An old tale in a new veil, giving me just enough information and inspiration to what a Hero should be (Campbell and Moyers). Bruce Wayne goes into the darkest recess of emotional pandemonium that a human being could possibly bear and comes out with that darkness not by evading but embracing it. "The hero symbolizes our ability to control the irrational savage," as Campbell opines (Campbell and Moyers 9), which Bruce Wayne does so bravely. He attains the illumination in his journey inwards and comes back with a purpose to serve. He is the balance between sanity and insanity, between chaos and order, between just and unjust. One may blame him to be as the one who nurtures the madness of Joker. Maybe that is true, maybe not, but whatever the case might be, one cannot escape the impasse that Joker will be there with or without Batman. It is our choice to embrace Batman as the answer or not. He is an autocrat but not like the ones we encounter in the real world. He does not kill Joker only because killing one will produce hundreds more like him. Also, if Batman kills, his admirers too will take up the task of 'cleansing the filth', which he certainly would not agree upon. He is a deontologist who will only interfere to bring order back to the system. He is the idea of a hero whom we not just aspire, but we need. Adoring this character only gives me hope that better things are out there in this world. Words like honour, justice, strength, self-restraint and so on, have meanings beyond the pages of a dictionary. His fiction enlightens me better about Buddha, Jesus, or Gandhi whom I might not have understood if not for him. Maybe that is my limitation, but if so, I am glad that I found this character and embraced him as a fan.

Notes

1. The children of the sixties and seventies were also the inheritors of so-called popular culture, which was part of what they were required to put in suspension when studying Jane Austen. But structuralism had apparently revealed that the same codes and conventions traversed both 'high' and 'low' culture, with scant regard for classical distinctions of value; so why not seize advantage of the fact that methodologically speaking, nobody quite knew where *Coriolanus* ended and *Coronation Street* began and construct an entirely fresh field of inquiry ('culture studies') which would gratify the anti-elitist iconoclasm of the sixty-eighters and yet appear wholly in line with 'scientific' theoretical findings? It was, in its academicist way, the latest version of the traditional avant-garde project of leaping the barriers between art and society, and was bound to make its appeal to those who found, rather like an apprentice chef cooking his evening meal, that it linked classroom and leisure time with wonderful economy. (Eagleton)

2. Those works alone will be considered works of art which convey feelings drawing people towards brotherly union, or such all human feelings as will be able to unite all people. Only such art will be singled out, allowed, approved and disseminated. But art that conveys feelings coming from obsolete religious teachings, outlived by the people – Church art, sensual art, art that conveys the feelings of superstitious fear, pride, vanity, the admiration of heroes, art that arouses sensuality or an exclusive love of one's own nation – will be regarded as bad, harmful art, and will be condemned and despised by public opinion. All the rest of the art, which conveys feelings accessible only to some people will be considered unimportant and will be neither condemned nor approved. And, generally, it will not be a separate class of rich people that appreciates art, but the whole people; so that for a work of art to be recognized as good, to be approved and disseminated, it will have to satisfy the demands, not of some people who live in identical and often unnatural conditions, but of all people, of the great mass of people who are in natural working conditions. (Tolstoy)

3. If interpretation has to cope with the liminal space resulting from something being transposed into something else, then interpretation is primarily a performative act rather than an explanatory one, although more often than not performance is mistaken for explanation. Whenever this happens, the mistake is one of category: for explanation to be valid, one must presuppose a frame of reference, whereas performance has to bring about its own criteria. The self-generation of criteria in interpretation allows first and foremost to participate in whatever is highlighted than to validate the results achieved. (Iser)

Bibliography

Batman Begins. Dir. Christopher Nolan. Warner Bros. Pictures. 2005. Film.

Bauman, Zygmunt. *Community: Seeking Safety in an Insecure World.* Cambridge: Polity Press, 2001. Print.

Bauman, Zygmunt. *Moral Blindness.* Cambridge, UK: Polity Press, 2013. Print.

Beck, Ulrich, and Johannes Willms. *Conversations with Ulrich Beck.* Trans. Michael Pollack. Cambridge: Polity Press, 2004. Print.

Beck, Ulrich. *The Cosmopolitan Vision.* Trans. Ciaran Cronin.Cambridge: Polity Press, 2006. Print.

Campbell, Joseph, and Bill D. Moyers. *The Power of Myth.* New York: RHUS; Anchor edition, 1991. Print.

Carroll, Lewis. *Alice's Adventures in Wonderland.* New York: The MacMillan, 1920. Print.

Covich, Anna-Maria. "Heroes with Issues: Fan Identification with Batman." *Fan Phenomena: Batman.* Ed. Liam Burke. Chicago: Intellect Books, 2013. 40-47. Print.

Danto, Arthur C. *What Art Is.* London: Yale UP, 2013. Print.

Eagleton, Terry. *Literary Theory: An Introduction.* Minneapolis: University of Minnesota Press, 2008. Print.

Fine, Robert. *Cosmopolitanism.* Oxon: Routledge, 2007. Print.

Iser, Wolfgang. *The Range of Interpretation.* New York: Columbia UP, 2000. Print.

Manning, Matthew. *The Batman Files.* Kansas, Missouri: Andrews McMeel Publishing, 2011. Print.

More Fool Me. Dir. Martin Lord. Perf. Stephen Fry. Kew Media Group. Netflix India.

Morrison, Grant, and Dave McKean. *Arkham Asylum.* New York: DC Comics, 2014. Print.

Morrison, Grant. *Supergods: Our World in the Age of the Superhero.* New York: Vintage Digital, 2011. Kindle file.

Pearson, Roberta. "Bachies, Bardies, Trekkies, and Sherlockians." *Fandom: Identities and Communities in a Mediated World.* Ed. Jonathan Gray, Cornel Sandvoss, and C. Lee Harrington. New York: NUP, 2017. 98-109. Print.

"Smoke Gets in Your Eyes." *Mad Men, Season 1.* Dir. Alan Taylor. Writ. Matthew Weiner. Netflix India.

"There's No Disgrace Like Home." *The Simpsons, Season 1.* Dir. Jen Kamerman and Jim Reardon.Writ. Matt Groening, James L. Brooks. Hotstar India.

The Dark Knight. Dir. Christopher Nolan. Warner Bros. Pictures. 2008. Film.

The Dark Knight Rises. Dir. Christopher Nolan. Warner Bros. Pictures. 2012. Film.

Todorov, Tzvetan. *The Limits of Art: Two Essays.* Trans. Gila Walker. Calcutta: Seagull, 2010. Print.

Tolstoy, Leo. *What is Art?* London: Penguin Books, 1995. Print.

Zizek, Slavoz. *Agitating the Frame.* New Delhi: Navayana, 2014. Print.

Further Reading

Rossi, Ino. "Reflexive Modernization." *Pioneer in Cosmopolitan Sociology and Risk Society.*Ed. Ulrich Beck. Munich: Springer, 2014. 59-64. Print.

Singh, Amar. "Hyperrealism and Christopher Nolan's Cinematic Texts." Thesis. Banaras Hindu University, 2015. Unpublished.

List of Contributors

Amar Singh is an Assistant Professor in English at Banaras Hindu University, India. His research interest lies in the area of Popular Culture, Film Studies and Cultural Studies. His Doctorate research is on *Hyperrealism and Christoper Nolan's Cinematic Texts*. He is currently pursuing Post-Doctorate research from Bergische Universität Wuppertal, Germany. He has been a visiting scholar at Osnabrück University and Wuppertal University, Germany.

Ashima Bhardwaj is a Fulbright-Nehru Postdoctoral Research Fellow from Naropa University, Boulder, Colorado, USA. She received her Doctorate from the Department of English and Cultural Studies, Panjab University, India. From 2012 to 2016, she was an Assistant Professor at UILS, Panjab University. Her areas of expertise include Beat Studies, Sub-cultural traditions, and Counterculture activism. Bhardwaj resides in Toronto, Canada, and is an independent researcher; she is currently working on the Drag-Cosplay traditions in Canada.

Himanshu Khosla is the Director Sales of Namco Asia, a private manufacturers' representative and trading firm in India. He is a post-graduate from Punjab Technical University, India with specialization in Pharmaceutical Chemistry on Quantification of *Plumbagin by HPLC*. Khosla is a former Professor at V.M.S. College of Pharmacy, Batala, Punjab (India). He has effectively contributed to research by presenting his articles and research papers in national and international conferences. With a keen interest in theater and production of films, he has observed the dynamics of the pharmaceutical industry and larger social foundations. Tracing how cinema is shaped, his writings focus on the narratives of Indian Cinema and Television; his current project investigates the gendered and racial perspectives in Bollywood.

Jamiel Ahmad is from the province of Kashmir (Jammu and Kashmir) and is currently working in the Department of English at North Campus, University of Kashmir (India). He completed his Ph.D. at the School of Languages and Comparative Literature, Central University of Jammu (India), where he also received his M. Phil. on the topic "Exploring *The Half Mother, Curfewed Night*, and *Haider*: A Biopolitical Study". Ahmad has published several research papers in journals, including *English Studies in India, Literary Herald, Langlit, Nuances*, and also published chapters in various books such as *Studies in Vijay Tendulkar's Silence! The Court is in Session* and *Studies in Amitav Ghosh's The Shadow Lines*. Two of his book chapters on *Kanthapura* and on "border-related trauma" are in press. Email: herespeaksjames@gmail.com

Priyanka Shivadas is a Ph.D. student at the University of New South Wales Canberra, located at the Australian Defence Force Academy. Her research focuses on global indigenous literary studies. She has published "The Bone People of New Zealand: Identity Politics in the South Pacific" in a book which is a collection of essays called *Homogeneity in Heterogeneity: Memory, Culture, and Resistance in Aboriginal Literatures from Around the World* (New Delhi: Authorspress, 2018) and "The Practice of Public Apology: Australia Says Sorry to the Stolen Generations" in *The Culture of Dissenting Memory: Truth Commissions in the Global South*, edited by Veronique Tadjo (Routledge, 2019).

Rajanikant Pandey teaches Anthropology and Tribal Studies at the Central University of Jharkhand, India. He has published several articles and book chapters with national and international publishers. His major areas of specialization are Environmental Anthropology, STS Studies, and Organizational Ethnography. Pandey has a keen interest in exploring the life-world of indigenous peoples of South Asia.

Ritika Pant is an Assistant Professor at the Department of Journalism, Kalindi College, University of Delhi (India). She has submitted her doctoral thesis at the School of Arts & Aesthetics, Jawaharlal Nehru University, New Delhi. A gold-medalist from the AJK MCRC, Jamia Millia Islamia, Pant is a recipient of the Junior Research Fellowship from the University Grants Commission, India. She has also worked as a media practitioner in the Indian television industry. She has presented papers at various national and international conferences. Her research interests include gender, transnationalism, stardom, fandom, television, and media studies.

Saket Kumar Bhardwaj is pursuing doctoral research on Human Trafficking and Media at the Department of Mass Communication and Journalism, Tezpur University, Assam (India). He has completed his five-year integrated M.A. in Mass Communication from the Central University of Jharkhand, and has qualified in Mass Communication and Journalism through the National Eligibility Test (UGC-NET). Bhardwaj has worked as an Assistant Professor in the Department of Culture and Media Studies, Central University of Rajasthan, and as a full-time news reporter for a Ranchi based English newspaper. His teaching and research interests include Communication for Social Change, New Media, Journalism, Advertising and Public Relations, Sociology of Communication Technology, and Media.

Shipra Tholia is an Assistant Professor at the Department of German Studies, Faculty of Arts, Banaras Hindu University, India. She is currently pursuing her Ph.D. as a DAAD research scholar from Bergische Universität Wuppertal, Germany. Her research interest lies in the area of German Literature and Culture Studies with a special focus on Narratology. Tholia's M. Phil thesis is on "Adventure of Tintin: An Intermedial Phenomena" from Jawaharlal Nehru University, New Delhi. She has been awarded several fellowships by the DAAD and the German Ministry of Education and Culture and has been a visiting scholar to Osnabrück University and Wuppertal University, Germany.

Uttam Kumar Pegu is currently an Associate Professor in the Department of Mass Communication and Journalism, Tezpur University, Assam (India). He has also taught at St Anthony's College and EFLU, Shillong. Pegu completed his doctoral research on "Information and Communication Technology Implications" at AJK Mass Communication Research Center, Jamia Millia Islamia, New Delhi. His research interests include ICT Implications, Political and Cultural Communication, Conflict Communication, Film Studies, and Social History. He has published articles in prestigious national and international journals. Email: uttamkp@tezu.ernet.in

Vishakha Sen is a creative writer and poet. Passionate about creative writing, painting, and traveling, she expresses deepest emotions fossilized in places and people. She is a lecturer by profession and recipient of the prestigious JNMF doctoral scholarship for her Indian Psychoanalysis research. A prodigy of the Department of English and Modern European Languages, University of Lucknow (India), her performance poetry is featured at VTS Contest, West Coast Tagore Festival, Richmond (Canada), Lucknow Society, 'Kavya-Sangoshthi' by Youth Eve, 'Arz Kiya Hai' by Lucknow Society (2019). Sen's critical writings have appeared in book chapters and reputed journals like *Muse India, Purakala,* and *Gnosis.* Her research areas are Indian Psychoanalysis, Psychoanalytic and Cyber Feminism, Cultural Studies in new media, films, Postcolonial Literature, and Indian Theatre. Email: vishakhacrusader@gmail.com

Ruchi Sharma is an Assistant Professor at Chitkara University, Punjab, India and teaches Culture Studies, Literary Theory, Aboriginal Literature, and Communications, with a specific focus on the impact of visual and textual literacy. She has also worked at the Department of English, St. Xavier's College, Jaipur. Sharma is currently the Secretary of Digital Humanities Alliance for Research and Teaching Innovations, India. Her research interests include Aboriginal Writing, Women's and Gender Studies, Star Studies, and Digital Humanities. She has contributed chapters to different books, published research papers in prestigious national and international journals, and has also been an invited speaker for All India Radio talk.

Index